MEDICAL
Muses

MEDICAL
Muses

Hysteria in Nineteenth-Century Paris

ASTI HUSTVEDT

BLOOMSBURY
LONDON · BERLIN · NEW YORK · SYDNEY

Bloomsbury Publishing Plc
36 Soho Square
London W1D 3QY

www.bloomsbury.com

Bloomsbury Publishing, London, Berlin, New York and Sydney
A CIP catalogue record for this book is available from the British Library

ISBN 978 0 7475 7633 4 (hardback edition)
ISBN 978 1 4088 1512 0 (trade paperback edition)

10 9 8 7 6 5 4 3 2 1

Printed in Great Britain by Clays Ltd, St Ives Plc

For Juliette

CONTENTS

LIST OF ILLUSTRATIONS

PART ONE

Charcot

During the decade of the 1870s, three young women found themselves in the hysteria ward of the Salpêtrière Hospital in Paris under the direction of the prominent neurologist Jean-Martin Charcot. All three—Blanche, Augustine, and Geneviève—would become medical celebrities. The stories of their lives as patients on the ward are a strange amalgam of science and religion, medicine and the occult, hypnotism, love, and theater. The illness they suffered from was hysteria. This disease was not an arcane preoccupation of the doctors that treated them, but an affliction that would increasingly capture the public imagination. Stories about hysterical patients filled the columns of newspapers. They were transformed into fictional characters by novelists. Hysterics were photographed, sculpted, painted, and drawn. Every week, eager crowds arrived at the hospital to attend Charcot's demonstrations of hysterics acting out their hysterical symptoms. And it wasn't only medical students and physicians who came to view the shows, but artists, writers, actors, socialites, and the merely curious. Hysteria had become a fascinating and fashionable spectacle. But who were these hysterical women? Where did they come from? What role did they play in their own peculiar form of stardom? And what exactly were they suffering from?

To answer these questions, I combed hospital records and munici-

3

pal archives. I read case histories, gathered testimony from the scientific and the popular press of the day, and sifted through visual documents. I read memoirs and letters written by those who spent time at the Salpêtrière in the late nineteenth century, including the young Sigmund Freud, who admired Charcot, and the enormously vindictive Léon Daudet, who did not. I pursued false leads and hit dead ends. History is filtered by subjectivity, and I repeatedly stumbled on the Rashomon effect of conflicting narratives. I relied heavily on the work of medical historians whose clarity in the face of so many bewildering accounts was enormously helpful.[1]

I first came across this material when I was a graduate student in French at New York University. I was writing my dissertation on a late-nineteenth-century novel, *The Future Eve* by Villiers de l'Isle-Adam. At that time, hysteria was a fashionable topic in literary theory, and I came across multiple references to various hysterical women, but they were usually in passing, in footnotes, or in evidence to support an argument. Long after I had finished my Ph.D. work, those tantalizing bits of information continued to haunt me, and I decided to write a book about the women themselves.

Hysteria was at least partly an illness of being a woman in an era that strictly limited female roles. It must be understood as a response to stifling social demands and expectations aptly expressed in paralysis, deafness, muteness, and a sense of being strangled. Blanche, Augustine, and Geneviève exhibited symptoms that physically illustrated their actual social conditions. They lived at a time when women were exclusively defined through their relations with men. Fatherless, unmarried, and poor, these three women found themselves in a world that had little use for them. I began writing with a preconceived notion: the hysterics were victims of not only their home lives, but of a misogynist institution led by the tyrannical Charcot. I would rescue them from that narrative and tell their stories, from their perspective. Despite my intention, the more I read, the more I found myself admiring Charcot's brilliance. I also became a reluctant fan of some—not all—of the members of his coterie, a group of physicians who worked with him at the Salpêtrière. Désiré-Magloire Bourneville's humanitarian compassion for the oppressed and Gilles de la Tourette's ferocious loyalty are both laudable. Instead of a clear-cut world of exploited women and exploiting men, I entered something far more nuanced. Blanche, Augustine, and Geneviève were undeniably victimized, both inside and outside the hospital. That said, they also participated in a hospital culture that was in many ways less oppressive than the world beyond it. The Salpêtrière provided a language—the language of hysteria—that allowed them to articulate their distress. Blanche, Augustine, and Geneviève mastered its vocabulary and were rewarded.

I set out to write a nonhysterical book about hysteria, to ground my work in something real. At first I found it unfathomable that these women really were suffering from the spectacular forms of illness recorded by their doctors, an illness that no longer exists. But now I believe that Blanche, Augustine, and Geneviève were indeed ill. They suffered from chronic debilitating symptoms. To what degree their disease was socially determined and to what degree it was physically determined is impossible to say. If they showed up at a hospital today, suffering from the same symptoms, they would probably be diagnosed with schizophrenia or conversion disorder or bipolar disorder. They would undoubtedly be diagnosed with eating disorders because they had bouts of willful starving and vomiting. However, if these women were alive today, they might not have become ill to begin with and no doubt would suffer from other symptoms.

I am convinced that Blanche, Augustine, and Geneviève were neither frauds nor passive receptacles of a sham diagnosis. They really did "have" hysteria. Located on the problematic border between psychosomatic and somatic disorders, hysteria was a confusion of real and imagined illness. In an era without demons and before Freud's unconscious, hysteria fell into a theoretical vacuum. The female body was viewed as the site of a disturbing and incomprehensible split between its inside and outside. The theatrical symptoms of the external body had no internal reference, no location. They did not reveal the workings of the unconscious. They were themselves only, baffling, alarming, but revelatory of nothing. Unable to find an organic source, Charcot tried to isolate and reproduce these symptoms. The hysterics who cooperated in this project became pure signs of their illness, divested of any interiority. Their symptoms pointed to no inner source. Charcot's goal was to transform his hysterics, with their bizarre fits and spasms, into ideal medical specimens—into living dolls.

Hysteria may be an illness of the past, but the medical and ideological notions of femininity that lie behind it offer insights into the illnesses of the present and the way they are perceived. And while modern medicine no longer talks about hysteria, it nonetheless continues to perpetuate the idea that the female body is far more vulnerable than its male counterpart. Premenstrual syndrome, postpartum depression, and "raging hormones" are among the more recent additions to a medical mythology that is centuries old. As I researched nineteenth-century hysteria, accumulating books, articles, notes, and images on the subject, a second pile of information—at first glance unrelated—had also piled up on my desk. Newspaper and magazine clippings, recently published books and downloaded information from the Internet on eating disorders, self-mutilation, chronic fatigue syndrome, multiple personality disorder, and outbreaks of rashes following the September 11 attacks on the World Trade Center competed for space in my already crowded office. Why has my study of a disease that is no longer officially a medical diagnosis compelled me to collect information on these new disorders? Why do the lives of three women who lived more than a hundred years ago feel so relevant today and resonate so strongly with the lives of women who are my contemporaries?

A partial explanation can be found in Freud, or rather, in his absence. When Freud was at the Salpêtrière, he had yet to invent psychoanalysis. Charcot and his colleagues worked in a pre-Freudian era. The dynamic unconscious was not a possible explanation for hysterical symptoms. Now, we seem to have entered a post-Freudian period. The brilliant founder of psychoanalysis has been attacked from all sides, and in the nature/nurture debate, nature is, at least for the time being, in the lead. Psychiatric disorders are increasingly understood to be "chemical imbalances" and are treated with drugs. Like their nineteenth-century predecessors, today's scientists are scrambling to find biological explanations for behavior, and everything from human mating strategies to homosexuality, from shyness to alcoholism, has been supposedly located in biology.

There is, however, a crop of bizarre new illnesses that, like hysteria, afflict mostly young women and stubbornly resist biological explanation. No drug exists to cure anorexia, bulimia, self-mutilation, chronic fatigue syndrome, and multiple personality disorder, and no genetic flaw has been found to explain them. Furthermore, as was true for hysteria, these contemporary disorders are thought to be contagious, spread by suggestion, imitation, and therapy. The numbers of women diagnosed with multiple personality disorder, for example, soared after the television airing of *Sybil*, the story of a twentieth-century medical celebrity. Accounts of bulimics entering treatment clinics for eating disorders and emerging as trained anorexics exist, as does a newsletter, the *Cutting Edge*, in which self-mutilators can swap trade secrets. And in yet another parallel to hysteria, discussion of these illnesses is not limited to medical circles, but has infiltrated every area of public discourse, from tabloid television to scholarly tomes.

The cultural and historical homologies between hysteria and these present-day diseases are so detailed and undeniable that it would be accurate to categorize them all as incarnations of hysteria. They are perceived as social and cultural diseases that express in some direct, if undetermined way social and cultural conditions. Moreover, I believe that they may be read as a metaphor both for women's position in society and for the image of the feminine in the history of scientific discourses. Hysteria, that bizarre rupture between symptom and source played out on the female body has resurfaced in our post-Freudian era in new but oddly familiar forms. My desire to write *Medical Muses* was not merely a desire to recapture a lost historical experience. I hoped to achieve an understanding of, and perspective on, ourselves and our social world.

Charcot: Art and Medicine

Jean-Martin Charcot's life spanned a period of radical political change in France as monarchists and republicans clashed in bloody battles for power. On November 29, 1825, when Charcot was born, the ultraroyalist Charles X was on the throne doing his utmost to suppress what remained of liberty, fraternity, and equality in France. The revolts of 1830 sent the reactionary king into exile, and the nation entered a period of relative stability under a more moderate monarch, the "citizen king" Louis-Philippe. The Revolution of 1848 led to the proclamation of the Second Republic, only to see democracy squelched by the 1851 coup d'état that ushered in the Second Empire when Napoleon III declared himself emperor. His authoritarian regime came to an end in 1870 following the humiliating defeat of the French by the Prussians. The Third Republic was declared, and gave rise to the Paris Commune. For two months, the official government army attacked the insurgents, killing an astounding 25,000 Parisians.

The Third Republic, in power when Charcot died in 1893, endured until 1940, when it was replaced by the Vichy Regime.

Charcot was the second of four boys born in a working-class family. His father was a carriage builder in Paris, a skilled artisan, and while not wealthy, the Charcots were by no means poor. According to legend, there was enough money to pay for the higher education of only one boy, and Charcot's father decided that his oldest would take over the family workshop, his two youngest would join the military, and his most studious son, Jean-Martin, would pursue a professional degree. A career in medicine was one route to upward social mobility in nineteenth-century France. Freed from the "Molièresque" tradition of the doctor as bumbling fool, physicians rose to new prominence in the nineteenth century. During Charcot's early childhood, doctors joined the republican opposition in the July Revolution of 1830 and, after the cholera epidemic of 1832, became public heroes. For a working-class boy, the medical profession offered not only an avenue to economic prosperity, but the allure of a noble cause. Charcot was a quiet child. He loved animals and preferred to spend time alone reading and drawing.[2] He never outgrew his love for animals, literature (his favorite authors were Shakespeare, Dante, and Rabelais), and art. Before he decided on medical school, he had considered a career as an artist, and he continued to draw throughout his life, both for pleasure and for work.

Charcot drew constantly. He drew landscapes, still lifes, and portraits. He drew when he traveled, when he saw patients, and when he smoked hashish. As one of his students wrote regarding his experiment with hashish: "The entire page was covered with drawings: prodigious dragons, grimacing monsters, incoherent personages who were superimposed on each other, and who were intertwined and twisted in a fabulous whirlpool."[3] In the large house in the Faubourg Saint-Germain where he lived at the end of his life, Charcot installed an art studio, where he painted. He used his artistic skills to narrow in on anatomical abnormalities wherever he came across them, whether he was in the hospital or traveling. One sketch he made depicts an old man he saw in North Africa. To my untrained eye, the drawing looks like a hand-drawn ethnic postcard: a bearded man sits in a caftan, framed by a Moorish arch. For Charcot, the portrait showed the joint deformities of a man suffering from Parkinson's disease. He was a gifted caricaturist and sketched strangers as well as people he knew—his children, professors, students, patients, and colleagues—sometimes with a great deal of wit.[4] During one of the many competitive examinations he sat for—the test to become a professor *"agrégé"* on the Faculty of Medicine, a high-level distinction—Charcot covered his test paper with doodles and sketches. Among them is a group portrait of the faculty of medicine, drawn in their formal caps and gowns, but with the faces of monkeys.[5] He failed the exam the first time he took it—maybe this less-than-reverential drawing was from that round. While he is often described as cold and proud, Charcot was capable of self-mockery as well. The Charcot Library has preserved self-portraits, or rather self-caricatures, in which he exaggerated his beakish nose. In one he drew himself as a parrot. Astute observation and an ability to pinpoint distinguishing characteristics, whether for humorous effect in a drawing or to diagnose the disease of a patient, were among Charcot's defining gifts. As his famous student Sigmund Freud later remarked, Charcot "had the nature of an artist." He was "a *visuel*, a man who sees."[6]

The Salpêtrière

In 1852, the twenty-seven-year-old Charcot spent a year of his medical internship at the Salpêtrière Hospital. The Salpêtrière, the name of which derives from its sixteenth-century origin as an arsenal for gunpowder (made from saltpeter), was first used as a women's hospital in the seventeenth century, but "hospital" is not a noun that applies well to its function. It was more of a warehouse for female outcasts: women who were mad, violent, crippled, chronically ill, mentally retarded, unmarried and pregnant, or simply old and poor. In the 1680s, Louis XIV built a prison on the grounds called La Force that added prostitutes and female convicts awaiting execution or transportation to the colonies to this mix of unwanted women. It is here that Manon Lescaut, the great femme fatale of Abbé Prévost's novel and Puccini's opera, was confined before she was deported to America. When the king repealed the Edict of Nantes in 1685, female heretics joined the ranks of women incarcerated at the Salpêtriére.

The grim notoriety of the Salpêtrière was further magnified when, during the September Massacres of 1792, a mob attacked the building and women imprisoned there were gruesomely murdered. After the French Revolution, the prison was shut down, the prostitutes and criminals were sent elsewhere, and the Salpêtrière became a fortress to house elderly and insane women. Three years after the September Massacres, Philippe Pinel became chief physician, the same position Charcot would later occupy, and applied more moderate revolutionary ideals to the hospital. Pinel freed the female inmates, now "*citoyennes*," from their chains. While his role as great emancipator has been overstated, he was undeniably important in bringing more humane practices to the hospital. All forms of physical violence, for example, were banned under his watch.[7] The next generation of doctors continued to implement reform at the hospital, but the Salpêtrière had yet to shed its reputation as a dismal repository for unwanted and incurable women.[8] The Salpêtrière still exists, and in a sad coincidence that seems oddly relevant to the story I am telling here, it is to this Parisian hospital that Princess Diana was taken after her fatal car accident.

When Charcot's internship ended, he famously resolved to return to the Salpêtrière and stay.[9] This was an odd ambition for a promising young doctor because the Salpêtrière was not considered a prestigious institution. It was an old-fashioned place without laboratories or teaching facilities. Charcot himself called it "that grand asylum of human misery." But where others saw a professional dead end, Charcot saw opportunity. As Freud recalled more than forty years later, Charcot was inspired by "the wilderness of paralyses, spasms and convulsions" he had seen at the Salpêtrière.[10] Ten years later, he returned as chief physician of medical services and began the long process of reorganizing the Salpêtrière, transforming the outdated hospital for epileptic, insane, and aging women into a modern medical institution, complete with laboratories, teaching facilities, and separate wards. The large population of old and sick women, many of them suffering from disorders of the nervous system and many of them admitted for life, provided Charcot with what he called a vast "reservoir of material." The ambitious doctor maintained that he was "in possession of a kind of museum of living pathology whose holdings were virtually inexhaustible."[11]

From Chaos to Classification

Charcot applied what he called the "anatomo-clinical" method, a research strategy that correlated clinical symptoms in the living patient with anatomical lesions found in his patients after their deaths. The fact that many of the women at the Salpêtrière were old and were there for life made this work possible in a way that it would not have been at other hospitals. He confronted this undifferentiated population of trembling and immobilized patients, this "pandemonium of infirmities," as he called it, and began the long process of cataloguing their symptoms and classifying their diseases.

Charcot's method differentiated between diseases that resembled each other: "It is a new means to bring together organic illnesses which are similar," wrote Charcot, "and to distinguish those which in spite of sharing similar symptoms are of a nature altogether different and which therefore belong to another order of illnesses."[12] As an animal lover, he never performed vivisection. By conducting research on his living patients and analyzing tissue samples after death, he avoided experimenting on animals. An old kitchen at the Salpêtrière was converted into a pathology laboratory equipped with microscopes to analyze brain tissue and cross sections of spinal cords. Charcot, wrote Freud, "never tired of defending the rights of purely clinical work, which consists in seeing and ordering things, against the encroachments of theoretical medicine." When he and other visiting students, educated in German physiology, challenged Charcot's clinical method, the French doctor responded: "Theory is good, but that doesn't prevent a thing from existing."[13]

Charcot's disdain for theory and emphasis on clinical observation led to his most important medical discoveries. He kept large dossiers for each patient that included histories, copious clinical notes, drawings, and handwriting samples. Charcot came up with inventive techniques to document real but imperceptible variations in tremors. The "sphygmograph," adapted from an apparatus used to take arterial pulses, graphically recorded a patient's trembling. He designed hats with long plumes attached. The oscillations of the feathers made visible slight variations in the quivering of one nervous system disease from the trembling of another, a whimsical solution that produced serious results. All of this data was preserved along with autopsy results, so that the patient's external symptoms could be correlated with internal lesions in her brain and spinal cord.

In this way, Charcot identified hitherto unknown diseases and greatly added to the definitions of those already known. He discovered the precise pathology of amyotrophic lateral sclerosis (ALS), commonly called Charcot's disease in Europe and Lou Gehrig's disease in the United States. He contributed to the description of multiple sclerosis; Parkinson's disease; and tabes dorsalis, a form of neurosyphilis; locomotor ataxia, called Charcot's joints; and, with his student Pierre Marie, Charcot described the inherited neuropathy known as Charcot-Marie-Tooth disease.[14] (Tooth refers to Howard Tooth, an English physician who also described the disorder.) Charcot's work is also responsible for advancing research on cerebral localization. Many doctors at the time thought of the brain as an unvaried organ, but Charcot's clinical method led him to argue that it was "not a single, homogenous organ, but rather a group, or if you wish, a confederation, composed of a number of different organs."[15] Charcot's superb work was recognized. In 1882 he was awarded a new professorial chair in the diseases of the nervous system and became known as "the founder of neurology."[16]

Charcot's discoveries drew students to the Salpêtrière and, as he had done with the old kitchen converted to a laboratory, he transformed a refectory into a classroom. As his reputation grew, the improvised kitchen was replaced by a new state-of-the-art laboratory for pathological anatomy, equipped with the latest microscope developed by Rudolf Virchow, the German physiologist who introduced cell theory. The crowded classroom was closed, and a large lecture hall or amphitheater was built to accommodate the growing number of students and doctors he attracted. Charcot had transformed the Salpêtrière from an antiquated hospice into a great teaching hospital.

During Charcot's tenure, the Salpêtrière was the largest medical institution in Europe, perhaps in the world. Located on Paris's Left Bank, in the 13th arrondissement, it housed approximately 5,000 patients and included more than 100 structures built in a variety of architectural styles, from seventeenth-century classical edifices to little Swiss chalet–style houses. The Salpêtrière was a self-contained "city within a city." It had its own narrow streets, sidewalks, and courtyards, and even a small trolley.[17] The hospital was largely self-sustaining: It had a vegetable garden, orchard, reservoir, stables, post office, firemen, and a cemetery. Patients provided much of the labor that kept the institution running. Workshops and studios were filled with women who mended sheets and sewed chemises, aprons, and bonnets. Patients worked in the kitchen as cooks, as nursing assistants or *"filles de services"*—"ward girls" in English—and did laundry in the vast washrooms that served not only the Salpêtrière but all the public hospitals in Paris. For the patients who were able, the work was mandatory, but they were allowed to choose their hours and were paid a nominal sum for their labor. The Salpêtrière had its own food market, bakery, general store, tobacco shop, café and even a wine merchant where patients could spend their earnings. There was a Protestant church and a Catholic church, a school, and recreational gardens with paths, benches, and boules courts. The basement of the old prison was converted to a gymnasium and a library. Concerts and dances were held, including the annual Bal de Folles or Madwomen's Ball, which was covered in the press.

Charcot was the charismatic and imposing leader of this city within a city, and he was referred to in the press as the "Caesar of the Salpêtrière" and the "Napoleon of Neuroses," an image he appears to have cultivated by posing for photographs in Napoleon's trademark position, with his hand in his waistcoat. (See Figure 1.) He controlled every aspect of life in the clinic; his critics found him an unbending tyrant; his disciples idolized him. Gilles de la Tourette, for example (known today for the tic disorder that bears his name), is said to have worshiped him "like a God." Charcot's reputation in the hospital helped his private practice flourish, and he became the consulting physician to the ruling class: emperors, princes, grand dukes, and czars were among his patients. The son of a carriage builder had become a member of Parisian society.

Figure 1. Jean-Martin Charcot. Charcot gave this photograph to Sigmund Freud in 1886. Getty Images.

Charcot at Home

At the age of thirty-nine, Charcot married Augustine Victoire Durvis, a wealthy widow. In a letter he wrote home to his fiancée, Freud commented on the match: "Madame is tiny, rather round, and lively with powdered hair. She is friendly but not very distinguished in appearance. It is she who has the fortune; her father apparently has millions, whereas Charcot was once a poor devil."[18] She had a daughter, Marie, from her first marriage, and went on to have two more children with Charcot. Both were named after their father: a girl Jeanne and a boy, Jean-Baptiste, the future polar explorer. In the same letter, Freud wrote that Jeanne Charcot bore an "almost ridiculous resemblance to her great father" and none too subtly added, "Now just suppose I were not in love already and were something of an adventurer; it would be a strong temptation to court her for nothing is more dangerous than a young girl bearing the features of a man whom one admires."[19] By all accounts, Charcot had a happy family life. He doted on his children and on his pets, the dogs Carlo and Sigurd, and his pet monkey Rosalie. The little monkey, a gift from Dom Pedro II, emperor of Brazil, had a place at the family dinner table beside Charcot. She sat in a high chair and wore a bib, and when Rosalie snatched food from his plate, Charcot responded with an indulgent laugh.

On Tuesday evenings, the Charcots held lavish parties in their magnificent home on the boulevard Saint-Germain. Artists, writers, architects, scholars, and politicians mingled there with physicians and Charcot's students. The latter, many of whom came from modest backgrounds similar to Charcot's, were dazzled by these elegant soirées. Even Léon Daudet, one of Charcot's most malicious critics, was impressed by these evenings:

The hospitality of Charcot was sumptuous and worthy of his high station. Adored by his family, his wife for whom he was a god, his handsome and intelligent children whom he cherished and loaded with favors and always surrounded by admirers, he wanted everything to be perfect: the food, the wine, the conversation, the gowns of the ladies, the service. One could write a captivating story just by recording the conversations that were held at the table and in the study of Professor Charcot. He was like Goethe, Montaigne, or Alphonse Daudet, like those men who radiate interest in everything.[20]

Charcot's granddaughter, however, recounted a potentially disastrous moment during one of these affairs. The guests of honor were French Prime Minister Léon Gambetta and the grand duke of Russia, who had been brought together to discuss international matters in a private setting. During the party, the mischievous monkey jumped onto the table and pulled apart the elaborate centerpiece on the dining room table. But rather than scuttling the negotiations between France and Russia, Rosalie's antics put both parties at ease and in good humor.[21]

Why did a neurologist receive so much attention? In part, because the second half of the nineteenth century was the heyday of positivism and the medical sciences had soared to new heights of power. In 1878, Claude Bernard, the founder of experimental medicine, was honored with a state funeral, a distinction previously reserved exclusively for military and political heroes. The public eagerly followed the latest medical developments, reported widely in the mainstream press. Charcot both encouraged the public's interest in medicine and opened the doors of the hospital to many. He established Thursday and Sunday as visiting days, when as many as a thousand friends and family members would pass under the arched gateway of the hospital. The status of medicine and Charcot's undeniable breakthroughs in neurology contributed to his public stature. But it was hysteria that made him famous.

Hysteria

When Charcot arrived at the Salpêtrière, hysteria was still a medical "trash can"—that is, the label where all medically inexplicable symptoms were dumped. It was considered exclusively a disease of women and was diagnosed when no other cause could be found for disturbing symptoms. Charcot described the typical trajectory taken by a doctor to diagnose hysteria:

> A little girl about seven years old begins to cough and goes on coughing for two months without any known cause. An experienced physician recognizes at once that he has not to deal with a case of bronchitis but with one of hysteria. Then the little girl is all at once affected with stiff neck . . . hysterical torticollis is made out. Or, again, a most characteristic symptom is observed. The child's leg becomes stiff and painful. This is hysteric contracture. . . . Things go along pretty smoothly till menstruation. Then the child begins to get peculiar—to have curious ideas. She is alternately sad or cheerful to excess. Then, one day she utters a cry, falls to the ground, and presents all the symptoms of an attack of hystero-epilepsy. She begins to assume various postures, to speak of fantastic animals, to mention words which are neither suitable to her age nor to her position in society. . . .[22]

Perhaps the most perplexing aspect of hysteria for nineteenth-century physicians was that it took so many forms. Among the most common symptoms were a predilection for drama and deception, excessive emotionality, paralyses of the limbs, temporary deafness and muteness, heightened sensitivity of the skin, willful starving, spontaneous bleeding, feelings of strangulation, hallucinations and somnambulism, and fits of contortions and seizures. Moreover, these symptoms were intermittent.

From the "wandering womb" of antiquity, in which hysteria was thought to be triggered by a uterus that refused to stay in its proper place, to the demonic possessions of the Middle Ages and Renaissance, to the "uterine fury," or nymphomania, of the Enlightenment, hysteria occupied an elusive position for the physician. And while nineteenth-century scientists made great advances in medicine, hysteria remained mysterious. The illness "is presented in a thousand different forms, and we cannot grasp any one of them," said Pierre Briquet, one of the nineteenth-century specialists Charcot admired.[23] The author of the entry "Hysteria" in a medical dictionary confessed to the daunting nature of his task when he wrote, "Without going so far as to compare our situation to that of Dante's hopelessness at not being able to describe the horrors of the ninth circle of Hell, we can say, without humility or coquetry, that it is the article in this dictionary that is the most difficult to write clearly and concisely."[24]

As a neurologist, Charcot took little interest in hysteria. It was considered an illness for the family doctor or, in its severe form, for an alienist—the nineteenth-century term for a physician who specialized in mental illness. Charcot's decision to focus on the disorder came about when a bureaucratic decision was made to restructure the hospital. The Salpêtrière building that housed patients suffering from epilepsy, hysteria, and insanity had become so dilapidated it had to be evacuated. The epileptics and the hysterics were sent to Charcot's service, and the insane put in another ward. "Thus," writes biographer Georges Guillain, "quite involuntarily and by force of circumstances, Charcot found himself engulfed in the problem of hysteria."[25]

Charcot met the "problem" head-on and brought hysteria, hitherto marginal, into the mainstream. He legitimized the disease by defining it as an inherited neurological disorder, not madness or malingering. He classified its many sensory deficits, such as hemianesthesia, or loss of feeling on one side of the body, and other sensory disturbances as hysterical "stigmata." Hysteria was a disease that vacillated from one extreme to the other. As Charcot's disciple Bourneville explained, "the hysteric always seems to be outside the rule: sometimes her organs behave in an exaggerated way, sometimes, to the contrary, her functions are slowed to the point of being completely suppressed." A hysteric, he noted, might suffer from anesthesia *and* hypersensitivity, from anorexia *and* bulimia, from constipation *and* diarrhea, from excessive urination *and* urine retention, from both depressed *and* heightened intellectual functions, from insomnia *and* "attacks of sleep."[26] They also collapsed in fits of violent seizures.

Charcot confronted this chaos of symptoms and applied his clinical method. As he had done in his descriptions of ALS and other diseases of the nervous system, Charcot relied on his powers of observation. "He used to look again and again at the things he did not understand," wrote Freud, "to deepen his impression of them day by day, till suddenly an understanding of them dawned on him. In his mind's eye the apparent chaos presented by the continual repetition of the same symptoms then gave way to order: the new nosological pictures emerged, characterized by the constant combination of certain groups of symptoms."[27] By looking, Charcot described what he called "grand hysteria," or major hysteria—a form of the disease that was characterized by episodic convulsions and isolated four distinct phases. First, the epileptoid phase of tonic and clonic seizures, preceded by an aura, or prodrome, mimicked the seizures found in epilepsy. Second, the phase of grand movements, or clownism, simulated the contortions and acrobatics of circus performers. The third phase was called the "*attitudes passionnelles*," or "passionate poses," during which the hysteric acted out emotional states such as terror, ecstasy, and "amorous supplication." The final and fourth stage of the hysterical attack was delirium.

Once the four phases of the "grande attaque" had been established as a paradigm for hysteria, Charcot was quick to clarify that there were many variations on this "archetype" and that the attack could appear in abbreviated versions. (See Figure 2.) What had once been viewed as a chaotic fit of random seizures and inexplicable flailing was now reformulated as a predictable progression of hysterical symptoms. "In the hysterical attack," wrote Charcot, "nothing is left to chance. To the contrary, everything unfolds according to the rules, which are always the same. . . . They are valid for all countries, for all epochs, for all races, and are, in short, universal."[28] Any doctor who had the schema could now diagnose the disease. But diagnosis and cause are distinct. The underlying illness that caused these myriad and baffling symptoms remained ambiguous.

The source of hysteria remained tenaciously equivocal. Charcot was unsuccessful in locating any lesions in the brains or spinal cords of hysterics postmortem, but he nonetheless asserted that there was an organic basis for the disease—he just hadn't found it yet. Charcot talked somewhat paradoxically about a "dynamic" lesion that he believed was located in the brains of hysterics but ended up admitting that hysteria was like "a sphinx that defies anatomy."[29] Without a source, there could be no cure. Indeed, Charcot rarely spoke of a cure for hysteria. Instead, he focused on both managing and visually documenting the disease. Visual representation was crucial to his study of hysteria. Not only was Charcot an artist, so were many of his interns. Hysterical symptoms were reproduced at the Salpêtrière in a number of ways—as staged reenactments, sketches, wax and plaster casts, and photographs. Art became a method to immobilize the tumultuous fits of his patients and order the savage thrashing into a sequence of static images. In his large new amphitheater, Charcot included live demonstrations. Blanche, Augustine, and Geneviève were his stars. These lectures were hugely popular and were attended not only by medical students and doctors but also by members of the general public. The Salpêtrière became a fashionable place to visit; it even became a destination for tourists.[30] Charcot's work as a neurologist had made him an admired physician, but his grand shows that depicted the bizarre symptoms of hysteria increased his renown and made him a figure of the popular imagination.

Charcot's lectures were memorable events. They began with a dramatic entrance: the master would arrive in silence, flanked by his students, and then his patients would be brought in, individually or in groups. Charles Féré, one of Charcot's students, recalled the feather demonstration as a particular crowd pleaser. "The long plumes provoked gaiety in the audience, but soon succeeded, by the variety of their movements, in making his point understood."[31] He lectured from a raised platform with footlights and incorporated large drawings, plaster casts, and wax models. As he spoke, he drew diagrams on a blackboard in colored chalk, and Charcot was among the first to use a photographic projector. To illustrate a point he was making, he mimicked the tremors, tics, spastic gestures, and hampered gaits of his patients. "Everything in his lectures," wrote another one of his students, Pierre Janet, "was designed to attract the attention and to captivate the audience by means of visual and auditory impressions."[32] Charcot's "positively fascinating" teaching style also made a deep impression on Freud, who wrote, "Each of his lectures was a little work of art in construction and composition; it was perfect in form and made such an impression that for the rest of the day one could not get the sound of what he had said out of one's ears or the thought of what he had demonstrated out of one's mind."[33] Charcot's lectures were two hours long, but given the fact that the Salpêtrière

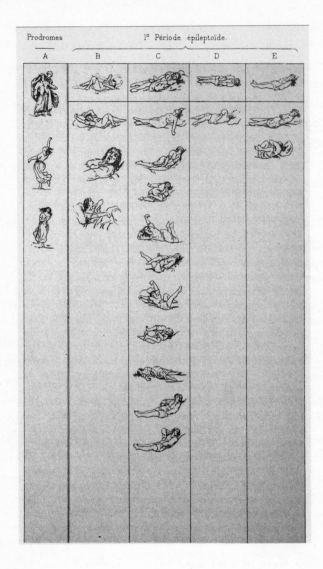

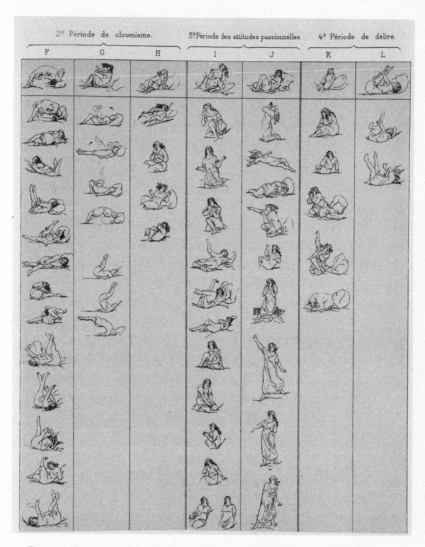

Figure 2. Synoptic table of the major hysterical attack. Drawing by Paul Richer. The top row represents the prototypical positions. The columns beneath each prototypical pose depict possible variations. From Paul Richer, *Études cliniques sur l'hystéro-épilepsie ou grande hystérie*, Paris: Adrien Delahaye et Émile Lecrosnier, 1881.

amphitheater was packed week after week, the audience did not find them tedious. One medical journal, only half facetiously, noted that Charcot's lectures were responsible for causing traffic jams in Paris.

Because Charcot believed that hysteria was a distinctive, universal pathology, he broke away from his predecessors who had located the disease in the female reproductive system. Being a woman had always been considered ground for the disease, and female puberty had often been cited as its original trigger. From adolescence onward, almost anything in the female reproductive cycle was regarded as a possible catalyst for a hysterical attack. Menstruation, amenorrhea, pregnancy, infertility, and menopause were all seen as principle causes, as were excessive sexual stimulation or its opposite, frigidity. One of Charcot's great advancements in the field was his official and adamant rejection of the uterine theory. He repeatedly insisted that hysteria could be found in men just as it could be found in women and hoped to separate the word from its etymology, arguing that its Greek origin—uterus—should be abandoned. Hysteria was a disorder of the nervous system, not the womb. This point, which he frequently reiterated in his lectures and writings, represented a radical departure from previous medical theory.

However, it was soon apparent that even though he emphatically emphasized that hysteria was a disease without gender—a claim that often prefaced his articles on the subject—he nevertheless proceeded as if it were a female condition, and not only because he worked in a hospital for women. Charcot discovered what he called "hysterogenic zones," which created a topography of the female body, a mapping that gave a privileged position to the ovaries and mammary glands. These regions, he claimed, functioned as mechanical buttons of sorts. When pressed, they could trigger or arrest a hysterical attack. Charcot also employed the "ovary compressor," an apparatus that was attached to the patient's abdomen and worked like a vice grip to apply pressure to the hysterogenic zone in order to elicit or suppress a hysterical attack. So while Charcot must be credited with understanding hysteria as a disease of the nervous system, not the uterus, his own adherence to his theory seems to have been ambivalent and vacillating at best. Charcot did provide case studies of male hysterics, but he argued that in men the disease was more often the result of a physical trauma or accident, and, using the metaphor of a seed in hostile soil, claimed that it did not have a very good chance of surviving.[34] Women's bodies, on the other hand, provided fertile ground.

The physical source of the disease may have remained undetected, but late-nineteenth-century Paris had been clearly established as the "hysteria capital of the world."[35] Hysteria was pronounced "the illness of the age" by the prominent journalist, novelist, and playwright Jules Claretie. "One encounters it everywhere. Everywhere one rubs shoulders with it." Guy de Maupassant went even further when he declared, "We are all hysterics."[36] In 1841 and 1842, of the 648 women who had been entered into the hospital's register, only 7, or a little over 1 percent, were diagnosed as hysterics. However, between 1882 and 1883 that number soared to over 20 percent; on average, this meant one new patient a day.[37]

Charcot's Death

Although hysteria made Charcot famous, it also, posthumously, damaged his reputation. On August 16, 1893, Charcot died of pulmonary edema, the complication of a heart condition, while he was on vacation in the Morvan, a region of picturesque villages southeast of Paris. Two of his former students, Georges-Maurice Debove and Isidore Strauss, as well as René Vallery-Radot, Louis Pasteur's son-in-law, were traveling with him. Over a lively dinner at the lakeside inn where they were lodging, Charcot held court, entertaining the younger men with his knowledge of archeology, history, botany, lit-

erature, and art. He then retired to his room, wrote a long letter to
his wife in which he mentioned that he was feeling ill, and went to
bed. In the middle of the night, his companions were called to his
room, where they found Charcot seated at the foot of the bed, desperately trying to catch his breath. "Under my pressing questions," wrote
Debove, "my poor Master told me that he was feeling a little better;
these were his last words. His breathing became slower and finally
stopped. Charcot was dead."[38] His body was brought back to Paris, and
his coffin was placed under the grand dome of the Salpêtrière, where
patients, students, nurses, colleagues, and politicians joined friends
and family to pay their last respects. According to his wishes, there
were no speeches or religious displays at the funeral. Charcot was
buried in the Montmartre Cemetery. The death of the great doctor
was reported in newspapers around the world, and his students and
colleagues created a fund to commission a statue in honor of their
mentor. A clear testament to Charcot's international stature can
be seen in the fact that half of the money raised for the monument
came from outside of France. Three years after he died, a life-size
bronze statue by Alexandre Falguière was unveiled at the entrance of
the Salpêtrière, where it stood until World War II. During the German occupation, the Nazis removed the sculpture and melted it for
scrap metal.

The process of tearing down Charcot, however, began long before
the German army assaulted his statue. His authoritarian rule over the
Salpêtrière for over thirty years and his dominance in the medical
world had inspired both intense loyalty and deep resentment among
his colleagues. He had overseen every step in his students' careers
and had carefully monitored their publications. Over the years, the
Salpêtrière School had become a monolithic institution. Its members were referred to as "Charcot and his disciples," or "Charcot and
his coterie." While he was alive, his "coterie" benefited greatly from
their association with Charcot. In fact, he was so powerful that it

was hard for anyone to gain an appointment to the Paris medical faculty without his approval.[39] But the paternalistic structure of the Salpêtrière also bred bitter conflicts and a kind of sibling rivalry. After his sudden death, disgruntled doctors vied to assert themselves and scrambled for positions of power, while Charcot's devoted students struggled to find their footing on the newly reconfigured academic and professional scene. Affiliation with Charcot, which had been so valuable while he was alive, had become a liability, and unswerving loyalty was no longer rewarded. Gilles de la Tourette, for example, floundered without his mentor and ended up with a marginal position in forensic medicine. Bourneville had already secured a hospital appointment, but his career as a publisher of medical texts foundered. In the new post-Charcot climate, his most successful journal, *Le Progrès Médical*, which had been the main organ for the dissemination of the Salpêtrière School's ideas, fell into financial ruin.

Other students quickly disassociated themselves from Charcot in general and from his description of hysteria in particular. Some of them were no doubt relieved to be free of the authoritarian figure that had dominated their academic and professional lives for so long. I find it interesting that many of these doctors, long after they had graduated from medical school, continued to be called "students," "disciples," and "protégés" of Charcot, terms that have been perpetuated by historians writing about the period. Many of these physicians must have chafed at the subordinate epithets. Charcot's "student" Joseph Babinski, still known in the medical literature for his description of the "Babinski reflex," led the attack on Charcot, but he was not alone. Charcot's theory of hysteria, he argued, was wrong. Babinski then proceeded to dismantle Charcot's description of the illness until it bore so little resemblance to his mentor's that he gave it a new name: "pithiatism." He announced this development in an article with the appropriately violent title: "Dismemberment of Traditional Hysteria: Pithiatism."[40]

Other former disciples joined Babinski in his rejection of hysteria.[41] In 1925, at a lavish celebration of the centenary of Charcot's
birth, his students spoke in glowing terms about their professor's work
until they arrived at his theories of hysteria, which they dismissed
as an embarrassing mistake. Hysteria became a "slight lapse" in an
otherwise brilliant career. George Guinon, Charcot's last chief resident, claimed that Charcot had taken him aside just days before he
died and confessed that his "concept of hysteria was obsolete. A total
revamping of this area of neurological disease is required."[42] Charcot
may very well have spoken these words, but Guinon may also have
invented them to rehabilitate his mentor's tarnished reputation.

Charcot died without finding a lesion for hysteria. Without an eti-
ology, hysteria remained ungrounded, and the diagnosis expanded to
accommodate virtually any pathological breakdown of bodily function that could not be attributed to an organic source. Charcot did
acknowledge the role of suggestion and emotions in the production
of hysterical symptoms and, by doing so, he paved the way for a psychogenic model of the disease. Two years after Charcot died, Freud
claimed that hysterics were suffering not from a lesion in their nervous
system but from repressed memories and ideas.[43] But, while hysteria
also made Freud famous, it ended up damaging his reputation, just
as it had Charcot's. The medical professionals who came after Freud
responded much like the professionals who survived Charcot: they
dismantled the diagnosis and then discarded it altogether. Jacques
Lacan noted the state of things in a playful lament: "Where are the
hysterics of former times, those magnificent women . . . ?"[44]

And while Lacan was surely right that the grand hysterics of Charcot's clinic and Freud's couch have mostly disappeared, hysteria has
survived, but in new incarnations. Many of the same questions that
stumped Charcot—what role does the mind play in the production
of hysterical symptoms, what specific neurological mechanisms are
at work—continue to be asked and have not been fully answered.

Cultural and psychological interpretations of "hysterical" illness, or illness that cannot be attributed to an organic cause, compete with biological explanations. Scientists continue to search for a source, probing brains and genes, but hysteria continues to resist biological explanations. The riddle of Charcot's sphinx has yet to be answered.

PART TWO

Blanche

In the spring of 1877, a frightened eighteen-year-old girl named Marie Wittmann was admitted as a patient to the Salpêtrière Hospital. She was suffering from a variety of symptoms, including convulsions, fainting spells, and temporary bouts of paralysis. Once inside the walls of the hospital, Marie would be diagnosed with hysteria, and this confused and timid teenager would eventually become "Blanche," one of Charcot's star patients, a medical diva whose fame spread throughout Europe, where she became known as "the Queen of Hysterics."

Exactly how she went from Marie, an ill young woman with a host of unpredictable symptoms to a model hysteric used by Charcot to demonstrate the nature of the illness called hysteria, is never addressed in the Salpêtrière's literature. There was, however, plenty of speculation elsewhere. Some of the hospital's most hostile critics claimed that she was merely performing a part written for her by Charcot. Others believed that she was herself the author of an elaborate hoax, deceiving not only a gullible public, but the great master himself. Still others claimed that she was working in cahoots with an intern or a group of interns, who had trained her to perfectly enact Charcot's detailed symptomology.

Charcot and his coterie were sensitive to this criticism, and were always on the lookout for any signs of fraud among his patients. A flair for drama and artful deception was written into the definition of hysteria, which was therefore, by its very nature, an illness that aroused suspicion within the medical community. Located on the problematic border that separated psychosomatic from somatic disorders, hysteria repeatedly defied medical expertise and threatened the specialist's authority. No form of trickery or deception was believed to be beyond the hysteric, and this gift for sham put her in an uneasy relationship with her doctor. Occupying the bizarre position of illness as fraud, hysteria seemed to elude and defy science.

The perceived chicanery of the hysteric prompted a range of responses. Charcot was impressed by "the ruse, the sagacity, and the unyielding tenacity that especially the women display in order to deceive . . . especially when the victim of the deceit happens to be a physician," while other doctors angrily ranted about this tendency for lying.[1] "Nothing pleases them more than leading their examiner down the wrong path, telling absolutely false stories that don't even qualify as embellishments of the truth, to enumerate what they have done and what they have not done with an incredibly luxurious allowance for details. These big lies are stated audaciously, bluntly, in a cold-blooded manner that is completely disconcerting. A doctor who examines hysterics must always keep in mind that they want to fool him, to keep the truth from him, to tell him things that never happened, and to hide from him things that actually did occur."[2] According to another physician, this urge to lie was the central trait of the disease: "One common characteristic unifies hysterics: instinctual simulation, an inveterate and incessant need to lie for no reason and for no end, simply in order to lie."[3] Charcot's loyal disciple Gilles de la Tourette also emphasized the hysteric's deceitful impulses: "The female hysteric represents an extraordinarily complicated type, of a completely particular and excessively versatile nature, remarkable for her spirit of duplicity, lying and simulation. With an essentially perverse nature, the hysteric seeks to fool those around her, in the same way that she has impulses that push her to steal, to falsely accuse, to set things on fire."[4] In order to separate the outright frauds from true hysterics, for whom fraud was an involuntary symptom, Charcot came up with a variety of tests. Needles were poked into arms to prove the veracity of an alleged anesthesia, limbs were placed in gravity-defying positions, bright lights were flashed at pupils. Not even a hysteric, with her remarkable capacity for deception, reasoned the neurologist, could fake physiological responses.

Significantly, Charcot's interest in hysteria coincided with Marie Wittmann's arrival at the Salpêtrière. While his first writings on the subject date from the early 1870s, this work was not particularly notable. During the first half of the 1870s, the Charité Hospital, not Salpêtrière, was considered the leading center for hysteria research. It was not until the mid-1870s that Charcot became known for his research on the disease. From that moment on, the neurologist focused almost exclusively on hysteria, a shift that put both Charcot and his clinic in the limelight. Marie arrived at this moment, and the timing is not irrelevant to the fact that she would become the working proto-type for his reformulation of the disease, something that would propel her, Charcot, and his clinic, to unprecedented medical fame.

Charcot's harshest critics are wrong when they claim that Marie was merely acting in a play directed by Charcot or, conversely, that Charcot was acting in a play directed by his star patient. Yet the Salpêtrière did become something of a school for hysteria.[5] Marie entered with a myriad of vague and difficult-to-diagnose afflictions, and emerged as Blanche, an exemplary hysteric whose symptoms per-fectly fit Charcot's schema. This transformation, I believe, was not a conscious act, but rather one that evolved slowly, shaped by a variety of social and medical conditions. Blanche was not a conniving fraud who deceived the great neurologist. Nor, however, was she the passive victim of a misogynist doctor.

A Hysteric in the Making

Most of the women who ended up at the Salpêtrière had nowhere else to go. The hospital was an enormous institution, and it still functioned as a warehouse for the women Paris no longer wanted. Many suffered from nothing more than extreme poverty and ended up at the Salpêtrière when every other option had disappeared. Blanche Wittmann was no exception. Her childhood was one of sadness, sickness, and deprivation. The only information I have about this period of her life, outside of a birth certificate found in the municipal archives, comes from the doctors who recorded her oral history.

Blanche Wittmann (then called Marie) was born on April 15, 1859, the oldest child of an impoverished Parisian couple. Her childhood was spent in the squalid living conditions prevalent among those at the bottom of Paris's working class. Her father, an unemployed carpenter, was an unstable and violent man. Her mother worked as a laundress, one of the lowest-paid and least-respected jobs available for women at the time. When Blanche was twenty-two months old, she suffered from convulsions that left her partially paralyzed and temporarily deaf and dumb, conditions that improved over time but that would periodically resurface. She also suffered from opthamalia, a chronic infection of the eye, and from such poverty-related conditions as infected scabs on her scalp and severe chilblains, painful sores caused by exposure.

On top of these physical torments, the young Blanche suffered extraordinary emotional pain. Five of her eight siblings died; four from convulsions and one from suspected epilepsy. Even with an infant mortality rate of around 20 percent in mid-nineteenth-century France, this number is extremely high. Her mother, who had nursed Blanche as a baby, and to whom she was particularly attached, was a frail woman subject to frequent "attacks of nerves." Moreover, her father's violence and unpredictable behavior escalated to the point that one day he attempted to throw Blanche out the window. Eventually, he went completely mad, ending up at the notorious Sainte-Anne insane asylum, where he would spend the rest of his life.

Blanche responded to her lot in life with rage. She was a difficult and willful child who would fly into fits of anger at the slightest provocation, rolling on the floor kicking and screaming, sobbing one minute and laughing uncontrollably the next. Her mother attempted, unsuccessfully, to control these outbursts by throwing water in her face. Because of her unruly behavior, she was rarely allowed in school, and this, combined with the developmental delays caused by her early illness, meant that when she first entered the hospital, her reading and writing skills were not at all well developed.

At twelve, she was sent to work as an apprentice for a furrier, and remained in his house for two years. Unfortunately for Blanche, her new environment did little to improve her situation. She continued to suffer from nervous symptoms, including bouts of deafness and muteness, only now they were more pronounced than before. At times she would lose consciousness and bladder control, but as this happened only at night, she was able to hide the severity of her condition from her employer and his wife. When she turned thirteen, the furrier began to pursue her relentlessly, cornering the young girl each time he found her alone, groping and kissing her. On top of trying to hide her illness, she now had to ward off unwelcome sexual advances. When he began to threaten her with beatings, the nervous symptoms she had experienced since early childhood increased both in severity and frequency. She started having tremors and began dropping things. "I would drop everything that I held in my hands," she told her doctors, "and my boss's wife, believing that I was doing it on purpose, or out of spite, made me pay for the things I broke."[6] One day, when she was fourteen years old, the furrier tried to beat her and she ran home to her mother. He made no attempt to get her back.

For the next year, Blanche lived at home with her two surviving brothers and her younger sister, working with her mother as a laundress. Parisian washerwomen worked from fifteen to eighteen hours a day, and many suffered from hernias and back problems caused by carrying heavy loads of wet clothing. In the murky environment inhabited by the lower rungs of French workers, laundresses occupied a particularly miserable position. Their presence near the Seine, where they hauled their loads of dirty laundry, brought them into constant contact with mariners and dockers, and the job was often perceived as a cover for prostitution. For Blanche, however, this period in her life was one of relative stability. With her father locked away at Sainte-Anne and the lecherous furrier no longer a threat, her nervous symptoms diminished. It was during this period that she had her first relationship with a young man named Louis who worked for a jeweler, and lost her virginity to him. Her happiness, however, would be short-lived. Blanche's mother, the only adult she had ever been able to depend on, contracted an upper respiratory infection and died suddenly, leaving the fifteen-year-old girl and her younger siblings alone. The two boys were placed in foster homes, and her little sister, who suffered from what the doctors simply refer to as "weaknesses," was sent to a foundling hospice. Blanche, too old for the state system, had nowhere to go but back to the predatory fur merchant.

It did not take long for the older man to coerce the girl into bed. For the eight months that she remained in his house, she had sexual relations with him on a regular basis. She told her doctors that she often had convulsions and lost consciousness following intercourse, and claimed that she once had an attack during the act itself. Eventually, she ran away and took refuge at the home of a female friend of her mother's. One week later, she left this woman and found work as a *"fille de service,"* or "ward girl," at the Hôpital Temporaire.

Women often turned to public hospitals as a last resort to work as ward girls when they had nowhere else to go. The job was miserably paid and the working conditions were horrendous. A ward girl worked long hours in the hospital as a nursing assistant, mostly cleaning up after the patients, doing the tasks no one else wanted to do. They were lodged in overcrowded barracks with no windows and fed inadequately. Not surprisingly, the job was a transient one: according to one hospital's records that I reviewed, during a one-month period, for every 100 positions, 167 women were hired, and 165 either quit or were fired. On top of the egregious working conditions, the poor women who sought such work suffered from a terrible public image. One journalist from the day wrote that they were "detestable, known for stealing the fruit and candy brought to patients on visiting day, only to try and sell it back to them later."[7] The only reason to go into the profession, he added, was religious devotion or extreme need. What the journalist failed to mention was that ward girls were often culled from the hospitals' own registers. Patients who were capable of working, hysterics in particular, were often hired, as Blanche herself would be later on at the Salpêtrière.

During this period, Blanche fell in love again, with a young man named Alphonse. She would see him on her day off, and after three or four months of working at the hospital, she quit to spend a week with him in the country. The relationship did not last long and, back in Paris, she found herself, yet again, with nowhere to go. She was now suffering from fits of convulsions and loss of consciousness almost every night and was granted asylum in a convent on the rue du Cherche-Midi. After a stay of two months, she was admitted as a patient to the hospital of Saint-Mandé. There she met and fell in love with another Louis, who was frequently with her during her attacks. Her case history does not elaborate any further about who Louis might have been, but it would not be unreasonable to conclude that he was a medical intern, since he was present during her fits, which took place in the middle of the night. Romantic and sexual relationships between hysterics and doctors or medical students were so common that they are casually noted in case histories of hysterics, suggesting that not only was there nothing unusual about the arrangement but no breech of medical ethics had occurred.[8]

An illustration of how nineteenth-century French hospitals turned to their female patients, especially hysterics, for a constant source of cheap labor, Blanche became a ward girl at the same hospital she had been admitted to as a patient. Two months later, while working in the laundry room, she had a hysterical attack, tore the linens, and was fired. She then turned to the Salpêtrière, where she was again hired as a ward girl. Her case history notes that this was done "in order to facilitate her admission to the special epileptic ward." She did her job for several days, sleeping in a bed in the infirmary, and was then admitted to what was called the "none-insane epileptic ward." The day was May 6, 1877. Blanche Wittmann had just turned eighteen. In her short life, she had witnessed the deaths of five siblings and her mother. She had watched her father go insane and be committed to the notorious Sainte-Anne's. She had had sexual relationships with at least four different men, and in one case with a man old enough to be her father who had forced himself on her. She was sexually active in a world that looked upon sexually active unmarried women as perverse and damaged. She had been a washerwoman and a ward girl, among the lowest-paying and most disparaged jobs in the city. When she walked through the gates of the Salpêtrière, little did she know that she would spend the rest of her life behind its doors.

An Unremarkable Beginning

One of the first transformations Blanche underwent at the hospital was her name. Her birth certificate and the hospital registry clearly state her name as Marie Wittmann. Throughout her case history, she is referred to as "W." However, in other medical documents and in the press, she is always called Blanche, Blanche Wit., Blanche Witt., Blanche Wittman, or Blanche Wittmann. Only one week after her admittance to the hospital, on May 14, the name Blanche appears for the first time. Marie herself uttered it, and she used it in the third person. During a fit of delirium following an attack of seizures, she repeatedly called out the name Blanche. The doctors explain that it was the name of her sister. While they use the present tense, her only living sister was named Suzanne, not Blanche, so perhaps it was the name of one of her deceased siblings. One week later, on May 21, she again called out the name: "Blanche! Blanche! Come quick! Blanche! Blanche!" (*Iconographie photographique de la Salpêtrière*, vol. 3, p. 8.)

I don't know why Marie came to be known as Blanche. Yet this inexplicable shift in nomenclature seems to foreshadow the transformation in her identity that would take place over the next decade at Salpêtrière. It is hard to resist speculating on the choice. Blanche, of course, means "white," but it also means "blank," as in a blank page. That Marie, with her messy history became Blanche, ready to receive any identity the doctors might give to her, seems too appropriate to have been merely fortuitous. Because Blanche is the name used most frequently, and the name that became famous, I too, from now on, will refer to Mademoiselle Wittmann as Blanche.

During her first years at the hospital, Blanche did not show any particular promise. She was, in fact, described as being quite ordinary; her habits, we are told, were "precisely those of all hysterics." Many of the traits that would later make her famous—the extraordinary predictability of her attacks, her highly sensitive "hysterogenic zones" (areas on the body thought to trigger hysterical fits) and, most important, her incredible ability to be hypnotized—were not initially present. Even her beauty, which was always mentioned in later accounts, was not noted early on. The first physical description of Blanche recorded reads as follows: "W. is tall (5'3") and corpulent (154 lbs.). She is blond and has a lymphatic complexion. Her skin is white and

Figure 3. "Normal State." Photograph of Blanche Wittmann by Paul
Regnard from Désiré-Magloire Bourneville and Paul Regnard, *Iconographie
photographique de la Salpêtrière*, Volume 3, Paris: Aux Bureaux du Progrès
Médical, Delahaye & Lecrosnier, 1879–1880, Plate 1. Yale University,
Harvey Cushing/John Hay Whitney Medical Library.

freckled. Her breasts are very large. There is a scar on the upper outside part of her left thigh." (See Figure 3.) (*Iconographie photographique
de la Salpêtrière*, vol. 3, p. 7.)

In her early days at the Salpêtrière, Blanche was often unpredictable and unruly. She would lie down in the courtyard and refuse to get
up, and at other times would run off and hide in the hospital's various
laboratories, gardens, or art studio. On June 22, 1878, she managed to
sneak out of the hospital but got no farther than the boulevard that
runs in front of the Salpêtrière before she was caught. For this infraction, she was punished by being put in a cell, a locked room used
to isolate the violent insane women and to punish unruly hysterics.
The last of the actual prison-style cells that had once existed in the
hospital basement was demolished in 1818, during the humanitarian
reforms of "the great emancipator" Philippe Pinel.[9] She could also be
childishly mischievous, and once she and a friend, another hysteric,
locked a group of visitors in the garden and ran off. In order to get out,
one of their captives had to climb over the gate to open the door. At
times she was destructive, grabbing objects and throwing them across
the room, ripping her clothes, and breaking windowpanes. The tar-
gets of her anger were not only inanimate: her case history notes that
she once slapped an epileptic patient and kicked an intern.

It is likely that during this early period in the hospital, Blanche
became addicted to ether. At the very least, she enjoyed its effects and
craved more and more of the drug. Ether, in the form of inhalations,
was among the preferred treatments at the Salpêtrière. It was used
as a sedative to manage the frenetic outbursts of hysteria. Often her
disruptive behavior was provoked by a doctor's refusal to give her as
much ether as she wanted. She kicked the intern because he refused
to give her another inhalation. A few days later, while in the gymnasium, she felt an attack coming on and hurried back to the ward.
Ether was administered, but not as much as she wanted. Once again
she lost her temper and as punishment was again sent to a cell.

A patient's addiction, or at the very least intense cravings for a drug, only enhanced the doctor's already enormous power over her. To a relationship that was already thoroughly unbalanced—the doctors were male, healthy, educated, and bourgeois; the Salpêtrière's hysterics were female, diseased, uneducated, and lower-class—another hierarchical bond can be added: drug dealer and addict. Nor were the doctors oblivious to their patient's increasing tolerance to and desire for the drug. "Initially ether succeeded," wrote Bourneville, the author of her case history, "but little by little its effect was attenuated to the point that, in order to arrest an attack, an enormous dose was needed, which meant a very long inhalation." (*Iconographie photographique de la Salpêtrière*, vol. 3, p. 35.) Blanche herself recognized some of its side effects. She claimed that her memory, previously quite good, had been dulled by her frequent use of ether inhalations.

Not only were some of the medications administered at the Salpêtrière creating addicts, but many of the symptoms Charcot attributed to hysteria may very well have been side effects from the drugs used to treat it. Sleep disorders, violent outbursts, hallucinations, vomiting, fluctuations in appetite, profuse sweating, agitation, listlessness, tremors, and convulsions were all part of Charcot's symptomology of hysteria. They are all also possible side effects from the most frequently administered drugs. In Blanche's case, the effects from ether included hallucinations, angry outbursts, and a ravenous appetite. Following inhalations, she would eat an "enormous amount, all the bread she can get her hands on." (*Iconographie photographique de la Salpêtrière*, vol. 3, p. 23.) Moreover, ether created strange cravings and "perverted" her taste—another symptom attributed to hysteria. Following a dose, she was repelled by meat and desired salad, onions, garlic, artichokes, herring, and she would douse "vinegar on just about all of her food." (*Iconographie photographique de la Salpêtrière*, vol. 3, p. 24.)

After a particularly violent episode on May 11, 1878, almost one year to the date after her arrival, during which she broke windows and tore linens, Charcot banished her from his ward. She was sent to the dreaded section of the hospital where the madwomen were housed. This transfer was not made because Charcot had second thoughts about her diagnosis, but rather to punish her for bad behavior. During her time there, she continued to see the same doctors as before and to receive the same treatments. Hysterics at the Salpêtrière enjoyed a certain amount of freedom within the hospital precisely because they were not considered insane. Since one of Charcot's most adamant claims about the disease was that its sufferers were inflicted with a neurological disorder, not mental illness, the hysterics, along with the old women housed in the hospice, were relatively free to move about the hospital grounds and were allowed to take walks unattended in the courtyard, sometimes even getting passes to leave the hospital for the day. Many of the depictions of the Salpêtrière written by visitors include descriptions of hysterics strolling about the grounds on their own or with friends, stopping by the photography laboratory or the art studio, taking classes in the gymnasium or chatting with interns, indicating a hospital policy that gave the hysterics a generous amount of freedom and choice. Once she was sent to the section for the insane, Blanche lost almost all of this freedom to move about and spent far more time confined to a cell than she did in the hysteria ward, where cells were used only for occasional confinements and punishments.

The threat of being banished to the ward for the mad was constantly present and, as hospital records show, not infrequently acted upon. Jules Claretie, who was invited by Charcot to spend time in the hospital, discussed this fear in his novel *Les amours d'un interne* (The Loves of an Intern) set in the Salpêtrière:

> To be sent to the ward for the insane! To cross that threshold! (. . .) To descend one degree further into that hell where human reason has been swallowed up in a black nothingness! This was the greatest fear of the hysterics, who were still free to

come and go, to sit on the park benches and take in the fresh
air, just like the old women, those who were "admitted" to the
hospital (not "committed" there.) To be transferred meant a loss
of freedom. (. . .) Only a thin line separated the wards, but
that line contained an entire world. On one side of it, sickness;
on the other, madness. On one side, free will—at least when
not in the throes of an attack. On the other, anything could
happen. It spelled the end. You disappeared, melting into madness and nothingness.[10]

Blanche would spend seven and a half months with the madwomen
before she was deemed sufficiently chastised and returned to the hysteria ward. This would be her one and only stay in the ward for the
insane. It was upon her return to Charcot's section that her behavior
began to change and with this change came increased attention and
interest. Her career as a successful hysteric had begun in earnest.

The Education of a Hysteric

Over the next decade, Blanche Wittmann would develop from an
ordinary hysteric into an exemplary one. She became a "queen" whose
talent and beauty were widely recognized. Her symptoms, which had
at first been unpredictable, became prototypical, medically perfect.
Blanche was held up as living proof of the Salpêtrière School's theories, the embodiment of Charcot's symptomology. As the prototypical
hysteric of the Salpêtrière School, she was also singled out by Charcot's critics as a prime example of the great neurologist's deception.
On the one hand, Charcot was accused of perpetuating a medical
fraud, and on the other, he was accused of being the dupe of a conniving hysteric.

Surrounded by physicians and medical students, Blanche was

chosen to demonstrate her symptoms before audiences. She was used as a living illustration and was photographed, sketched, painted, and reproduced in wax and plaster. She was featured in newspaper columns, magazine articles, and fictionalized in plays and novels. If hysteria was not actively "manufactured" at the Salpêtrière, as some claimed, it was most definitely cultivated. Charcot's hysteria must be understood, at least in part, as an iatrogenic illness, that is, one that was created in the clinic, forged between patient and doctor. Blanche arrived with a set of symptoms, Charcot did not fabricate them. However, over the years, her symptoms were molded, altered, and tweaked to fit his elaborate nosology. Human beings, as a rule, adapt to fit social norms, and patients adapt to medical standards.

Freud's frequently repeated comment, that his French mentor Charcot was a "*visuel*," is accurate. Charcot described the physical characteristics of hysteria in great detail, and repeatedly produced visual representations of its various poses in photographs, drawings, wax casts, as well as staged reenactments. Blanche and the other hysterics were surrounded by these images and therefore, even if no one was verbally coaching them, they most certainly knew what was expected of them. The walls of the amphitheater, of the laboratories, even those in Charcot's office, were filled with images of Charcot's various stages of hysteria. One visitor, the Belgian philosopher Joseph Delboeuf, described the clinic as a kind of museum:

> [The] walls, and even the ceiling, were decorated with anatomy drawings, paintings, etchings and photographs depicting patients alone or in groups, naked or dressed, seated, lying down or standing. Sometimes the images depicted one or two legs, a hand, a torso or another body part. There were cabinets all around, filled with skulls, spinal columns, tibias and humeri presenting one anatomical peculiarity or another. A pell-mell of bottles, instruments and apparatuses were scattered here and

there, on tables and in vitrines. There were wax images not
yet finished, an old nude woman spread out on a kind of bed
and busts, among them one of Gall [Franz Joseph Gall was the
founder of phrenology], painted green.[11]

For a young woman like Blanche, it would have been apparent
that there were rewards to be had by providing the appropriate symptoms, and as she knew all too well, punishments for not cooperating.
Even by Charcot's own reasoning, then, it would have been quite
natural for a hysteric to simulate the desired symptoms, so prominently displayed. Yet, since simulation and suggestibility are written
into Charcot's very definition of hysteria, what outsiders might consider outright fraud was simply labeled "symptom" inside the clinic.
Blanche's transformation into a model patient was a resounding success. A productive collaboration between doctor and patient occurred
and Blanche emerged from the encounter as the prototypical hysteric.
She was repeatedly held up as the ideal specimen of hysteria, one to
which other hysterics presented endless variations.

Mapping the Hysterical Body

What would later become known as Blanche's remarkably responsive
"hysterogenic zones" were not particularly sensitive during her early
years at the hospital. "Hysterogenic zones," spots on the hysterical
body charted by Charcot, would trigger or arrest an attack when they
were pressed. (See Figure 4.) In any medical investigation, the body
becomes a kind of map. Diagnosis creates new routes and previously
undistinguished areas are reclassified and given new significance. The
female body, that "dark continent" of the nineteenth century, was
presented to doctors as uncharted territory in need of scientific exploration. Charcot confronted the chaos of the hysterical female body

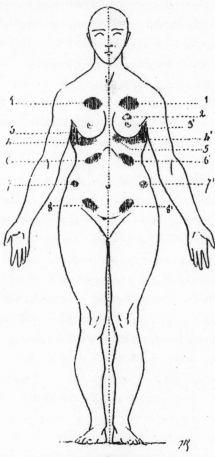

Fig. 9. — Principales zones hystérogènes
Face antérieure du corps.
1, 1'. Zones sus-mammaires.
2. Zone mammaire.
3, 3'. Zones sous-axillaires.
4, 4', 5. Zones sous-mammaires.
6, 6'. Zones costales.
7, 7'. Zones iliaques.
8, 8'. Zones ovariennes.

Figure 4. Hysterogenic zones. Drawing by Paul Richer from *Études cliniques sur l'hystéro-épilepsie ou grande hystérie*, Paris: Adrien Delahaye et Émile Lecrosnier, 1881.

and created a new topography, one that included a map of "hysterogenic zones," mechanical buttons of sorts. These zones were located
on the trunk of the body and privileged the ovaries and, to a lesser
degree, the breasts. By focusing on the ovaries, Charcot shifted attention away from the uterus, the traditional locus for hysteria. However,
by doing so he also undermined his own claim that hysteria should
not be thought of as a disease of the female reproductive organs.

When she first arrived at the Salpêtrière, Blanche's hysterogenic
zones are described as follows: "W . . . presents several hysterogenic
regions found on the outer edge of each breast and at the level of the
intercostals. They are two to three centimeters in diameter. According
to the patient, there is no difference between the two sides; pressing
on one of these areas alone does not produce an attack, but makes her
swallow. Simultaneous energetic pressure immediately produces a
convulsive crisis. Pressure is painful on each side of the fifth dorsal
vertebra, but does not bring about an aura. Both ovarian regions are
hyperaesthesiac." (*Iconographie photographique de la Salpêtrière*, vol. 3,
p. 25.) Nor were her responses to compression particularly consistent.
On May 21, two weeks after her arrival, Charcot was unable to stop
an attack with ovarian compression. Even two years later, pressing
one of her hysterogenic zones did not trigger convulsions: "Today,
even strong pressure is powerless to bring about an attack." (*Iconographie photographique de la Salpêtrière*, vol. 3, p. 26.)

Applying ovarian pressure presented quite a physical challenge
to the doctor. "The best position for a successful demonstration,"
explained Charcot, "is for the patient to be stretched out horizontally on the floor, or if possible, on a mattress. . . . Then the doctor,
with one knee on the ground, plunges his closed fist into [her ovarian
region]. Most important, he must call on all of his forces in order to
vanquish the rigidity of the abdominal muscles."[12] Perhaps the act
of plunging a clenched fist into a prostrate female body too closely
resembled a sexual assault, or perhaps the task was simply too ardu-

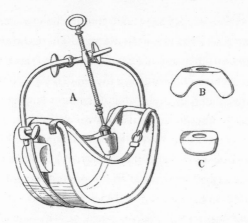

Figure 5. Ovary compressor. Drawing from Désiré-Magloire Bourneville and Paul Regnard, *Iconographie photographique de la Salpêtrière*, Volume 2, Paris: Aux Bureaux du Progrès Médical, Delahaye & Lecrosnier, 1878. Yale University, Harvey Cushing/John Hay Whitney Medical Library.

ous for the doctors, for Charcot had a Dr. Poirier develop a device called an "ovary compressor." (See Figure 5.) This bizarre apparatus was attached to the patient's abdomen and worked like a vice grip with a descending knob that applied pressure to the ovary. In spite of its resemblance to something that might have been used in medieval torture, it was not unusual for hysterics to request it. One day in the early fall of 1879, Blanche felt the usual phenomena of an aura that signaled an attack was coming on: pain in her left ovarian region, the famous "globus hystericus" (the sensation of a ball rising up in the throat felt by most of the Salpêtrière's hysterics); heart palpitations; visual and aural disturbances; intestinal rumbles; and fluctuation between extreme pallor and flushness. Along with these physical sensations, Blanche would also experience bizarre mood swings in which she would laugh one minute and cry the next. Not wanting to miss out on a session of physical education taking place in the hospital gymnasium, she asked for the ovary compressor. After her request was granted, she was able to participate in the class, even with the bulky compressor attached. Once the class was over, she returned to her bed, removed the compressor and her attack began.

Blanche eventually became the hospital's most responsive patient to the device. Paul Richer, a doctor at the Salpêtriére and a professor of artistic anatomy at the École des Beaux-Arts in Paris, wrote that she would wear it "for twelve, twenty-four, even forty-eight hours at a time in order to ward off an impending attack. An attack never appeared during the compression. It was when we stopped the compression that her attacks reappeared."[13] In time, she became so responsive to ovarian compression that Richer speaks of her as a mechanical toy, a kind of "music box" that could play several tunes, always in the same order. "This order is so invariable," he writes, "that if by ovarian compression one suppresses attack #1 at its onset, attack #2 begins. Allow me a somewhat banal comparison, but one that seems to me to express what happens here: our patient resembles one of those music boxes that play several different tunes, but always in the same order. If we successively stop one, two or three attacks, it is as though we have skipped one, two or three notches in the music box, and if we let the next attack follow its course, it is the following motif, #4, that is carried out. This occurs to such a degree in this patient that we can choose to let one or another of her attacks unfold."[14]

Joseph Delboeuf also used a musical metaphor in describing the remarkable precision of Blanche's responses: The doctor "played her as though she were a piano, and . . . he played any tune."[15] In repeatedly enacted scenarios, performed before live audiences in the clinic's amphitheater, Charcot and his students would transform Blanche into a mechanical doll that would respond appropriately when her "buttons," or hysterogenic zones, were pushed.

Dermagraphism: Inscribing the Hysterical Body

Blanche's body was molded to respond appropriately in a variety of ways, including the bizarre medical art known as "dermagraphism."Indeed, Charcot's plans for Blanche were literally spelled out on her body in an early experiment. Dermagraphism involved the literal inscription of words and images on the patient's skin.[16] Given that some hysterics were known to have extreme cutaneous sensitivity, their skin would become red and raised when lightly traced with a blunt object, the marks lasting anywhere from three hours to three months. A doctor described the amazing facility and success he had in drawing shapes and writing words on his hysterical patients' bodies: "If we lightly trace a name or a figure on the shoulders, chest, arms, or thighs of our patient, we see, almost instantly a bright red line appear. Two minutes later, the letter or the inscription appears in the form of a pale pink line (. . .) We have on numerous occasions obtained inscriptions that are distinct enough to read from a distance of twenty meters."[17] Physicians marveled at the endless creative possibilities the blank page of the hysteric's body offered: "We can vary the experiment in thousands of ways, producing the most varied drawings on her skin."[18] At times the doctor's diagnosis—for example, *"démence précose"* (dementia praecox)—was recorded on the back of a patient, a striking example of how medical authority fixated the female body.[19] In other cases, the vocabulary of demonology appeared, pointing to an intersection of positivism and the occult. The words "Satan" and "démoniaque" were written on the backs, arms, and chests of hysterics. At times her body was a canvas on which images or decorative ornaments were drawn; indeed, doctors frequently dated and signed their names on their "works of art."[20] (See Figure 6.)

In one case, a doctor dermagraphically "programmed" his patient:

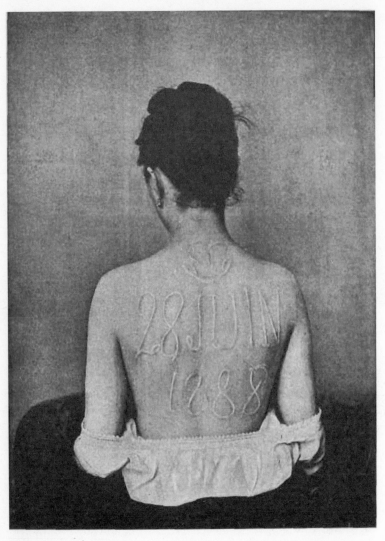

Figure 6. A dermagraphic experiment. Photograph from Ernst Mesnet, "Autographisme et stigmates," *Revue de l'hypnotisme experimental et thérapeutique*, 1889–1890. Courtesy of the New York Academy of Medicine Library.

he traced his name on the hysteric's arms with a rubber stylus and instructed her to bleed from the letters he had drawn at four o'clock that afternoon. At the appointed hour, his name appeared on her skin, with several drops of blood, and remained visible for more than three months.[21] The idea of "possession" could hardly be dramatized better than this: of course this "possession" is that of a patient by her doctor. To emphasize his ownership, the man signed her. And, like a member of some Satanic cult, the physician inscribed himself on the body with the victim's own blood. Such grotesque examples prompt the critique that here is sadism masquerading as science. At the very least, the science of hysteria articulated a desire to possess and immobilize women.[22]

In August of 1878, Blanche had her destiny literally inscribed on her body. The authors of the *Iconographie* explain: "We used the point of a stylus to trace the name of the patient on her chest, and on her abdomen, we traced the word 'Salpêtrière.' This produced a red stripe that was several centimeters high, and on this band the letters appeared in relief, about two millimeters wide. Little by little the redness disappeared, but the letters persisted." (*Iconographie photographique de la Salpêtrière*, vol. 3, p. 19.) The next day, Blanche slept until noon. The words, though less prominent, were still visible and resembled scratches. Two days later, Blanche was overcome by an attack in the courtyard. She was brought back to the dormitory, where the compressor was applied and chloroform administered. Once again the doctors experimented with dermagraphism: "We write the name of the patient with the point of a pin across the upper part of her chest, the word 'August' on each leg, and 'Salpêtrière' on her abdomen. A quite large reddened stripe develops promptly; then, the letters appear in relief. This phenomena appears more slowly on the legs than on the chest or the abdomen." (*Iconographie photographique de la Salpêtrière*, vol. 3, p. 19.)

The following day, the words on her chest and abdomen were still legible, but the date inscribed on her legs had almost completely disappeared. The date, which isolated the incident in time, faded, leaving behind only "Blanche Wittmann" and "Salpêtrière." Her role as prototype, as the Salpêtrière mascot, had literally been inscribed on her body. Her medical notes for that day, end as follows: "W. hid in the gardens until 11:00 at night." (*Iconographie photographique de la Salpêtrière*, vol. 3, p. 19.) It is hard not to read this as a last defiant moment of resistance to her sentence in the hospital, one that was not merely given her, but, like Kafka's prisoner, written *on her body*; a last-ditch effort to escape her fate, a fate that she would eventually yield to and even embrace.

Hypnotism

Hypnotism played the most significant role in Blanche's metamorphosis from an unstable sickly child to a proud medical diva. Shortly after her arrival at the Salpêtrière, Charcot began to incorporate hypnotism into his practice. The year was 1878, and at that time this "science of magnetic fluids" or "animal magnetism" was a medical taboo. Ever since Franz Anton Mesmer had theorized, more than a century earlier, that an invisible "universal fluid" yielded a cosmic influence on living organisms, connecting man and the universe in ways that resembled the attraction between magnets and metallic objects, hypnotism had been soundly denounced by the scientific community. Disease, claimed Mesmer, was caused by a corporal imbalance of this fluid and could be cured by restoring harmony. Forced to leave Vienna, Mesmer settled in Paris, where he conducted highly theatrical "group healings" in which his participants, mostly women, were "mesmerized" by the wand-wielding, purple-robed master into hypnotic trances from which they awoke refreshed and healed, cured of whatever had ailed them. Louis XVI appointed a royal commission to

determine the validity of "animal magnetism," and the committee—
which included Benjamin Franklin—came to the verdict that no
such thing existed.[23]

In spite of repeated and unqualified rejections by the scientific
community, hypnotism, or magnetism, or animal magnetism, as it was
also called, survived. Nevertheless, it was held in such contempt by
the medical establishment that physicians who persisted in research-
ing the phenomenon did so in secrecy. But when the world's leading
neurologist began to take the subject seriously and incorporate it into
his practice, the Academy of Science, which had on three separate
occasions officially condemned the entire field, reversed its position.
Charcot had succeeded in legitimizing a thoroughly discredited field,
and magnetizers of all kinds, both inside and outside the scientific
community, once dismissed as charlatans, enjoyed a new status. During the 1880s, publications on the phenomenon numbered in the
thousands. Hypnotism in all of its manifestations, from the hocus-
pocus of traveling stage shows to Charcot's "medical" demonstrations,
became enormously popular.

Just as Charcot had provided a rational framework for the irratio-
nal symptoms of hysteria, he systematized hypnotic phenomena into
three main categories that he considered to be versions of their hysterical counterparts: lethargy, catalepsy, and somnambulism. Charcot
rejected Mesmer's notion of occult forces and postulated that hypnosis was an induced neurosis that was only possible in hysterics. He distinguished between what he called "auto hypnosis," which occurred
when these phases erupted spontaneously, that is, during a hysterical
attack, and "artificial hypnosis" in which they were induced by a hypnotist. "Between hypnotic lethargy, catalepsy and somnambulism,"
explained Gilles de la Tourette, articulating his master's position,
"and hysterical lethargy, catalepsy and somnambulism, there is only
one difference, which is that these first states are provoked, and the
others are spontaneous."[24]

Charcot's position that hypnosis imitated hysteria, and that there-fore the susceptibility to be hypnotized was a symptom of hysteria, was not accepted by the medical community without a fight. Because the hypnotic state had no anatomical basis, yet was capable of producing physical symptoms, it belonged, Charcot insisted, in the symptomol-ogy of hysteria. His most outspoken critics came from the Faculty of Medicine at the University of Nancy. Ambroise-Auguste Liébeault, Jules Liégeois, and especially Hippolyte Bernheim argued that the ability to be hypnotized was a normal and universal phenomenon. They insisted that they had successfully hypnotized many healthy subjects. Bernheim also claimed that he had never seen the three stages of "artificial hysteria" except in a patient who had spent three years at the Salpêtrière. He accused the Parisian of conditioning his patients to play a role, which was all part of what he dubbed Charcot's "hystero-culture." The Nancy School maintained that any influence exerted by hypnosis was entirely psychological, a claim that would later be supported by Freud. Charcot and his supporters, among them Gilles de la Tourette and Joseph Babinski, struck back, attacking the research conducted at Nancy as being unscientific, and a bitter and very public debate ensued. Initially, the Salpêtrière School won most of the arguments. However, the Nancy School gradually gained adherents and Charcot's position became increasingly untenable. Fol-lowing his death in 1893, the Nancy School claimed full victory.

Blanche found herself at the center of this controversy. She had become Charcot's most hypnotizable hysteric and that, combined with the predictability of her hysterogenic zones, meant that she was the one most often chosen for public demonstrations. Blanche, however, had not always been an ideal candidate for hypnosis. An attempt to hypnotize her on an early fall morning in 1877 had not been an unqualified success. While she was successfully hypnotized and several muscles were contracted, the doctor was unable to release those that held her tongue and larynx muscles. Even when awakened and then put back under, her tongue and larynx remained frozen, rendering the young woman completely unable to speak. Eventually, the doctor successfully released her tongue, but her larynx remained contracted. Only after administering chloroform did her larynx relax and her vocal chords function. Later, however, she would become Charcot's most hypnotizable patient. Frederic W. Myers, the British founder of the Society for Psychical Research, who like so many others came to visit the Salpêtrière, described Blanche to his readers: "Blanche Witt- is one of the best known personalities—or groups of personalities—in Paris. A hystero-epileptic of the most pronounced type, she has never been able for long together to meet the stresses of ordinary life. She has long been an inmate of the Salpêtrière; and some of my readers may have seen her exhibited there, at Prof. Charcot's lectures, or by the kindness of Dr. Féré or other physicians, as the type—I may almost say the *prototype*—of the celebrated 'three stages' of lethargy, catalepsy, and somnambulism, of which she realized every characteristic detail with marvelous precision."[25] Other visitors would not be so generous in their assessments. Blanche's remarkable ability was used by the Nancy School and other critics as proof that these demonstrations were staged, that Blanche and the other hysterics on display were merely highly trained actresses. Charcot fought back, insisting on the scientific veracity of his experiments.

Contemporary medical thought regarding hypnosis has certainly sided with the Nancy School in this argument. In fact, Charcot's ideas about hypnosis are largely responsible for the precipitous decline in his reputation following his death in 1893. Many of his former disciples could not distance themselves enough from their former hero and master. Yet, while Charcot certainly deserves some of this criticism, it is wrong to completely discredit his work with hypnosis. In an era before Freud's major work, Charcot's writings on hypnosis are brilliantly prescient. Freud understood this, and his admiration for Charcot can in part be explained by a sense of indebtedness. By equating hysterical symptoms with hypnotically induced symptoms, Charcot did nothing less than pave the way for psychoanalysis. He understood, for example, that a hysteric might suffer paralysis following an accident even when there was no physical explanation for that paralysis. According to Charcot, the very *idea* of physical trauma that accompanied the accident was enough to create the paralysis. It was this "auto suggestion" that Charcot equated with hypnotic suggestion, an equation that led him to misjudgments, if not out-and-out mistakes, but an equation that also pointed the neurologist toward a psychological explanation for physical suffering, years before Freud. More than a century later, the relationship between the somatic and the psychological remains mysterious.

My intention here is not to support the Salpêtrière School as opposed to the Nancy School, but rather to look at the ways in which Charcot used hypnotism to create an artificial and improved version of Blanche. Unlike the Nancy School, which focused on hypnotic suggestion as a treatment, the purpose of the experiments at the Salpêtrière was never explicitly therapeutic. Hypnosis was not used to cure or even alleviate Blanche's or any other patient's hysteria. Rather, it was used to create an artificial world in which hysterical symptoms could be reproduced and transformed, a world in which the hysteric could be completely mastered. Once hypnotized, the physician would instruct, or "suggest" that the hysteric follow his orders, an arrangement that worked beautifully in the artificial world created through magnetism, but which was rarely successful in the real world. As Charcot himself noted, if suggestion functioned in the natural hysteric in the same way that it did in her artificial version, all the physician need do in order to cure hysteria would be to suggest to the patient that she was healthy. Hypnotism, then, was not used to cure the patient of a natural disease, but rather to create an "artificial" hysteric in whom doctors could reproduce symptoms at will, and then just as easily, make them disappear. "Between the normal functions of the organism and the spontaneous disorders that the illness causes," wrote Charcot, "hypnosis becomes a kind of open path to experimentation. The hypnotic state is nothing but an artificial nervous state . . . , whose multiple manifestations appear and disappear according to the needs of the study. . . ."[26] Unlike the symptoms of natural hysteria, which often manifested themselves in what Charcot referred to as "*formes frustes*"—that is, unpolished or crude forms— artificial symptoms produced in hypnosis were impeccable. Depending on the stage of the hypnotic trance, the physician could provoke an exemplary anesthesia or a perfect paralysis, modify it according to his desires, and then with a single word or gesture, erase it. "A paralysis created through suggestion," Charcot continues, "can be altered in any way we like, and through suggestion, can even be completely undone."[27]

Hypnosis was the first step in a transformation from natural to artificial and was used effectively to turn the "natural" hysteric, with all her unpredictable symptoms and deceptions, into an artificial woman whose corporal and mental plasticity rendered her completely malleable, ready to be reinvested by science. Once hypnotized, the hysteric was under the complete control of her magnetizer. Charcot used hypnosis in order to better analyze his specimens, to control them and prepare them for medical probing and mechanical reproduction, and ultimately, to reconstruct an ideal specimen, embodied by Blanche Wittmann.

Catalepsy: Statues and Automatons

Just as Charcot imposed order on the chaos of the hysterical attack, he structured the hypnotic state into his "celebrated" three distinct phases: catalepsy, lethargy, and somnambulism. In Charcot's three-part schema, a new topography of the hysteric's body was mapped out in which specific regions responded to different stimuli, triggering the desired result.

According to Charcot's schema, the hypnotist could bring about the cataleptic state through a variety of means, such as shining a bright light in the subject's eyes, brandishing an incandescent strip of magnesium before her, or by sounding a gong, a whistle, a drum, or a tuning fork. These stimuli prompted the patient to go limp and numb; she felt no physical sensation.

During catalepsy the subject's eyes remained open but unblinking, giving her the appearance of being awake. She was also endowed with what the doctors speak of as "waxen flexibility," and could maintain any position she was "molded into." (See Figure 7.) This condition gave rise to innumerable comparisons between the cataleptic hysteric and a wax doll, or in Charcot's words, "a kind of statue." In fact, the image of the doll or the statue crops up again and again in the medical descriptions of the cataleptic patient, an altogether appropriate trope for the artificial and idealized forms the physician created.

One of the many American physicians to visit the Salpêtrière, W. J. Morton, uses a slightly different image—that of a wax figure—to describe Blanche, or "Witt.," as he refers to her. "Body and limbs now maintain any position in which they are placed; in short, we have the condition familiarly known as catalepsy. If the arm is raised to a right angle with the body, it remains so; if the leg is placed in a similar position, it does not fall. The patient may be moulded at will like a waxen figure, into any pose one pleases, and the position will be retained. The patient is totally anaesthetic, whether so previously or not. She makes no response to questions, nor in any way gives any sign of being in communication with the external world; the eyes are wide open."[28] In order to prove she was completely anesthetized, physicians pierced her with needles. With pins poking through her body, the patient clearly, if gruesomely, manifested her status as an artificial woman, with no organic interior. The photographs docu-

Figure 7. "Catalepsy: Provoked Pose." Photograph of Blanche Wittmann by Paul Regnard from Désiré-Magloire Bourneville and Paul Regnard, *Iconographie photographique de la Salpêtrière*, Volume 3, Paris: Aux Bureaux du Progrès Médical, Delahaye & Lecrosnier, 1879–1880, Plate 9. Yale University, Harvey Cushing/John Hay Whitney Medical Library.

menting these experiments show no blood that would suggest the
woman's corporal reality. As Paul Regnard, a student of Charcot and
the photographer of the *Iconographie photographique de la Salpêtrière*
writes, "We can cut them, prick them, and burn them, and they feel
nothing. Even better, these completely numb spots are so poorly irri-
gated that when we wound them, there is not one drop of blood. The
hysterics are very proud of this immunity and amuse themselves by
passing long needles through their arms and legs."[29] In an engraving
made from one of Regnard's photographs, Blanche appears to have
been transformed into an object, from a flesh and blood woman into
a doll. (See Figure 8.)

Claretie, in his Salpêtrière novel, provided a fictional account that
differs little from the medical descriptions. In fact, if a difference in
tone can be found, it is that the novelist's passage is more "scientific,"
filled with more medical terminology than the physicians' passages
quoted above. In the following description, a doctor has just hypnotized the hysteric Lolo: "Lolo is in a state of catalepsy. The physician
touches the skin near her neck very lightly, just above the sterno-
cleido mastoid, and right away the tall girl seemed to be afflicted
with torticollis, given the tilted position of her head. . . . It seemed as
though the cataleptic's brain had been shaped, just like a wax mould,
to give the impression that the doctor desired (. . .) [He] was the
master of this lump of flesh, of its thoughts and feelings, which had
become even easier to shape between his fingers than a lump of clay
is beneath the hands of a sculptor."[30]

Like the fictional Lolo, the cataleptic Blanche could be molded as
though she were a lump of clay into any desired form, and unlike her
natural state, in which her body manifested disorder, her artificial version displayed complete synchronicity between her physical gestures
and her facial expressions. All the physician needed to do to create
a particular expression was to "sculpt" the appropriate gesture. As
the American doctor who visited the Salpêtrière explained: "There

Figure 8. "Hysterical Anesthesia." Engraving from a photograph of Blanche Wittmann by Paul Regnard from *Les maladies épidémiques de l'esprit. Sorcellerie, magnétisme, morphinisme, délire des grandeurs*, Paris: E. Plon, Nourrit et Cie, 1887.

exists but one method of producing in her any external evidence of intellection. This constitutes the curious phenomenon called 'suggestion.' If, for instance, the now waxen limbs are placed in a pose which indicates aversion, i.e. with the arms fully extended in front and the palms of the hands turned outward, the muscles of the face at once contract, and its whole expression is that of aversion. If again, her hand is placed at the lips, as in the act of throwing a kiss, the face at once breaks into a smile."[31] The stormy female body has been transformed into a predictable machine.

Hypnosis, then, was not used at the Salpêtrière, as it is often used today, to discover a hidden truth and reunite the subject with some notion of an original but forgotten self or an earlier history, but rather to completely erase inner content. "Magnetic sleep" pushed the rupture, the dislocation between organic source and physical symptom that characterized the disease to such an extreme that the original vanished entirely. In repeated demonstrations, Charcot sought to bypass this rupture and externalize it completely. This process— less a question of "turning the inside out" than of eradicating the inside altogether—turned the hysteric into a kind of pure sign of her illness.

In her unnatural hypnotized state, Blanche no longer menaced medical authority by blurring the categories of real and unreal. Her original contradiction was replaced by unity. Unlike her original, this representation of illness was a demystified image. Her symptoms were completely ordered. Obscurity and chaos were replaced by clarity and harmony. Once hypnotized, Blanche became a smoothly running woman-machine whose inscribed gestures were in complete harmony with her expressions. Gilles de la Tourette and Richer referred to the hypnotized hysteric as "an actual automaton who obeys each and every order given by her magnetizer."[32] Significantly, the physicians employed the verb "imprint" to describe their actions, and the noun "operator" to describe their role: "One of the main characteristics of the state of hypnotic catalepsy," wrote Gilles de la Tourette and Richer, "outside of the lightness of the limbs and their ability to maintain any given position, consists in the harmony, in the perfect coordination that always presided over the variety of positions that we imprint on the subjects. (. . .) The movements imprinted on the diverse parts of the body, in as much as they are expressive, are followed to a fatal degree by secondary movements destined to complete the primitive expression started by the hand of the operator."[33]

These imprinted gestures and their corresponding expressions could be infinitely varied, from the most banal (such as wiping her nose) to the most sublime (kneeling, with hands pressed together in ecstatic prayer): "When these poses are expressive, the face harmonizes with them and has the same expression. Therefore, a tragic pose imprints a sad look on the face, the eyebrows contract. To the contrary, if we place both hands in an open position on the mouth, as if in the act of blowing a kiss, a smile immediately appears on the lips. In this circumstance, the gesture's action on the facial expression is very gripping and comes about very precisely. In this way we can vary the positions infinitely. Ecstasy, prayer, humility, sadness, defiance, anger, fear . . . can all be represented."[34] In short, the possibilities were endless, limited only by the doctor's imagination.

This woman automaton, with her infinite capabilities, ran so smoothly that the physician, or "operator," could even run it in reverse, creating facial expressions to produce the corresponding gesture. However, because of the obvious difficulties in molding the face, a new technique of electrical stimulation, created by Charcot's close friend and colleague Duchenne de Boulogne, was used. Incredibly, Blanche, the woman-machine, was animated by electricity. An electric probe was applied to her face that would set in motion an entire repertoire of facial expressions. By stopping the current once the desired look appeared, the expression would remain indefinitely imprinted, and the appropriate gesture would follow mechanically.[35]

As Charcot explained: "Once produced, the movement imprinted on the facial features cannot be erased, even when the source, the electrode, is taken away. The expression remains immobile in catalepsy, and the same is true for the attitude and gesture that accompany it."[36] Blanche and the other hysterics who participated in these experiments did not actually experience any of these emotions, as Gilles de la Tourette and Richer pointed out. Through hypnosis, the doctor could annihilate the natural woman's content and turn her into an empty shell.

The hypnotized Blanche had been effectively changed into a machine. Moreover, this desire to render the organic mechanical was explicitly articulated. Charcot spoke of his artificial hysteric as an incarnation of La Mettrie's "man-machine": "In her utter simplicity, what we have before our eyes is an actual version of the man-machine dreamed up by La Mettrie."[37] However, Charcot's woman-machine was no ordinary toy; she was not one of the crude dolls created by Vaucanson, the eighteenth-century inventor of the automaton. Gilles de la Tourette and Richer insisted on the extraordinary sophistication of their creation. Catalepsy "transforms the patient into *a perfectly docile automaton*, without any stiffness, on which one can imprint, with the greatest of ease, the most varied positions. Moreover, these positions are always harmonious, making our automaton something more than a simple mechanism à la Vaucanson. Her expressions harmonize all by themselves with the gestures that are imprinted, and vice versa."[38]

In his description of the cataleptic hysteric, Dr. Foveau de Courmelles, one of the pioneers of electrotherapy, blended all of these various images—the statue, the wax figure, and the automaton: "Although at first an inert, plastic mass of flesh and bones . . . the cataleptic subject allows herself to be molded at the will of the operator. She becomes a soft wax figure on which the most fantastic emotions can be imprinted, she is an automaton capable of being animated."

And, unable to resist the obvious, he adds: "Like another Pygmalion, the hypnotizer gives life to Galatea, and the living marble becomes an impulsive and active being."[39] An impulsive and active being whose impulses and actions are not her own, but those of her Pygmalion.

Lethargy: The Petrified Woman

According to Charcot, the lethargic state was induced by closing the cataleptic subject's eyes. In lethargy the hysteric went into a deep, sleeplike state in which her eyes remained closed. She was now, claimed Gilles de la Tourette and Richer, like "a cadaver before rigor mortis had set in."[40] In this deep sleep, the lethargic subject's arms and legs would fall back heavily when raised, unlike the cataleptic's waxen limbs, which would maintain any position they were molded into. In lethargy, pressure on a given muscle would create a contracture of incredible rigidity. A body part could be manipulated into an artificial contraction that perfectly replicated the contraction brought on by a hysterical attack, and in its artificial form, it could be maintained indefinitely. It could be "petrified" for close study, or reproduced in a photograph or wax model. Dr. Morton described an experiment he attended in which Blanche, "a helpless subject for experimentation," was placed into a lethargic trance:

> The left sterno-cleido mastoid is rubbed several times with the point of the finger, and straightaway this muscle stands out like a rigid column in the neck producing at the same moment its usual action of turning the face around to the right; we have a perfect torticollis which left to itself, would persist for at least a number of days. But the opposite sterno-cleido mastoid is now rubbed and contracts until the face looks directly forward, and the torticollis is resolved. The flexors of the forearm are pressed

Figure 9. "Lethargy: Zygomatic Contraction." Photograph of Blanche
Wittmann by Paul Regnard from Désiré-Magloire Bourneville and Paul
Regnard, *Iconographie photographique de la Salpêtrière*, Volume 3, Paris: Aux
Bureaux du Progrès Médical, Delahaye & Lecrosnier, 1879–1880, Plate 40.
Yale University, Harvey Cushing/John Hay Whitney Medical Library.

upon and rubbed, and they at once become rigid, flexing of course at the same time, the hand upon the arm. If the irritation be continued, the muscles become extremely hard, and the bystander, by any force which he can reasonably exert, cannot overcome this flexion. But it may be at any moment resolved by rubbing the corresponding extensors. Or a number of muscles may be contracted at once—the flexors of the forearm, and we have flexion at the wrist—the biceps, and the forearm flexes on the upper arm—the pectorales, and arm and shoulder draw inward and forward, recalling in features the contracture seen in hemiplegia. But all this may be resolved at once, if the bystander or operator chooses, by simply exciting in turn the natural antagonistic muscles.[41]

Like the body piercings, these unnatural positions were used to authenticate the hypnotic trance, since even the most skilled impostor could not simulate the feats of the hypnotized hysteric. Not only was she able to achieve such a position; she could maintain it indefinitely—beyond the capacity of the most accomplished acrobat.

Again, Blanche excelled as a lethargic subject, outdoing the other hysterics. Delboeuf provided the following description: "It is enough to lightly stimulate any of her muscles with the point of a pencil for them to instantly contract completely. And by touching her in this way in different spots, she can be given a torticollis, made to grimace, open or close her hand, or activate any function. In short, one can do with her an exploration of the human body as detailed as, and more demonstrative than, one can do with a cadaver."[42] (See Figure 9.) In order to revive a subject from lethargy, the hypnotist would simply open her eyes in a brightly lit room, or he might blow in her face or press on her ovary, which in hysterics functioned as an ON-OFF switch.

Somnambulism: The Suggestible Woman

The third phase, the somnambulic state, was brought about by pressing on the top of the hysteric's head or by reopening her eyes when
she was in lethargy and gazing directly into them. In this state, the
patient was "suggestible"—that is, she would hallucinate on command and obey the hypnotist's orders.

The power of the magnetizer over his subject is described as
absolute. Catalepsy and lethargy were tools with which the doctors
isolated and froze symptoms so they could be analyzed. Through hypnotic suggestion, the physician altered the unruly hysteric into a com-
pliant patient. In fact, he could change her entirely and bring about
the most miraculous, albeit temporary cures: the paralyzed walked,
the deaf heard, and the blind saw.

Most of the physicians' suggestions, however, had nothing to do
with the patient's health. Elaborate scenarios were staged with the
hysterics in starring roles. Poorly educated working-class women were
turned into elegant and educated aristocrats. Women were turned
into men; indeed, gender switches were quite popular, and the doctors took particular delight in transforming their female patients into
priests and army sergeants. Alfred Binet, one of the physicians at the
Salpêtrière known today as a pioneer of IQ testing, (he's the "Binet"
in the Stanford-Binet test), described some of these alterations: "Put
to sleep and subjected to certain influences, [the women] forget their
identity; their age, their clothing, their sex, their social position,
their nationality, the place and the time of their life—all this has
entirely disappeared. . . . They have lost the idea of their late existence. They live, talk and think exactly like the character suggested
to them." He described this in words that evoke what a century and
a half later would be called method acting: "Instead of imagining a
character simply, they realize it, objectify it, . . . rather like an actor

seized with passion, who imagines that the drama he plays is a reality, not a fiction, and that he has been transformed, body and soul, into the personality that he sets himself up to play."⁴³ When one of the hysterics was given the suggestion that she was an army general, she immediately got into character, shouting in a rough voice: "Give me my field glasses. . . . The enemy! I see them coming up the ravine. . . . My horse and sword!" Her extraordinary enactment ended tragically: "She makes a gesture of buckling her sword in her belt. 'Forward! Ah! I'm hit!'"⁴⁴ According to Binet, this enactment was "not a simple dream, it [was] a living dream."⁴⁵

Giddy with power, the doctors saw no end to the possibilities. Much of the time, however, their suggestions lack imagination, borrowed directly from clichéd images of femininity and the hackneyed acts of stage magnetizers. The squeamish, fragile female appeared regularly. On numerous occasions, Blanche is described as holding up her skirts and stamping in terror at suggested rats or snakes crawling below. (See Figure 10.) Other suggestions partook of the stuff of amateur side shows: Blanche, with evident pleasure, smelling ammonia she was told was rose water; eating sour lemons as though they were sweets. Suggestions were not limited to a single species. Hysterics became animals: dogs and birds were among the doctors' favorites. Another common suggestion involved telling the subject that she was somewhere else. Blanche was frequently transported to the countryside, to meadows, woods, and riverbanks where she saw a little bird. (See Figure 11.)

The parameters of what constituted professional behavior on the part of a medical staff in nineteenth-century Paris were obviously very different from what they are now. Keep in mind that under Charcot's direction, the Salpêtrière was perhaps the most respected medical institution in the world at the time. The frankness with which these stories are related reveals how accepted these practices were. Gilles de la Tourette wrote how, in June of 1884, Charcot and the other

Figure 10. Drawing of Blanche Wittmann from Désiré-Magloire Bourneville and Paul Regnard, *Iconographie photographique de la Salpêtrière*,
Volume 3, Paris: Aux Bureaux du Progrès Médical, Delahaye & Lecrosnier,
1879–1880. Yale University, Harvey Cushing/John Hay Whitney Medical
Library.

Figure 11. Drawing of Blanche Wittmann from Désiré-Magloire Bourneville and Paul Regnard, *Iconographie photographique de la Salpêtrière*,
Volume 3, Paris: Aux Bureaux du Progrès Médical, Delahaye & Lecrosnier,
1879–1880. Yale University, Harvey Cushing/John Hay Whitney Medical
Library.

physicians at the Salpêtrière were gathered in the laboratory when their star patient happened to stop by: "She had barely crossed the threshold, when we put her into a cataleptic state with the bang of a gong. *From that moment on she belonged to us.*" The physicians then induced somnambulism by rubbing the top of her head, and Blanche is asked where she is. "Why in the laboratory, of course!" she responded. "What a question!" One of the physicians suggested that they were not in the clinic at all, but in the Bois de Boulogne, sitting under a bower, enjoying the scenery. Blanche immediately began to relish the country air and mentioned how happy she was with the change of scenery, that she was "beginning to get bored" at the Salpêtrière.[46]

Other suggestions, however, went beyond banality and reveal more about individual doctors than they do about nineteenth-century medicine. In 1885, Delboeuf was again invited to the Salpêtrière, along with the historian Hippolyte Taine. "Towards the end of December, I went to Paris and through Dr. Binet I asked Mr. Charcot if I could visit the famous somnambulic hysterics of the Salpêtrière." Permission was granted, and Delboeuf attended a demonstration conducted by Binet and Féré, in which "they were going to exhibit for me the famous Wittmann . . . known throughout the world." Blanche, adds Delboeuf, had "a richly endowed poitrine."[47]

Much of what he witnessed was frankly erotic, or at the very least, titillating. What is surprising for today's reader, is how these burlesque experiments are described matter-a-factly, side by side with the more "scientific" experiments conducted to produce or remove an "exemplary paraplegia." Delboeuf recounted how Blanche was hypnotized and when in a somnambulic state, instructed upon awakening to kiss the green bust of Franz Joseph Gall, on view in one of the hospital's laboratories. Delboeuf explained that that ridiculous suggestion was chosen "in order to show us just how far the power of hypnotism can go." Blanche, he wrote, "obeyed punctually." She nonchalantly walked across the room, "with the air of someone who simply wanted to stretch her legs a bit." She then paused to examine various bones and instruments on display in the glass vitrines, and then went over and lifted the veil covering a wax model of a female nude in progress. Finally, she came to the "green man." At first she simply passed by, but then returned and picked it up, only to put it back down again. "Her ploy," wrote Delboeuf, "was most amusing. She was visibly in the grip of an inner struggle. She finally gave in and amorously kissed the plaster on both of its cheeks. Afterwards, she returned and went back to sleep in her armchair." When Dr. Féré awakened her, he asked about what she had just done. She gave an exact, detailed account of the various objects she had examined and how she checked on one of the unfinished wax models to see how the "old lady was progressing." However, she neglected to mention the kiss, and when told what she had done, she adamantly denied it. "What a thought! That ugly plaster man, why would I kiss him?! I'm not that crazy!" Delboeuf thought that she was simply ashamed of the kiss; however, Dr. Féré assured him that her denial was sincere.[48]

Gilles de la Tourette recounts a similar experiment conducted at the Salpêtrière in which a doctor ordered his hypnotized patient, whose name is not given, to kiss the hospital priest at a specific time upon awakening. However, in a rare moment of self-consciousness over the frivolity and risqué nature of the command, he also ordered her not to reveal the doctor's name. The appointed hour arrived and the patient announced that she was off to find the priest in order to kiss him. When prevented from doing so by the hospital staff, she became obsessed with carrying out the doctor's orders, struggling violently in an effort to break free. Her obsession did not diminish, and she steadfastly refused to reveal the name of the physician who had hypnotized her—the only one capable of "reversing the spell." The silly request grew into a full-blown crisis. Eventually, the situation was explained to the priest, who graciously allowed the patient to carry out the command and kiss him: "Only then was order restored."[49]

The woman in question was probably not Blanche, since she was known for being something of a prude and was the object of frequent teasing by the doctors. Binet told of one occasion when Albert Londe, head of the photography laboratory at the Salpêtrière, played an off-color practical joke on her. While in a state of somnambulism, he showed her a photographic plate that depicted some donkeys in the Pyrenees. He pointed to one of them and remarked, "Look, here's your portrait; you are stark naked." The suggested image of her naked self persisted long after the session was over, and the interns delighted in teasing the modest Blanche by holding up the plate. One day, in a gesture that is hard not to admire, she managed to grab it from their hands and smash it on the floor. Two photographs, however, had been taken from the plate and these were carefully preserved. Even a year later, when one of the doctors taunted her by holding up the picture, she would see herself naked.[50]

In another episode that expands the definition of medical research, Gilles de la Tourette described how he and some of the other doctors hypnotized Blanche and asked her to undress in front of them. They told her that it was unbearably hot out, and that they should all take a bath together:

> She did not seem very convinced; yet, she began to remove her blouse. However, when it came to taking off her corset, her entire body stiffened, and we barely had time to intervene in order to avoid an attack of hysteria, which in her case always begins in this fashion. We should add that W. is quite modest. Obviously, it is for this reason that an almost unconscious revolt manifested itself, ending in the above result, for, in the same cir-

cumstances, Sarah R . . . [another, less modest, hysteric in the ward] would not hesitate to remove all of her clothes and take an imaginary bath.[51]

Another skit, titillatingly called "*mariage à trois*" was performed for Delboeuf. The skit, he claimed, was "always a great success" and, not surprisingly, "a favorite among the interns."[52] The day he witnessed the experiment, it was not Blanche but a "vivacious brunette" who was the subject. She was put into a somnambulic state and then "divided in two." She was told that each side of her body, her left side and her right, had its own husband and was reminded that it was her duty to be faithful to both of them. Two men were chosen to play the roles of the husbands: in this instance they were Delboeuf and Féré. "We could each caress our side," wrote Delboeuf, "and she received our caresses with marked pleasure. But if one dared encroach on the side of the other, watch out! When I ventured too far, I received a whopping slap. Mr. Féré received a slightly more timid slap. As soon as one of us approached the precise median line of her body, her defiance was awakened, and her hand was positioned to return the rash fellow to reason."[53]

The fact that such experiments were conducted in the name of science at one of the world's leading medical institutions by world-renowned physicians before audiences that included respected figures in many fields, in this case Hippolyte Taine, reveals an enormous amount about nineteenth-century medicine and the role of hysterics. It is to Charcot's credit that he worked to remove the sexual stigma traditionally associated with hysteria. Yet, these experiments were conducted openly with the stated purpose of demonstrating "medical facts" about hypnotism and hysteria. Blanche and other women were repeatedly hypnotized to perform erotically charged scenarios, ones that reveal more about the physician's fantasies than the patient's illness. While unruly and threatening in her natural state, the hysteric, in her hypnotized form, embodied the promise of perfection since once she was rendered artificial, she could become any woman.

Legal Implications

As these anecdotes illustrate, the magnetizer exercised tremendous power over his subject, and an entire medicolegal discipline devoted to hypnosis rose during the last part of the nineteenth century. French courts addressed the question of liability when crimes were committed under the influence of hypnotic suggestion and became the subject of countless medical and legal articles. In the hands of unscrupulous practitioners, hypnotism was thought to be a dangerous means for inducing otherwise law-abiding subjects to commit robbery and even murder.

Once again, Blanche found herself at the center of a highly public debate. Repeatedly, before audiences of medical and legal experts, Blanche would be hypnotized to commit what Gilles de la Tourette called "laboratory crimes"—from petty thefts to cold-blooded murders. In one experiment, Blanche was given the posthypnotic suggestion to steal a photograph she had coveted for a long time. She was also instructed not to remember who had given her the order to steal it, even if she was put back into a trance and questioned: "When you wake up, you will take a photograph from this drawer: I am giving it to you; however, take care that no one sees you because it's not mine. But, listen well: you will not remember that it was me who gave you this order, and, moreover, even if you are put back to sleep again, you will not remember that it was me who put you under."[54]

The drama was staged so that Albert Londe (the Salpêtrière photographer who suggested that the donkey was her nude portrait) would walk into the room and catch her red-handed. All unfolded according to plan. Blanche crept into the photography laboratory at the appointed hour and stealthily opened the drawer. Just as she fingered the desired photograph, Londe entered the room and grabbed her arm. "Aha!" he exclaimed, "I have caught you red-handed; so you are the one who has been stealing my photographs." Blanche vehemently denied that she was stealing it, insisting that it had been "given" to her: "Monsieur, this photograph is mine; it was given to me." When asked who had given it to her, she responded, "that's no concern of yours. Besides, it's mine and I want it." Then "she was suddenly hypnotized by a gong," and according to plan, refused to name the one who ordered her to take the photo.[55]

Blanche's laboratory crimes did not stop with petty theft. In a frequently repeated suggestion, she was hypnotized and ordered to murder someone. In a newspaper column dated July 11, 1884, Jules Claretie recounted how he was "murdered" by Blanche Wittmann at the Salpêtrière:

> I myself was poisoned by a patient at the Salpêtrière who had been given the suggestion to kill me. Mr. Gilles de la Tourette (. . .) placed Blanche W., a young woman with delicate, soft features and tranquil, kind, blue eyes, into a somnambulic state before my eyes. In this state, Blanche W. automatically obeyed any suggestion that was imprinted on her brain.
>
> "This gentleman here (pointing at me), do you see him?"
> "Yes."
> "Well, he has killed Réné!"
> "Réné?" (the name of an intern)
> "He killed him?" repeated the young woman. And her features expressed the deepest horror for the assassin, which was I.
> "Do you want to avenge Réné?"
> "Oh yes! Yes!"

"Well, in a moment you will give him this glass to drink. It has poison in it."

"Good!"

They wake up Blanche W. She smiles, not seeming to remember what was said to her. Then, gently, with perfect grace and the feminine smile of an adorably treacherous female, she hands me the glass that this poor unconscious one believes to be poison and says:

"It's quite hot, don't you think? Don't you want something to drink?"

"Yes, thank you."

She breaks into a joyful smile that she quickly represses. She brings the glass to her own mouth and pretends to moisten her lips with it, and then hands it to me.

"Pretend to get sick," an intern whispered to me. "If she believes that the poison has no effect, she is likely to become enraged and have a fit!"

I then say, out loud, that I don't know what I'm feeling, that the glass of water has made me feel sick, that it is burning me. I am brought into the next room and one of the people present asks the young woman:

"What did you give this gentleman to drink? He is poisoned!"

Then, with an unforgettable expression of fright—I was peeking at her through a crack in the door—she let out a scream and recited with such alarmed volubility that an actress, even a Sarah Bernhardt, would have had difficulty rendering as eloquently:

"Ah! But it wasn't me! You seem to be accusing me! It wasn't me! It wasn't me! I drank out of it first! You saw me! I took the first sip!" She was just like a guilty woman, struggling and terrified before a judge. And don't think that this entire scene was merely drama. I have proof of the absolute sincerity of the observed facts.

A noisy explosion, for example, has the ability of making hysterics fall into catalepsy! Well! They placed a newspaper, a bit of paper, in between Blanche W.'s fingers while she was in a somnambulic state and told her: "This is a pistol. Pull the trigger!" Awakened, she pulled the imaginary trigger, she pulled the newspaper that she believed to be a pistol, and, actually hearing a shot that didn't exist, she fell, completely stiff, into a state of catalepsy. The stiffness of her limbs, in an unbelievable position, could not be simulated.[56]

Another journalist, Hugues Le Roux told of a similar experiment in his newspaper column. In it he moved effortlessly from discussing a real crime story that was a sensation in Paris to the mock crime committed by Blanche that he had witnessed at the Salpêtrière: "I will never forget the emotions I felt that morning when I visited the photographic laboratory of Mr. Londe. I was there to see the curious photographs of one of the in-house patients, Mademoiselle Blanche W." While the journalist was in Londe's laboratory, Blanche happened to stop by. "Nothing in her manner or appearance," wrote Hughes Le Roux, "would make one suspect the illness she suffers from." He then went on to recount how Gilles de la Tourette, in the presence of Charcot, hypnotized the young woman and suggested she murder one of the interns. With amazing sangfroid, Blanche, "a big, beautiful, blond girl with blue eyes and a fresh and rosy complexion" carried out the crime.[57]

Gilles de la Tourette, in his book *L'hypnotisme et les états analogues au point de vue médico-légal* (Hypnotism and its Analogue States from a Medico-Legal Point of View) recounted yet another "murder" committed by Blanche. Only this time, she initially resisted the suggestion and needed to be persuaded. The intended victim, Mr. G., she argued, was a very "nice fellow." She then categorically stated, "I will not poison him. I'm not a criminal, after all." However, when she is told that Mr. G. was the one responsible for a falling-out she had had with a friend, her resolve is weakened, and the next step is the selection of a murder weapon. After some discussion, "poison" is chosen and is poured into a glass of beer.

Gilles de la Tourette provides a wonderfully evocative description of what transpired next. His account reveals a hospital culture in which doctors and hysterics mingled together socially and in which clinical experiments strayed far from today's parameters of scientific study. After Blanche was woken from her trance, she engaged in small talk with the group in a manner that revealed absolutely nothing about the murderous suggestion. She chatted with Jules Claretie about a recent "*concert de folles*" they had both attended, one of the so-called madwomen's concerts that took place at the Salpêtrière, and reminded him to thank his wife for the lovely flowers. She then proceeded to converse with the group about the latest developments in medical photography. "Nothing," recounts Gilles de la Tourette, "betrayed the thoughts that were troubling her." Blanche was so good at concealing her intentions that the doctors feared their experiment had failed. Just then, she approached Mr. G. "with the most nonchalant attitude in the world," and offered him a drink. "My God it's hot in here!" she exclaimed. "Aren't you thirsty? Me, I'm dying. I'm sure you must be thirsty." Mr. G., toying with her, insisted that he was not at all thirsty, but he might be persuaded to have the beer she was offering him if she kissed him. Blanche's initial reaction revealed a fleeting revulsion, but she quickly recovered her composure and acquiesced to the unwanted kiss: "W.," recounts Gilles de la Tourette, "flinches as though revolted; but she is obliged to smile through it all, to smile at the one she must poison. She cannot refuse him a kiss; she would sacrifice anything in order to accomplish the fatal order." He then adds, with more than a touch of salacious glee, "We remain convinced that she would have gone all the way, giving herself completely, if that was the price to pay in order to accomplish the suggestion." The scene unfolded with more back-and-forth banter, a cat-and-mouse game with Blanche feigning to drink from the "poisoned" glass in order to coax the reluctant doctor. G. finally drank the beer, but, in an effort to prolong the suspense, nothing at first happened. "He finished the drink but did not fall down dead! The order was therefore not carried out to the very end!" Eventually, the "poisoned" G. collapsed on the floor and was quickly carried into another room, lest Blanche catch on to the fact that he was only pretending to be dead. The doctors spared no trouble in the production of their drama and had kept a man whom Blanche has never seen before hidden in the wings. This stranger was brought in to play the role of a judge who just happened to be passing by. "Here he is . . . , right when we need him, a judge. (. . .) We will let him shed some light on this affair! No one leave the room!" Blanche initially held up remarkably well under the judge's questioning, but, as the interrogation continued, she became overly excited. "Fearing that our play might end in a hysterical attack," the doctors "judged it prudent to put her back to sleep with the beat of a tom-tom drum."[58]

Blanche's "laboratory crimes" were more than entertaining skits. The repercussions were felt outside of the clinic and touched on issues no less important than free will and accountability. The alleged powers of the hypnotist raised questions of legal liability when a crime was supposedly committed as the result of posthypnotic suggestion. In fact, Charcot was frequently summoned to testify as a medical expert in real court for real criminal cases. As mentioned earlier, according to the Salpêtrière School, only hysterics could be hypnotized, so in order for someone to be found not guilty due to posthypnotic suggestion, he or she would have to be diagnosed as a hysteric. One such case, tried on November 8, 1885, involved Annette Gaudin, a twenty-six-year-old woman, who was found guilty of stealing an old blanket from a man named Varenne. She was sentenced to three months in

prison for her crime. However, while in prison, she came to the attention of a doctor when she ended up in the prison infirmary suffering
from morphine withdrawal. This doctor discovered hysterical symptoms and found that he was able to hypnotize her. Given this new
information, information the doctor believed might have affected the
outcome of her case, he encouraged Gaudin to appeal her sentence.
Charcot was called in as an expert witness, and did indeed confirm
the prison doctor's diagnosis: she was a full-fledged hysteric, capable
of being hypnotized. Under the weight of Charcot's testimony, there
was no way to prove that she had not been hypnotized to commit the
theft, and she was released. Subsequently, she entered the Salpêtrière
as a patient.[59]

In a far more famous case, one that became known as the "Gouffé
Affair," a twenty-two-year-old woman and her lover were accused of
robbing and brutally murdering a bailiff. The facts of the case were not
disputed: Gabrielle Bompard, the young woman, had lured the bailiff,
Alexandre-Toussaint Gouffé, to an apartment where she seduced him
into a position the two had plotted in advance. Gouffé reclined on a
chaise longue with the cord of Bompard's peignoir strategically draped
around his neck. Meanwhile, her lover, Michel Eyraud, who was waiting behind a curtain, jumped out and strangled the unsuspecting
Gouffé. The murder weapon: the sash from his lover's robe. The two
robbed their victim and fled to America. Bompard, however, had a
change of heart and came back to Paris to turn herself in. Her defense
rested on the claim that Eyraud (who was later captured in Havana)
had hypnotized her and that she had therefore been powerless to resist
the suggestion that she entice Gouffé and act as an accomplice in his
murder. An eager public followed each and every turn of the case, a
delectable combination of sex, murder, and hypnotism. Eyraud was
quickly found guilty and guillotined. Bompard's trial, however, was a
drawn-out affair. Not only was her case presented to the court and the
public, so were the opposing schools of hypnotism. The Salpêtrière

School insisted that only hysterics could be hypnotized, while the Nancy School claimed that any suggestible person could be hypnotized. Liégeois, representing the Nancy School, testified as an expert witness on behalf of the defense. Bompard, he argued, should be found not guilty because she had committed her crimes as a result of posthypnotic suggestion and had been powerless to do otherwise. The Salpêtrière was represented by Dr. Paul Brouardel, dean of the Faculty of Medicine as well as a professor in the new discipline of legal medicine. Brouardel was also a friend of Charcot's. He argued for the prosecution, claiming that while Bompard suffered from "*petite hystérie*," a very mild and common form of the disease, she did not have the major hysteria required in order to be hypnotized. She was therefore, according to Brouardel, responsible for the crime. The case demonstrated which school of thought had more credibility at the time: with the authority of Charcot and Salpêtrière on its side, the prosecution won, and Bompard was sentenced to twenty years.[60]

Hysteria's Theater

As is often mentioned in the literature about the Salpêtrière, not only by recent scholars but also by Charcot's contemporaries, demonstrations of hysteria, especially in its artificial or hypnotic form, were highly theatrical. Hysteria was a spectacular disease. With the sound of a gong, the wave of a hand, the beat of a tom-tom, or the push of an anatomical button, a physician could create a cataleptic woman and pierce her body with needles; a lethargic woman, capable of being "petrified" into astounding postures; and for the grand finale, a somnambulic woman, open to any suggestion. Not surprisingly, Claretie was not the only fiction writer to be inspired by Charcot's demonstrations at the Salpêtrière. Hysterical characters appeared in the novels, plays and short stories of other writers who attended these public lectures.[61] Whether in the scientific amphitheater of the Salpêtrière or in the pages of a novel or a play, the hypnotized hysteric was an amazing spectacle. During these demonstrations, science exploded into something else altogether.

The diagnosis of hysteria identified it as a "theatrical" illness, an illness of surface and illusion, as a form of fiction. This diagnosis produced in turn further layers of fiction and theater. The enactments of hysteria in front of audiences furthered the theatrical quality. Along with Claretie and Taine mentioned above, Daudet (both father and son), Guy de Maupassant, J. K. Huysmans, Théodore de Banville, Henri Bergson, and Emile Durkheim all attended performances. Actors, artists, architects, musicians, visiting royalty, politicians, the prefect of police, and other members of high society also came to witness the phenomenon.[62]

Before rapt audiences, Charcot's patients were ordered to enact degrading and fascinating scenarios. Axel Munthe, a Swedish doctor who studied for several years at the Salpêtrière, provided a critical firsthand account: "I seldom failed to attend Professor Charcot's *Leçons du mardi* in the Salpêtrière, just then chiefly devoted to his grande hystérie and to hypnotism. The huge amphitheatre was filled to the last place with a multicoloured audience drawn from *tout Paris*, authors, journalists, leading actors and actresses, fashionable *demimondaines*, all full of morbid curiosity to witness the startling phenomena of hypnotism almost forgotten since the days of Mesmer and Braid. It was during one of these lectures that I became acquainted with Guy de Maupassant." Munthe continued with a scathing critique insisting that "these stage performances of the Salpêtrière before the public of *tout Paris* were nothing but an absurd farce, a hopeless muddle of truth and cheating." According to Munthe, many of the "performers" were out-and-out frauds, duping not just the audience, but also the doctors with "the amazing cunning" of hysterics. Munthe repeated the oft-circulated criticism that the famous stages of the hysterical attack had been invented by Charcot, and were "hardly ever observed outside the Salpêtrière." On the other hand, the Swedish doctor accused Charcot of exploiting vulnerable women, who were indeed hypnotized. Not only did he object to the inherent humiliation they underwent on stage, but he also charged Charcot with driving the poor girls mad.

Some of them smelt with delight a bottle of ammonia when told it was rose water, others would eat a piece of charcoal when presented to them as chocolate. Another would crawl on all fours on the floor, barking furiously when told she was a dog, flap her arms as if trying to fly when turned into a pigeon, lift her skirts with a shriek of terror when a glove was thrown at her feet with a suggestion of being a snake. Another would walk with a top-hat in her arms rocking it to and fro and kissing it tenderly when she was told it was her baby. Hypnotized, right and left, dozens of times a day, by doctors and students, many of these unfortunate girls spent their days in a state of semi-trance, their brains bewildered by all sorts of absurd suggestions, half conscious and certainly not responsible for their doings, sooner or later doomed to end their days in the *salle des agités* if not in a lunatic asylum.[63]

I was unable to find any records that corroborated the accusation that repeated trances resulted in any hysteric being driven mad. It should also be pointed out that Munthe had personal reasons to depict Charcot in a negative manner. When he first arrived in Paris, he had sought out the famous neurologist, who welcomed him into the Salpêtrière. Their relationship, however, was strained when Charcot accused him of leaking information to the press and ended in a scandal.

Alphonse Daudet, however, had less reason to disparage Charcot, who was his doctor, neighbor, and a dear friend to whom he dedicated his novel *The Evangelist*: "to the eloquent and learned professor." However, three years following Charcot's death, he also described these demonstrations as highly theatrical in a memoir. Blanche (under the pseudonym Balmann) is viewed as a self-centered and temperamental leading lady, unwilling to settle for anything less than center stage. He recounts a demonstration in which "Daret," another hysteric, less beautiful and less talented than Blanche, is brought out first to be hypnotized before the usual audience. Worried that the inexperienced hysteric may become overtaxed, Charcot asked that the pro, Wittmann/Balmann, be brought in instead. "But the intern," explained Daudet, "returned alone. Yes indeed, Balmann refused to go on, furious that Daret had been brought out first. Between these two cataleptics, leading ladies of the Salpêtrière, there was the jealousy that exists between stars, between divas. And sometimes angry rows would break out in the laundry room, sprinkled with salty words, and send the entire ward into a ruckus. Given Balmann's refusal, Fifine was summoned. She entered with a sour face. She was taking Balmann's side and refused to work. The intern tried in vain to put her to sleep. She was crying and resisting. 'Don't bother with her,' said Charcot, and he returned to Daret, who was now rested and was only too proud to continue the session. Ah, the mysteries of cataleptic sleep."[64] Hypnosis at the Salpêtrière was a tool to direct the hysteric's talent, to determine her roles, scenes, and lines.

The dramatic character of Charcot's demonstrations was reinforced by the fact that the hysterics were treated as actresses. The best performers attracted large audiences and their shows even went on the road, traveling to other hospitals and amphitheaters. Blanche was lent to the Hôtel Dieu Hospital in Paris, where she worked with another doctor. Since an instinctive flair for drama was part of the definition of hysteria, once the patient's disorderly symptoms had been tamed through hypnosis, this predilection for performance served her well. Charles Richet, one of Charcot's interns at the Salpêtrière, discussed the hysteric's love for theater, writing that "everything for her becomes the subject of a drama. She is constantly playing a role, as successful with comedy as she is with tragedy, on the dull stage of reality."[65]

By all accounts Blanche was the most gifted actress. According to Gilles de la Tourette and many others, her performances were brilliant. Blanche's talent was frequently compared to the great nineteenth-century actress Sarah Bernhardt. In a newspaper column, "Chroniques Parisiennes," published on July 11, 1884, in *Le Temps*, Jules Claretie wrote that an actress "such as Sarah Bernhardt" would have had "difficulty rendering as eloquently" the scene he had witnessed Blanche perform. Delboeuf went even further: "Never has an actor or a painter," he wrote, "never a Rachel or a Sarah Bernhardt, Rubens or Raphaël, arrived at such a powerful expression. This young girl enacted a series of tableaux that surpassed in its brilliance and power the most sublime efforts by art. One could not dream of a more astonishing model."[66] In fact, as the historian Alain Corbin has noted, hysterical gestures found their way onto the stage. Actresses and opera divas borrowed from Blanche and other hysterics. "Sarah Bernhardt mimicked the great doctor's patients, or perhaps one should say the great director's actresses. The great divas of opera strove to outdo the now universally famous stars of the Salpêtrière, from the Wagnerian Kundry's display of remorse in 1882 to the long vindictive cry in Richard Stauss's Elektra (1905.)"[67] We know that Sarah Bernhardt came to Charcot's demonstrations and, while preparing for her role in *Adrienne Lecouvreur*, a play by Eugène Scribe, one of France's most popular dramatists, she did more than simply attend a lecture. In an interview she gave to *La Chronique Médicale*, she discussed how she spent time locked inside of one of the Salpêtrière's cells in order to prepare for the role.[68]

Not only were Blanche's performances at the Salpêtrière celebrated, she became a character in the theater. In a play by André de Lorde

called *Une leçon à la Salpêtrière* (A Lesson at the Salpêtrière), Blanche
was the inspiration for "Suzanne," a beautiful young hysteric who has
learned to simulate the various stages of hypnotism in exchange for
small bribes such as candy or money to buy a new corset. Charcot
appeared as Marbois, the arrogant physician in chief who foolishly
believes he is in control of his clinic. André de Lorde wrote the play
in 1906, thirteen years after Charcot's death. It is dedicated to Alfred
Binet: "In acknowledgement and gratitude of our deep friendship."
Not only were de Lorde and Binet friends; they collaborated on other
medical dramas. That Binet could participate in this kind of an attack
on his old mentor is yet another indication of how far Charcot's reputation had fallen after his death.

Jane Avril

Jane Avril, the famous dancer portrayed in the Moulin Rouge paintings by Toulouse-Lautrec, spent time at the Salpêtrière as a patient—
not as a spectator at Charcot's demonstrations, as has sometimes been
reported. She wrote about her stay at the clinic in her memoirs, which
were published in serial form in 1933. Her recollections, written in a
colorful fairy-tale style, offer the reader a rare glimpse of the hospital
from the perspective of a patient.[69] In 1882, when she was fourteen
years old, she was admitted to Charcot's ward for what appears to have
been a hodgepodge of social and physical reasons. Jeanne Beaudon—
Jane Avril was her stage name—was the daughter of an unmarried
courtesan and a decadent Italian marquis who had fled his austere
Catholic family to pursue a life of pleasure in Paris, where he fathered
the infant Jeanne and squandered his fortune. Jeanne's mother played
the role of devoted parent in public, but in private, she brutally beat
her daughter. At fourteen the girl ran away from home to throw herself into the Seine, but her nerve didn't hold and instead of suicide

by drowning, she ended up on the doorstep of one of her mother's "benefactors." This man and his wife took pity on the girl and agreed to hide her from her abusive mother. When she developed a nervous condition, "Saint Guy's Dance," ("Predestination!" she wrote about the diagnosis, displaying her sense of humor), her rescuer brought her to the Salpêtrière, where she lived "among the great stars of hysteria, who were at that moment all the rage."[70]

Jeanne Beaudon stayed on the ward for eighteen months.[71] The Salpêtrière served as a sanctuary for her, an "Eden" where she was safe from her mother's violence. Charcot's head nurse, Mademoiselle Bottard, nicknamed "Babotte," took a special interest in the girl. When Babotte noticed that the mother's visits exacerbated the daughter's illness, she concocted a story about how Jeanne had misbehaved and was no longer allowed to go outdoors. This meant that all future visits from "the wicked mother" (Jeanne's own description) took place under the watchful and protective eyes of a nurse.[72] In her memoir, Jeanne recalled Sarah Bernhardt's exciting visit to the Salpêtrière, pleasant walks in the hospital's magnificent gardens, and the evenings when she entertained her ward mates and the interns in the nearby laboratory with her songs, as well as the gymnastic lessons she attended three times a week. She quickly became a favorite of her gymnastic teacher and developed the skills that would later make her famous as a dancer at the Moulin Rouge. The Salpêtrière, as Jeanne remembered it, had its own social hierarchy, one in which the hysterics were the "aristocrats" among the hospital inmates, housed in the grand Duchenne de Boulogne Room on the ground floor. The epileptics, on the other hand, were deemed "the humble folk" and relegated to more modest quarters upstairs. One evening that made a deep impression on her was the annual masquerade ball. Dressed in an elaborate Mardi Gras costume that Charcot's daughter had given her, Jeanne heard the music begin to play and then she danced. She twirled and kicked and leapt, and by her own account dazzled the

other revelers. Not only patients attended the ball, but members of
the whole staff. The medical elite had turned their gaze on the young
woman and they applauded her performance. Jeanne Beaudon was
cured, and she was on her way to becoming Jane Avril. Before she was
sent home, a meeting was held about her case. Charcot was present
while a physician warned Jeanne's mother that if she ever mistreated
her daughter again, the girl had permission to return immediately to
the Salpêtrière and enroll in Bourneville's nursing school.[73] "I have
bittersweet memories of the time I spent in that establishment," she
recalled fifty years later. "Its buildings and gardens . . . exuded a gran-
diose majesty, as does everything in the style of Louis XIV. I was
happy there and pampered by everyone. The nurses thought of me as
the child of the house, a house filled with quaint charm that pleased
my romantic soul."

Jeanne Beaudon also described the petty rivalries among the
clinic's "stars," who competed with one another for lead parts in Charcot's demonstrations. She wrote that the women delighted in deceiving the doctors and reported that they deliberately faked symptoms
"in order to capture attention and gain stardom." When Charcot and
his entourage would approach them (Beaudon mentioned Gilles de
la Tourette, Richer, Babinski, Poirier, and another disciple, Gilbert
Ballet), one of the hysterics would collapse in a sham fit and execute
"extravagant contortions." The women had instructed Jeanne that
once the men entered the room, she was to press on the ovary of
her fitful fellow patient. In this way the flailing hysteric became not
only the center of attention but, with Beaudon's ovarian compression,
recovered her composure so that she could carry on a calm conversation with the doctors. More than fifty years later as she puzzled over
the "secret" the older hysterics had let her in on, she had come to
believe that "the great Charcot was not in the dark."

This of course was not the first time the Salpêtrière hysterics had
been accused of fraud—that was a common allegation—but this time

it came from a patient inside the ward. Hysteria was a disease that unwittingly imitated other diseases. But, as Charcot acknowledged, hysterics also willfully feigned symptoms:

> It is a matter of simulation, no longer the imitation of one disease by another . . . but of intentional and deliberate simulation, in which the patient exaggerates real symptoms or creates an imaginary symptomology from scratch. Everyone knows that the need to lie, sometimes without anything to gain, a kind of art for art's sake, sometimes with the goal of causing a stir or gaining pity, is common, especially in hysteria. We encounter it with every step we take in the clinic of this neurosis and there is no denying that this accounts for the low opinion that is at times attached to the study of hysteria.[74]

Even at their most authentic, hysterical symptoms were imitations of the symptoms of "real" diseases. In this situation, Jeanne Beaudon recalled, hysterics, prey to the peculiarities of their disease, also imitated the imitations.

While Charcot's hysterics undoubtedly veered close to the depictions by de Lorde and Jane Avril, the Salpêtrière's critics are nonetheless on shaky ground in their accusations of "staged performances." According to Charcot, theatricality was integral to hysteria, and the hysteric was by nature an actress with a predilection for drama and an amazing talent for simulation. And while the degradation and the cruelty inherent in these performances are unquestionable, they were not necessarily contradictory and fraudulent as some of Charcot's critics have claimed. As Charcot conceded, the hysteria doctors were confronted at every step with willful deceit. What he did not admit was that they must have, at least on occasion, mistaken a sham imitation for a genuine one.[75]

Medical Fiction and Fictional Medicine

The French medical world intersected with other literary forms as well. Naturalism, Zola's doctrine that fiction should be a human or social case study with the writer a kind of scientist, engendered an enormously popular subgenre of medical novels, whose main characters typified newly defined pathologies. While most of these works are not important for their literary value, they are fascinating as cultural artifacts. Dubut de Laforest's long series called *Les derniers scandales de Paris* (The Latest Scandals in Paris), an attempt at a fin-de-siècle *Human Comedy*, is populated with pathological types. Each novel is devoted to a different kind of "degenerate": the nymphomaniac, the alcoholic, the lesbian, and of course, the hysteric. Armand Dubarry's collection of narratives *Les déséquilibrés de l'amour* (Unbalanced by Love) also extensively catalogued pathological syndromes, and his choices were even more rarefied than Dubut de Laforest's. Each title in the series announced a perversion: *Coupeur de nattes* (The Braid Snipper), *Les femmes eunuques* (Female Eunuchs), *Les invertis: le vice allemand* (Inverts: The German Vice), *Le plaisir sanglant* (Bloody Pleasure), *L'hermaphrodite* (The Hermaphrodite), and, of course, *Hystérique* (The Hysteric.)[76]

Léon Daudet, the son of Alphonse Daudet, also wrote a medical novel, or rather, an antimedical novel that portrays a thinly disguised Salpêtrière called *Les morticoles*. The Daudet family and the Charcot family were close, their lives intertwined in various ways. They were neighbors and Alphonse Daudet and Charcot were good friends. Charcot was also Alphonse Daudet's doctor. Their sons, Jean-Baptiste Charcot and Léon Daudet, born the same year, were best friends growing up. Léon, however, grew up to be a rabid conservative, a devout Catholic, and an anti-Semitic monarchist, and he came to detest the progressive, republican, anticlerical Charcot. Besides his political and religious convictions, there were also complicated personal reasons for his resentment. Before his career as a journalist, Léon Daudet had been a medical student, and when he failed his exams, he accused Charcot of turning his instructors against him in order to advance his own son, Jean-Baptiste, who was in the same class. Léon Daudet also insinuated that Charcot had a vendetta against him because he had jilted his daughter, Jeanne, in order to marry Jeanne Hugo, the grand-daughter of another famous man, Victor Hugo. Léon and Jeanne were divorced after only a few years of marriage, and she later married Jean-Baptiste, who by that time had left medicine to embark on a career as a polar explorer. That marriage, too, ended in divorce. Besides this complicated love triangle, there has been speculation that the younger Daudet blamed the elder Charcot for the painful treatments his father underwent. Alphonse Daudet was suffering from tabes dorsalis, a form of syphilis that progressively destroys the spinal column, a disease that, coincidentally, Charcot had described. Léon Daudet also resented Charcot for his inability to cure his father of the slow and painful illness that eventually killed him.[77] The younger Daudet was haunted by fears that his father's illness had been passed down to him, and to his offspring. Many years later, when his fourteen-year-old son ran away from home and committed suicide, the press speculated that he had inherited his grandfather's disease in the form of dissociative fugue states and epilepsy.[78] Whatever the reasons, Léon Daudet never lost the opportunity to attack Charcot in the press.

Léon Daudet claimed he wrote *Les morticoles* in order to "lift the veil" from the fraudulent medical world. In the novel, medicine has risen to such power that doctors rule the land. Disguised in name only, the Salpêtrière's most famous hysteric, Blanche (called Rosalie), Charcot, (called Foutange) and Charcot's chief resident and interns are all characters in the book. Bourneville is "Cloaquol," the editor of *Le Tibia Brisé* (The Broken Tibia), the most powerful and influential medical journal of the day. "Rosalie" was also the name of Charcot's beloved pet monkey, a fact that Léon Daudet was well aware of. She is described as "a quite young and quite pretty creature, with disheveled blond hair, and a little nose stuck up in the air."[79] Like Blanche, Rosalie draws crowds to the hospital to witness her extraordinary performances: "The one and only Rosalie, the one who has been used in all of those experiments, talked about in the press . . . , the one and only Rosalie on whom our extraordinary muscular-cerebral-cutaneous-sensitivity system is based; the one and only Rosalie, the landmark of so many marvelous studies. . . . Salute her, for she has made more ink flow than filth through our sewers."[80] In Daudet's version, not only Blanche, but the hospital interns, plot behind the back of the Charcot character.[81] In one scene that takes place in the hospital staff lounge, Rosalie and a group of interns stage a mock scene of one of Charcot's demonstrations. The chief resident, named Gigade, a fictionalized Babinski perhaps, climbs on top of a rickety chair and pontificates in the manner of Foutange/Charcot: "Now how about some passionate poses! Take a look, gentlemen, ecstasy, prayer . . . and, now anger, see how her fists clench, see her furious expression."[82] Before an audience of interns doubled over in laughter, Rosalie, "dressed in a flashy manner" and "intoxicated by her success, took on each position indicated by the booming professor. As she writhed on the floor, her comb fell out and her beautiful golden hair fell freely, her upturned skirts revealed delicate calves."[83] In Daudet's malicious parody, Rosalie has been taught how to simulate hypnotism and hysteria by Gigade, who wants to play a practical joke on his boss Foutange. "A great favor you did me, my old chap," she quips. "That Foutange is a sucker like nobody else."[84] Les morticoles, published the year after Charcot died, was a best seller.

The relationship between nineteenth-century French medicine and literature was one of mutual fascination. Fiction writers eagerly employed the latest medical terminology in their descriptions of pathological characters. The hysteric as a type appears in many works,

from the minor narratives mentioned above, to the great novels of
Flaubert, Zola, Huysmans, the Goncourts, and many others that borrowed descriptions directly from Charcot's symptomology. However,
very little has been written about the fact that there was a good deal
of influence in the other direction as well. Prominent physicians held
cultural salons and wrote for literary journals. Charcot was an avid
reader and spent time with many writers. He invited Jules Claretie
and other novelists to the Salpêtrière, including his friend Alphonse
Daudet. "When I chat with Daudet," wrote Charcot, "I feel I am
under a microscope." "A beautiful mind," replied the writer, "respect-
ful of literature. His analytic sense is close to mine."[85]

During this period, literature and medicine were so intertwined
that in one case a gynecologist wrote the preface to a novel, and in
another a gynecologist appealed to a novelist, Alexandre Dumas fils,
to write the preface for his medical thesis.[86] Besides Binet, who wrote
plays with André de Lorde, Claude Bernard, the famous physiologist, wrote prose for the literary magazine *La Revue des Deux-Mondes*,
and Richet analyzed Zola's *L'assommoir* in this same journal.[87] Richet
also wrote poetry and fiction under the pseudonym Charles Epheyre.
Two of his books, *Possession* and *Soeur Marthe* (Sister Martha), are
about women who become ideal love objects through hypnosis. The
descriptions of hysteria in these works of fiction differ little from
those found in medical texts. Unlike medical language today, with
its jargon that to a large extent excludes the lay reader, nineteenth-
century physicians wrote in a way that was and remains accessible to
the general reader. In fact, the lines that divide fiction from nonfic-
tion in late-nineteenth-century France were blurry at best, and often
disappear altogether when the subject is female. When writing about
hysteria, doctors even referred to novelists for information. Richet,
for example, published an account of hysteria in 1880 in *La Revue
des Deux Mondes*. In the article he cited the usual scientific sources:
other physicians, medical journals, and the case histories of patients

at the Salpêtrière. However, he also repeatedly referred to novels as documentation to support his medical claims, completely erasing the lines that separated the two disciplines.[88] Richet appropriated descriptions and quotations of female characters from fiction by Anatole France, Edmond and Jules de Goncourt, Gustave Flaubert, and others as medical case studies and as "precise descriptions that complete what we have just said concerning the psychological state of nervous women."[89] Indeed, a quotation from Madame Bovary takes up an entire page. According to Richet: "In several lines, Flaubert characterizes hysteria, and in his precise and seductive description, it is hard to decide whether we should admire him more for his artistic talent or for his scientific observation."[90]

When writing about the female condition, medical prose becomes surprisingly "literary." The cold, analytical style of medical discourse is abandoned in favor of a flowery, metaphorical language with an appeal to artists and poets. Hysterics, as we have seen, are "played" like pianos and have hysterical fits that unfold like the music from a music box. Binet, in his descriptions of the hypnotized hysteric cited above, uses a language more philosophical or literary than medical: "Only a single idea remains—a single consciousness—it is the consciousness of the idea and of the new being that dawns upon their imagination."[91] At the very least, this conspicuous shift in prose style indicates the place occupied by the hysteric in the discourse. The movement in style is a lapse into the lyricism of fiction, as though the language of science—the sober particularity of medicine—cannot properly express its subject. The articulation of female hysteria within the discourse strays from the goals of the discipline itself. The desire to observe, locate, identify, predict—in short the aims of scientific method—are derailed, careening off into the ambiguous territory of poetry the moment the subject is a hysteric. Charles Richet, a Nobel Prize winner for his research on anaphylaxis, turned to the fiction writers for help with the science of hysteria.

While doctors embraced novels by citing them as medical case history or by writing reviews of them in literary journals, or prefaces for them, or by actually writing them, they nonetheless accused literature of breeding hysteria. Parents were warned to keep books out of the hands of their daughters, and husbands were admonished to make sure that their wives were kept away from novels. Like Madame Bovary, Blanche read popular romance fiction. In fact, she recited scenes from the books she was reading during hysterical deliriums. In May of 1878, a year after her arrival at the Salpêtrière, her case history recorded, "She speaks in a low voice reciting scenes from a novel: 'Fabrice has killed Madame de la Rivière.' Her face expresses fear." During the night, she repeated the above statement over and over again, "chattering non-stop." The following morning her delirium continued: "her face is a bit drawn, her eyes sunken and her pupils dilated. 'I am going to the cemetery. . . . A child under a stone. . . .' She sees scenes from *La Fille Maudite* (The Cursed Girl): 'Ah! They hit her, that woman!' She cries out in pain: 'They must let that boy leave!. . . . He's lying down on the gravel at the back of the cemetery." (*Iconographie photographique de la Salpêtrière*, vol. 3, p. 14.)[92] A comment the philosopher Delboeuf made while defending the rights of entertainment hypnotists revealed how well accepted was the "threat" posed by novels. According to Delboeuf, it ranked side by side with prostitution and alcohol: "Should we forbid drinking establishments and places of prostitution, theaters and café concerts, newspapers and novels? And yet, think of the evils they have caused! One work of literature has all by itself created more neuropaths than all of the actual and alleged neuropaths put together that public hypnotism is blamed for."[93] Reading any book was thought to tax the already frail female system; reading novels was a sure way to send it careening over the edge.

Brouillet's Painting

Blanche's fame reached its pinnacle when a group portrait by the painter André Brouillet was exhibited at the Salon of 1887 (only one year after the famous Impressionist exhibition). The painting, entitled *Une leçon clinique à la Salpêtrière* (A Clinical Lesson at the Salpêtrière) depicts one of Charcot's famous demonstrations of hypnosis. (See Figure 12.) It is enormous, measuring 9 by 13 feet, as though anything smaller would not have been able to capture the supposed grandeur of the event. The almost life-size Blanche appears partially undressed, her blouse removed, revealing a chemise that has slipped off her shoulders, and a laced corset. She is leaning submissively against the doctor, Joseph Babinski (1857–1932), the son of Polish immigrants, who is known today primarily for "Babinski's sign," a deformation of the toe reflex that continues to be diagnostically significant. Babinski's starring role in the portrait can no doubt be attributed to his status as one of Charcot's most brilliant students and, at least in part, to the fact that he was strikingly handsome. Gilles de la Tourette might also have been an obvious choice, given his status as a favored disciple; however, unlike the tall good-looking Babinski, he was decidedly unattractive. "An ugly Papuan idol covered in hair," said the caustic Léon Daudet. Gilles de la Tourette himself said he was "as ugly as a louse." Brouillet nonetheless managed to depict him in a flattering manner: seated in the center foreground, we see him in profile, leaning in attentively to better view the scene unfolding before him. Babinski's artistically pleasing features are subtly lit, while daylight from the window behind Blanche sharply illuminates her exposed chest and neck. Her face is completely without expression, blank and beautiful. If one focuses only on this relatively small section of the painting, the detail that includes Blanche and Babinski, they look for all the world like a pair of lovers, Blanche swooning into

Figure 12. André Brouillet, *A Clinical Lesson at the Salpêtrière* (1887). Oil on canvas. Musée d'histoire de la médecine, Paris. Getty Images.

her adoring partner's arms. The rest of the painting, however, quickly belies that perception. Blanche's contracted hand, bent at an odd angle from her body, indicates a pathological state, in this instance one of hypnotically induced lethargy. The presence of the nurses, of Charcot, and of the audience, places the lover's tryst into another context. Babinski is no longer amorous, but merely a concerned and gentle doctor; Blanche, though seductive in her state of semiundress, is a patient. The medical setting, however, does little to undermine the erotic charge of the painting. Babinski's hand rests precariously close to Blanche's breast, and the spectacle unfolds before an audience of twenty-seven men who are leaning forward in attention, gazing intently at the woman's body.[94] Besides Blanche, the only other women in the scene are two nurses; the head nurse Mademoiselle Bottard, who at the time the portrait was painted had been at the Salpêtrière for forty-seven years, and Mademoiselle Ecary, a young nurse in Charcot's service for two years. Charcot's disciples are also depicted—Paul Richer (shown with his sketchbook and pen), Charles Féré, Gilbert Ballet, Georges Guinon, Romain Vigouroux, Albert Londe and Désiré-Magloire Bourneville—as are the novelists Jules Claretie and Paul Arène, the philosopher Théodule Ribot, and the politician Victor Cornil. The art critic and collector Philippe Burty is there as well, probably a self-serving decision on the part of the artist.[95]

The painting was an enormous success. Group portraits were very much in vogue, and Charcot and the Salpêtrière were certainly considered worthy, indeed heroic, subjects. The painting also draws the viewer into its scopophilic fantasy: like the men depicted in the painting, the viewer can ogle Blanche's partially undressed and receptive body while also engaging in admiration of medical science. In a review of the Salon, the art critic for Le Temps writes about Gallery 23, where Brouillet's painting was hung: "It is in this gallery that Brouillet's painting is found, by all accounts the greatest success of the Salon."[96] His comments are meaningful: Le Temps was one of the largest and most reputable dailies in Paris, and the 1887 Salon included more than 5,000 paintings by more than 2,500 artists.[97] The Salon took place in the Palais de l'Industrie and was widely attended. More than half a million visitors came during the two months the exhibit was open.[98] The painting was bought by the state and was then donated to a museum in Nice. For many years the painting itself was held in a storage room, but due to a lithograph edition printed by Pirodon, the image of Blanche, Charcot, and the Salpêtrière became well known. Freud kept one of these lithographs in his office, a treasured souvenir from his days at the Parisian clinic. In 1965 the painting was brought out of storage and transferred to Lyon, where it was displayed in the Neurological Hospital. Today the painting is back in Paris, where it hangs in the Musée d'Histoire de la Médecine. André Brouillet went on to become a moderately successful but quickly forgotten artist, who earned a living mostly as a portrait painter. There is a school in Poitiers, a city where the painter spent many years, named after him: the Collège André Brouillet.

The Clinic and the Carnival

The compelling spectacle of the hypnotized hysteric found many venues outside of the hospital. Not only was she portrayed in paintings, plays, and novels, but shows featuring a male hypnotist "à la Charcot" and his female subject "à la Blanche," were extremely popular throughout Europe. The most famous pair, as well as the pair that conducted experiments that most closely resembled those done at the Salpêtrière, was the Belgian hypnotist Alfred Dhont (sometimes written d'Hont), who went by the stage name Donato, and his partner Mademoiselle Prudence, who was later replaced by Mademoiselle Lucille. They traveled extensively in Europe, attracting large crowds to their performances. Donato, by all accounts a skilled hypnotist, would put his female subject through Charcot's three stages of catalepsy, lethargy, and somnambulism, exploiting the particularities of each phase. Writing about Donato's performances, Gilles de la Tourette noted, not without sarcasm: "The plastic poses of catalepsy are a huge success. Fear mixes with enthusiasm when, with a long needle, this modern Mesmer pierces the arm of his victim from one side through to the next and graciously invites someone from the lovely audience to come up and see that his subject is completely insensible."[99] Donato was also adept in the "stiff as a board" act in which the lethargic subject would be suspended by her head and toes in that alarming pose between two chairs. A journalist, describing Donato's show, wrote: "He hypnotized members of the audience. . . . He made one become as stiff as a board. Two chairs are brought out and her head was placed on one, her feet on the other, and the rest of her body is held up by nothing. . . . These experiments are almost exactly like the ones that Dr. Charcot conducts at the Sainte-Anne asylum [journalist's error]."[100] And not unlike Charcot's demonstrations at the Salpêtrière, the somnambulic state, in which the subject obeyed any and all commands, was one of the showman's highlights. According to Gilles de la Tourette, "the audience bursts into frenetic bravos while watching the unfortunate victims eat potatoes as fruit, drink water as though it was a delicious nectar, burst into tears and then laughter, beings riveted by an invisible force emanating from the eye of the magnetizer."[101] The irony is that Gilles de la Tourette never applied the same criticism to the public spectacles offered by the Salpêtrière. The most significant difference between Donato's shows and those at the Salpêtrière was context. Donato and other showmen did everything they could to minimize the differences between their acts and medical hypnosis, borrowing techniques and terminology from the neurologist, and costuming themselves and their subjects to look like doctor and patient, even advertising their shows as being "à la Salpêtrière."

The medical establishment heaped scorn on what it labeled grotesque and dangerous mimicry. From a perspective of outrage and superiority, it cast Donato and his kind as illegitimate interlopers on medical terrain. Doctors were fighting for exclusive control of hypnotic power. Charcot explicitly articulated this argument as a battle for territory: "In the name of science and of art, medicine has only recently taken definitive possession of hypnotism; and this is completely justified, for medicine alone has the knowledge to apply it properly and legitimately, either as a treatment for patients, or for physiological and psychological research. In this recently conquered domain, medicine will from now on reign as the absolute and jealous mistress of its rights; it formally rejects any intrusion."[102] Medicine's conquest of hypnotism was not, however, as absolute as Charcot claimed it to be.

Indeed, the two worlds overlapped in myriad ways, sharing subjects and techniques, and exercising mutual influences.

Gilles de la Tourette, in his extraordinary book *L'hypnotisme et les états analogues*, published in 1889, painstakingly lays out the Salpêtrière's case against the lay hypnotists. And while he never wavers in his criticism, his research reveals a remarkable overlap between the clinic and the carnival.[103]

There were hysterical patients at the Salpêtrière who shuttled back and forth between commercial hypnotism and the hospital. Gilles de la Tourette, who treated several of them, credited these women for providing him with some of his best inside information about the world of nonmedical hypnosis. The rest he gathered on his own by going undercover to the various shows and by sending in "spies," recruited from medical students, who pretended to be part of the regular audience.

The commercial magnetizer, he discovered, was almost always male and came from all classes. The skill often ran in families, and was handed down from father to son. Many lay hypnotists were also in some way connected to the fringes of the medical establishment: pharmacists, failed medical students, dentists, and even renegade doctors, whose "purse grows as their honor disappears."[104] The subjects, or somnambulists, were almost exclusively female, and usually quite young.[105] And like the hypnotists, this profession often ran in families, passed down from mother to daughter. Subjects were sometimes recruited from the audience. Following Charcot, Gilles de la Tourette believed the somnambulists were all hysterics, even when they were unaware of their condition.

Significantly, medical hypnotists objected to Donato and the other showmen not because they believed they were charlatans hoodwinking a gullible public, but rather because they thought they were abusing a very real power and therefore constituted a threat to public

health. Articles about unsuspecting audience members, latent hysterics, becoming sick after watching a performance by Donato or one of
the other lay hypnotists, filled the press. "The curtain rises," writes
Gilles de la Tourette, "and the 'doctor,' dressed in black with a white
tie, begins a series of experiments on his subject that provoke enthusiastic bravos from the crowd of imbeciles who have brought to this
repugnant spectacle their wives and daughters, as though hysteria does
not spread quickly enough with ordinary day to day provocations."[106]

Gilles de la Tourette was not alone in disparaging the lay hypnotists. Almost every issue of the *Revue de l'Hypnotisme*, one of the
more than twenty French journals that specialized in hypnosis during this period, ran a column devoted to the dangers of *hypnotisme
extra-scientifique*, dangers that included everything from the onset of
hysteria in latent hysterics, to outbreaks of mass hysteria, to suicide
attempts. Hospital admissions, the journal pointed out, would spike
significantly when Donato was in town.

At the 1889 International Congress of Hypnotism, held in Paris,
which featured Blanche as its star subject, a Swiss physician named
Dr. Ladame argued that these public shows should be outlawed. After
a hypnotist comes through town, argued Ladame, one of the medical
pioneers of hypnotism, he leaves behind disaster: "an enervated and
agitated population, reeling under the influence of a true psychic epidemic, recalling the great mental epidemics of the Middle Ages, with
their convulsionaries, their witches and their superstitions."[107]

In Claretie's novel *Les amours d'un interne*, a fictional account differs little from the medical accounts. One of his heroines, the young
Mathilde, accompanies her lover, a sculptor of medical wax models,
to a hypnotism show where an intern from the Salpêtrière decides to
use what he has learned at the clinic for some extramedical entertainment. Before an audience of friends, he hypnotizes "the great Lolo"
and, applying the techniques he has learned from Doctor Fargeas (a
Charcot-like director), puts his subject into catalepsy, lethargy and

somnambulism. Like the hysterics at the Salpêtrière, she fawns over a hallucinated bird and shrieks at a hallucinated snake. Under the "unhealthy" influence of this bizarre spectacle, Mathilde becomes deathly pale and begins to laugh nervously and uncontrollably. Not long after, she experiences her first full blown hysterical attack and ends up being admitted as a patient to the Salpêtrière hysteria ward.

Besides the threat of provoking hysteria, doctors were quick to point out another danger inherent in lay hypnosis: rape. In the lethargic state, a woman was rendered completely unconscious, making it easy for an unscrupulous hypnotist to take advantage of her. The newspapers of the day reported cases of young women who were raped after being hypnotized. Gilles de la Tourette held Donato personally responsible for the rape of one young girl. Her attacker, one of Donato's spectators, "studied the hypnotist's techniques and applied them to his victim in order to put her in a state of lethargy and rape her."[108] There were many hypnosis-rape cases that were taken to court. In what became known as the "Marguerite A. Affair," an eighteen-year-old young woman who consulted a magnetizer-healer found herself pregnant but had no recollection of how it had happened. The court concluded that she had been hypnotized and then raped by her "healer."

While Charcot and his colleagues kept an indignant distance from lay hypnotists, Donato openly acknowledged his debt to science, both past and present, and even wrote an article praising the medical masters of hypnotism and listing his own scientific contributions to the field.[109] Joseph Delboeuf, for one, took him seriously and came to his, and other lay hypnotists', defense. Accusing the medical establishment of arrogance and hypocrisy, Delboeuf pointed out that until recently medicine had denied the very existence of hypnotism, only to change its mind and claim that, yes, indeed it existed, but exclusively for them. He went on to attack the doctors for trying to monopolize hypnotism for mercenary reasons, remarking that it was quite lucrative for any successful practitioner, both inside of the clinic and out. Delboeuf also insisted that the medical hypnotists were indebted to the lay hypnotists for many of their techniques, and claimed that Dr. Ladame, mentioned above, had plagiarized Donato's techniques. In fact, one of the chapters from his book *Magnetizers and Doctors* is entitled "Why Mr. Ladame Owes Everything He Knows to Donato and Why He Is Not Afraid to Bite the Hand that Feeds Him."[110]

Pierre Janet, a student of Charcot's, shared Delboeuf's conviction that stage magnetizers had had a significant effect on doctors. Medical students, he pointed out, attended lectures given by the famous theatrical hypnotists and then brought this information back to the Salpêtrière with them. One stage hypnotist, the Marquis de Puyfontaine, was even brought to the hospital, where he worked with Charcot's pupils and patients.[111]

Charcot had reasons other than public health for wanting to discredit Donato and suppress his appearances. Donato, who successfully hypnotized healthy members of his audience, men included, inadvertently added support to the Nancy School's claim that the ability to be hypnotized was a universal phenomenon, not one present only in hysterics, as the Salpêtrière School insisted. Donato also openly supported Bernheim's claim that Charcot unknowingly created his famous stages of hysteria through hypnotic suggestion.[112]

No matter how much Charcot tried to distance himself and his hysterics from the carnival hypnotists, the rest of the world refused to oblige. Not only did the popular press compare his "lectures" to the carnival shows, so did professional journals. The British medical journal *The Lancet*, for example, speaks of Donato and Charcot in the same breath: "On one occasion [Charcot] gave a regular 'séance' at the hospital, in the presence of Gambetta and other political celebrities, when he made the patients, all females, fall into convulsions, jump, laugh, cry; and he produced other phenomena which one may witness any day at the 'salle de conference' of M. Donato, who is not a medical man." Later in the same article, the journalist, discussing Charcot's stages of hypnotism, writes: "in fact, M. Donato, the public magnetizer . . . has obtained the same results, as may be witnessed by his public 'séances' or conferences, as he pleased to call them, to give them more of the character of scientific meetings."[113]

Besides their shows, lay hypnotists set up consultation booths, where the somnambulist acted as a clairvoyant and, for a price, would predict the future, find lost objects, or lost loved ones. Scams, not surprisingly, were quite common. Blanche's friend Gabrielle Caill., a Salpêtrière patient who also worked in the carnivals, tells of a trick in which the somnambulist would "see" a buried treasure, and then for a fee of 1,000 francs, showed the client where it was. Somnambulists sometimes acted as mediums to contact the dead, summoning everyone from Plato to Marie Antoinette to a deceased loved one for their client. That they were able to convince a naïve public of their special power did not surprise Gilles de la Tourette. The somnambulic state of the hypnotic trance, he argues, often heightens intelligence. "I have known somnambulists, poor girls who are badly educated and of very ordinary intelligence, who, once put to sleep, completely change their manner. From the glum girls that they were, they become lively and joyful, even spiritual. In the somnambulic state, the senses become highly developed—hearing, touch and sight take on a remarkable acuity, and in this state of mind, it is easy for her to pass as a prophetess."[114]

The highest fees, not surprisingly, went to somnambulists who claimed healing powers. Trained by her magnetizer, who would set her up in a room deliberately designed to look like a doctor's office, the somnambulist saw patients for a fee. "There are somnambulists," writes Gilles de la Tourette, "who, during their sleep, respond in monosyllables to the questions they are asked and remain gloomy. If they are aiming for commerce, they will certainly not make a fortune. There are others, however, whose minds are very malleable, very flexible: these are the ones magnetizers are looking for. They educate them, telling them how they must be in order to satisfy the clientele, furnishing them with medical terms borrowed from popular books that they always have copies of, train them as one trains for any profession."[115] By 1889, there were more than five hundred of these "*cabinets somnambulists*" in Paris, promising to treat disorders resistant to traditional medicine. Some pharmacists worked as accomplices. The somnambulist would prescribe a certain herb or medication and then send the client off to a specified pharmacy, one that was only too happy to fill the prescription. As Gilles de la Tourette pointed out, if the "patient" got better, he or she, not recognizing the fact that most ailments heal naturally, would proclaim the extraordinary powers of the somnambulist, and recommend her to friends and family members. However, if their condition stayed the same, or worsened, they would in all likelihood see a real doctor and be ashamed to mention that they had ever consulted a somnambulist. He concluded that for the most part the somnambulists were in authentic hypnotic trances but added that, after years of practice, they were good at feigning the somnambulic state and could easily get away with simulating now and then without damaging their reputation. Curiously, he never made the same claim about Blanche and the other hysterics at the Salpêtrière.

He did, however, mention three of his patients who spent time in both clinic and carnival. While undercover in the world of stage magnetism, he happened to bump into one of them, an ex-patient named Jeanne, who had become a professional somnambulist. Remembering that she was highly suggestible, he jokingly told her, "Look, there's a man with a nose as long as a donkey." She looked and gasped, actually seeing the long nose on the man he had pointed at. "Oh, leave me alone," she complained, "I'm too tired. Every night I'm put under, and I no longer know what I'm doing, or what I've become. I believe everything I'm told and I do anything they want. I no longer know where I am. I don't have a shred of will power left. I'm convinced that I'll end up mad."[116]

According to Gilles de la Tourette, the path between the carnival and the clinic was a well-traveled one. As entertainment somnambulists, hysterics were well paid, received a cut of the night's profits, as well as food and lodging. When they needed a break from the pressures of their professional lives, or their hysterical attacks became too disruptive, they would return to the Salpêtrière. He tells an amazing story about Blanche's friend Gabrielle Caill. She was working as a consulting somnambulist when she met a magnetizer who asked her to perform with him. She agreed to become his partner, but before embarking on a trip to America, where they had scheduled a grand tour, she had second thoughts and fled, escaping with her down payment of 200 francs and her elaborate sky-blue costume, which she sold in order to buy clothes "more appropriate for ordinary life."[117] When she discovered that part of their performance involved her being put under hypnosis and instructed to walk into a cage of wild beasts, she became understandably alarmed. Even Delboeuf, who enthusiastically supported the rights of lay hypnotists, objected to this practice, which had become very popular, calling it "stupid and immoral."[118]

Gilles de la Tourette related another story that demonstrates the conjunction of carnival and clinic. A Salpêtrière medical student who had studied under Charcot was struggling financially, so the other students all pitched in to help him meet his expenses. One day he disappeared, and it was discovered that before he ran off, he had committed a series of thefts in the hospital. One of his victims was none other than Gilles de la Tourette. However, out of pity for the desperation that drove the poor student to steal, no one pressed charges. They later discovered that he had become a dentist, a fact which, Gilles de la Tourette remarked, "is very regrettable for that profession."[119] While at the Salpêtrière, the thief became romantically involved with one of the hysterics, referred to as Mig., and later came back for her. The two left the hospital together and formed a team with himself as magnetizer and Mig. as somnambulist. While they enjoyed some success, Mig. ended up back in the hospital. What became of the unscrupulous dentist is unknown. However, he received a comeuppance when the young girl told the hospital doctors everything, revealing all the tricks of the trade.

In *L'hypnotisme et les états analogues*, Gilles de la Tourette recounted a tale of yet another unsavory dentist, one he had gone to school with when they were boys. Unsuccessful at dentistry, he went into business with his brother, a doctor who practiced hypnotism. Together they published a medical journal, and while only one issue was printed, Gilles de la Tourette gives the reader an insight into his character by noting that the publication was deceptively labeled "Vol. 5, number 22." No more successful at publishing than he had been in dentistry, the ex-dentist and his mistress, a hysteric, tried their luck at public hypnotism shows, having learned the trade from his brother the doctor, and they enjoyed some success. However, following an argument, his somnambulist ran off and left him. The man then had the audacity to show up at the Salpêtrière, hoping to use his connection to his old schoolmate to procure another hysteric. When the physician threatened to have him thrown out, he reluctantly left the hospital and was not heard from again.

The Supernatural at the Salpêtrière

These anecdotes reveal the remarkable fluidity between the carnival and the clinic. Despite the fact that Charcot actively campaigned against the public displays of hypnotism practiced by stage magnetizers and amateurs, the spectacles at the Salpêtrière had much in common with the traveling shows he fought to ban. In the somnambulic state, the hysteric, on top of all of her other talents, was thought to be capable of supersensory powers. And while Charcot was careful to never categorize this phenomenon as supernatural, the research conducted at the clinic did seem to prove that her senses were developed to an otherworldly degree. In one case, a patient was able to hear conversations taking place behind closed doors hundreds of meters away and could feel the hand of her doctor even though he never touched her.[120]

Delboeuf described a hypnotized Blanche, "La Wittman" as "a veritable piece of living laboratory." She was so highly sensitized that it was "not even necessary to touch her, it is enough to move one's hand above the region in which one wants to produce a movement to see her nerves swell, her limbs move, the back of her hand curl into a ball, her eyes slide in all directions beneath her closed eyelids."[121]

Not only did the hypnotized hysteric have extraordinarily developed physical senses, she became clairvoyant, capable of perceiving a hidden world, either real or imagined. Charcot did not regard the phenomenon as the hallucinations of a madwoman but insisted on the reality of these perceptions. Experiments in telepathy, clairvoyance, and what was called "*sommeil à distance*," or "telepathic communication," were conducted to demonstrate the veracity of these "occult" phenomena. Once again Blanche proved incredibly gifted. When in a somnambulic state, tests were conducted to show that hallucinated objects appeared closer when Blanche peered at them through a pair of opera glasses, were multiplied when she viewed them through a prism, and were reflected by mirrors held before her eyes. However, as the always-suspicious doctors realized, the possibilities of being hoodwinked in these particular instances were great—Blanche would only need to claim that she had experienced these visual effects. In order to scientifically establish the reality of these hallucinations, another kind of test was required.

One of Charcot's favorite experiments, done to verify these perceptions, was to show Blanche a card from a completely blank deck on which he would suggest that there was a specific picture—usually a portrait of someone she knew and liked. The deck was then reshuffled, but not before the card with the suggested image was marked discreetly in back so that the physician, but not the patient, would be able to identify it. Blanche was then able to pick out the "picture card," even though it was as blank as all the others. She kept an entire collection of these portraits that she would take out from time to time to look at and admire. They gave her, claims Gilles de la Tourette, the greatest pleasure.[122] Joseph Delboeuf witnessed an experiment during which Charcot told Blanche that the blank card was a portrait of himself. This time he also marked it discreetly, not only to distinguish it from the other blank cards, but to show which end was the top of the "portrait." Blanche then gave a detailed description of what she saw: Charcot was in profile, turned to the left, wearing a hat, with one hand in the pocket of his overcoat. When the card was mixed in with the other blank ones, she was able to locate it immediately, and, to hold it right side up. In fact, she liked it so much that she begged to keep it, and when Charcot agreed, she "lovingly" placed it in her pocket. Like the other "portraits" she kept, this one lasted for some time. However, as Delboeuf notes, the image would eventually begin to fade, a fact that Blanche explained by stating that it must have been "a photograph of poor quality."

The boundary that separated these experiments from the world of spiritualism and what was then called "psychical" phenomena was not well defined. Charcot never explicitly labeled any of the hypnotic phenomena "supernatural." They were merely symptoms, albeit extraordinary ones, of hysteria. However, others, even from within the scientific community, were more willing to entertain otherworldly possibilities. Charles Richet, for example, Charcot's fellow doctor and colleague, as well as a Nobel Prize winner for medicine, was a member of the Society for Psychical Research, an organization that continues to exist, and is devoted to examining paranormal experience in a scientific manner. Dr. Jules Luys, who had been at the Salpêtrière before moving to the Charité Hospital, respected the eccentric Dr. Gérard Encausse, who went by the name of "Mage Papus" and became a figure in occult circles. Luys himself became well known for a series of bizarre experiments in what he called the action of "medication at a distance." Hysterics were hypnotized and then shown various drugs in sealed test tubes. The contents of the test tubes were not revealed, but the hysterics nonetheless responded appropriately when the small vial was held near them, even when held behind them. Ipecac produced vomiting, nitrobenzole created convulsive shocks through the whole body, while alcohol produced "merry or furious drunkeness." Other reactions were also noted: the pleasant-sounding oil of cherry laurel brought about "ecstasy and piety" and valerian made the woman crawl about on all fours with "feline movements."

Cesare Lombroso, a towering figure of nineteenth-century science, openly acknowledged the supernatural in hysteria. In his book, *Hypnotisme et spiritisme*, Lombroso stated what the neurologist repeatedly denied: "The truth is that we cannot provide a truly scientific explanation for these facts, which are on the threshold of a world that must rightfully be labeled occult, because it is inexplicable."[123] What follows, in typical Lombrosian fashion, is a bombardment of case histories, endless lists of "scientifically verified accounts" of what today would be called psychic phenomenon. Like Charcot, he claimed that these bizarre phenomena occured most readily in hypnotized hysterics, and like Charcot, he insisted on the reality of these experiences. However, unlike Charcot, Lombroso believed that science could not account for these experiences. When in a state of somnambulism, not only do hysterics hallucinate images that function as real objects, they are able to "see" actual events occurring miles away. They are able to "read" minds and predict the future. Lombroso backed up these claims with data: accurate predictions of illness, death, and murder are all cited. Time and space are no longer obstacles to the hysteric's supersensory perception.

Frederic W. H. Myers was another nineteenth-century man who did not hesitate to label the bizarre behavior of hypnotized hysterics supernatural. Trained as a classics scholar at Oxford, Myers left his university post after he experienced what he believed to be contact from his dead wife. From that time on, he devoted his professional life to the research of psychic occurrences, and it was he who founded the Society for Psychical Research, with William James as president. Myers was a frequent visitor to the Salpêtrière, and he published many of the clinic's experiments in the society's journal. In fact, some studies done on Blanche were included in the first volume of his enormous work entitled *Human Personality and Its Survival of Bodily Death*. The Society for Psychical Research counted scientists, such as Cesare Lombroso, and many doctors among its members, including Charles Féré, Pierre Janet, and Charles Richet from the Salpêtrière.

Hysteria's "magic"—its clairvoyance, its transformations, its telepathy—took place during its artificial stage, during hypnosis, thus removing it from its raw, unguided state. The desire on the part of the physician-hypnotist to reveal hysteria by recreating it as a controlled spectacle is, in the end, a wish of absolute separation. "Species" similarity, to use the language of the day, disappears. Women are made to bark like dogs, hold impossible positions, see what isn't there. They do what isn't human, what is seemingly beyond natural boundaries.

Metals and Magnets

Another area of research at the Salpêtrière that at times blurred the boundaries between science and science fiction was "metallotherapy," or the use of metals and magnets to treat hysterical symptoms. Charcot was introduced to this phenomenon by a doctor named Victor Jean-Marie Burq. Burq had discovered, quite by accident, that certain metals restored sensation to the anesthetic limbs of his hysterical patients and had been experimenting with various metals for decades. In 1876 he presented his findings to the open-minded and progressive Société de Biologie, which formed a committee, with Charcot as president, to verify Burq's results. Charcot successfully repeated the experiments on hysterical patients at the Salpêtrière, and metallotherapy became part of the hospital's arsenal of treatments for hysteria. Blanche and other patients suffering from hemianesthesia, a loss of feeling on one side of the body, had metals and magnets applied to their skin and tactile sensibility returned. Each patient reacted differently to the various metals: Blanche responded well to copper and gold. An entry in her medical observation on December 13, 1877, notes that two copper plates applied to her leg restored her sense of touch in a small area of 4 to 5 centimeters. Charcot added electricity and magnets to Burq's metals, and he gave these healing agents the name "aesthesiogens."

Doctors soon began to notice a bizarre phenomenon. When an aesthesiogen had restored sensation to one part of the patient's body, the corresponding part on the other side of her body *lost* its sensation. For example, if copper plates temporarily restored hearing to a hysteric's left ear, her previously healthy right ear became deaf. If a gold bracelet brought back feeling to a previously numb left arm, it was immediately substituted by a loss of sensation in the same area of the right arm. This process was labeled "transfer" by a physician named Dumontpallier, who deliberately used a term borrowed from the vocabulary of finance. Story has it that one day, while he was transferring funds from one bank account to another, he realized the action was analogous to his patients' response to metallotherapy. Blanche Wittmann was again at the center of a new medical practice, and again proved most gifted.

According to Charcot, magnets produced the best transfers. Given the inherent tendency for hysterics to deceive, especially when the victim of their deceit was their doctor, Charcot insisted that these experiments be conducted while the patient was hypnotized. As Binet and Féré explained, while a hysteric in an awakened state could simply pretend that a transfer had occurred, it would be "impossible for an awake person to imitate even one of the physical phenomena of hypnotism."[124] Therefore, in order to verify transfer, the patients were first hypnotized. Even then, always alert to the possibility of being tricked, Charcot would from time to time substitute a sham magnet for a real one, and when no transfer occurred, was satisfied the results were genuine.

Joseph Delboeuf wrote that it was mainly his desire to inspect the phenomenon of transfer that brought him from Liège to Paris and the Salpêtrière. There, on October 15, 1886, he witnessed a series of extraordinary experiments conducted by Dr. Féré and Dr. Binet on Blanche. Blanche the "placid and quite delectable Alsatian" was, writes Delboeuf, "not only accommodating, but visibly happy to participate in anything that was asked of her."[125] (Blanche, due to her Germanic surname, was sometimes referred to as "the Alsatian.") He watched as Blanche was hypnotized and saw the usual transfers of insensitivity and paralysis from her left leg to her right, as well as far more extraordinary occurrences. In one experiment, Blanche was placed in a designated position, seated at a table with her head resting on her right hand and her left leg crossed over her right. Under the influence of the magnet, she took the opposite position: resting her head on her left hand, and crossing her right leg over her left. This same experiment on Blanche had already been published in the *Revue Philosophique* one year earlier and was used to show that transfer could occur even with voluntary movements— that is, when the subject was awake. In this instance, Blanche was not hypnotized, but merely asked to sit in a specific position. When,

quite naturally, she wanted to know why, she was told that she was
sitting for a portrait, and cheerfully complied.[126] Delboeuf also witnessed an experiment in which the magnet transferred movements
from one side of Blanche to the other. For example, when she was
asked to write a series of numbers, she, being right-handed, naturally
wrote them with her right hand. However, when a magnet was held
up to her left side, she moved the pen to her left hand and continued
writing. Moreover, she wrote the numbers backward, as they would
appear in a mirror.[127] By the time Delboeuf witnessed this demonstration, Blanche had done it so many times that she was able to write as
well with her left hand in mirror writing as she was with her right.[128]
Indeed, she became so good at it that the doctors could move the
magnet back and forth quickly and repeatedly and she would effortlessly switch the pen from her left hand to her right, with no break
in her transcription. Once again, the doctors appeal to a mechanical image—that of a pendulum—to describe the fluid and automatic
motions of their hypnotized hysteric.[129]

Another Salpêtrière experiment in transfer appeared in the *Revue
Philosophique*. Blanche was put into a somnambulic state, and again
the green bust of Gall figured as a character. This time, however, she
wasn't asked to kiss it, but rather to thumb her nose at it, and she was
told to execute this motion with her left hand. All unfolded according
to plan. Blanche enthusiastically thumbed her nose at the founder of
phrenology. When a magnet was held near her right side, the con-
temptuous gestures her left hand was making slowly came to a halt
and her right hand began to tremble. She stopped, suddenly aware of
her actions and, as though to justify her behavior, said, "He's disgust-
ing, that man."[130] She then began to thumb her nose at him again,
only this time with her right hand, and continued to do so for ten
minutes.

Through the use of various stimuli on different body parts, the
doctors were able to turn Blanche into a divided woman, cataleptic

on the right side, lethargic on the left, a person literally split in two, "a curious example of dualism."[131] Delboeuf was also present when the doctors put Blanche in two simultaneous hypnotic states. As he remarks, "the young girl was, so to speak, cut in two, one half of her body being in lethargy, the other in catalepsy." Then, using a magnet, they successfully reversed this double state, turning her left side cataleptic and her right lethargic. The doctors accomplished a different kind of division by putting all of Blanche into catalepsy, but then giving each half of her its own emotion. For example, Delboeuf watched as Blanche displayed "love on the left side and hate on the right . . . one side of the face smiling, the other threatening. (. . .) sadness and gaiety . . . admiration and terror."[132] These expressions were no more connected to her inner state than those imprinted by Duchenne's electrical probes. They had no relationship to any actual emotions—they were merely masks, covering an emptiness. The doctor's act of dividing Blanche in two and giving each side a contrary expression emphasized her artificiality. Her expressions became pure signs that signified emotions but expressed nothing.

The magnet could also transfer hallucinations. Blanche, in a state of somnambulism, was told that she had a pigeon perched on her hand but that she was only able to see it with her left eye. When she awoke, she did in fact see the pigeon, but only with her left eye; when the doctors closed it, she no longer saw the bird. However, when the doctors held up a magnet to her right side for several minutes, she was able to see the pigeon again, but only with her right eye, not her left. In another experiment, Blanche was again told that she was holding a bird. This time the doctors had discreetly placed a magnet on a table located to her right. While stroking the bird, she wandered away from the table, and to her dismay, the bird suddenly disappeared. As she walked back toward the table, the doctors were able to deduce that the hallucinated bird had reappeared, since they could hear her scolding: "Now is that any way to behave? Leaving me like that!"[133]

In the doctors' hallucinated tableaux, birds are cast more frequently than other animals. As is obvious from the range of experiments performed at the Salpêtrière, this can't be from a lack of imagination. One possible explanation is that Blanche was fond of the winged creatures. She loved the birds in the courtyard and had made friends with one in particular, whose feathers she had marked to recognize it. The creature ate from her hand.

Hallucinated colors could also be transferred. When Blanche was given the hypnotic suggestion that everything in the laboratory was red, she saw green—red's polar opposite—when a magnet was held up to one side of her body. Likewise, she saw purple when yellow had been suggested, or rather, given her partial color blindness, she saw purple as she always did: it appeared as black. The doctors loved this particular experiment. They assumed that Blanche and the other hysterics did not have the education to know complimentary colors, so they believed it proved the authenticity of their results.

The magnet's power was not limited to physiology. In a process labeled "psychic polarization," it was capable of transferring emotions. For example, a magnet held behind Blanche's head would turn her happiness to sadness, "benevolence" to hatred, and anger to indulgence. "In short," concludes Delboeuf, who witnessed the transfers, "it changes one's mind, it makes black white and white black." In an experiment recounted by Binet, Blanche was hypnotized and told that when she awoke she would want to beat Mr. Féré. Sure enough, as soon as she woke up, she acted on Binet's suggestion, and his colleague just managed to jump away and catch her arm before being slapped. "I don't know why," she said, "but I want to hit him." A magnet was then held up behind her and her expression suddenly changed, becoming "soft and sweet." Once again she threw herself at Féré, only this time it was to hug and kiss him.

Féré and Binet admit that it was easier to successfully enact a psychic polarization on a hypnotically induced emotion than on a genuine one, illustrating once again how the artificial hysteric was easier to control than the natural one. For example, no matter how long they held the magnet up, they were unsuccessful in their attempt to get Gabrielle Caill. to change her mind about a person she had detested for years. Blanche, however, always the perfect subject, was successfully polarized, and her hatred for this same person was transformed to fondness.

The magnet could turn memory into forgetfulness. The doctors labeled the magnet's ability to erase memory an "anesthesia of memory" or "magnetic amnesia." In one experiment, Blanche, in a state of somnambulism, was given a false memory: she was told that Albert Londe, the hospital photographer, who had recently left his post at the Salpêtrière, had come by the day before and had taken pictures in the courtyard of Gabrielle Caill., dressed in a musketeer costume. Blanche was awakened and asked: "What's new?" She responded: "You know Albert X the photographer has left, but, I can tell you that he came back yesterday and resumed his old position. He took pictures of Gabrielle, and she was wearing a costume that really suited her, she was dressed as a musketeer and she looked so adorably chic. Albert Londe was the best, but then he left. Oh! I am so upset, I do like him so much." At that moment the doctors held a magnet up, and Blanche changed her mind, stating: "Oh! I never liked him." She then forgot the false memory altogether, and, when asked what time he had stopped by, she responded that she had absolutely no idea what the doctors were talking about. In another instance of magnetic amnesia, one that no doubt pleased everyone involved, Blanche was asked to think about Charcot, and then a magnet was applied "until her memory of Mr. Charcot [was] completely abolished." Then, the great man himself, who had been hiding behind her chair, stepped out in front of her, and while Blanche was perfectly aware that she was seeing a man, she had no idea who he was.[134]

Transfer was not restricted to a single subject. Joseph Babinski, the doctor featured in Brouillet's portrait supporting the lethargic Blanche, conducted a different kind of experiment with magnetic transfer at the Salpêtrière. Two hysterics referred to only as "A" and "B" were seated back-to-back, both suffering from hemianesthesia. Babinski was then able to use a magnet to transfer the hemianesthesia of A to B, leaving one fully anesthetic and the other with complete sensation. By moving the magnet, he was able to reverse this transfer. While Babinski was initially excited by the therapeutic applications of this discovery (transferring a hysterical paralysis from a woman to a pig, for example), he later backed away from the study, and significantly, it is nowhere to be found in his later published collected works.[135]

Blanche's Double Personality

Blanche's uncanny ability to be transformed was pushed to a new level in 1888 when she was "on loan" to another hospital, the Hôtel-Dieu. Here she was studied by Dr. Jules Janet—the younger brother of Pierre, a doctor at the Salpêtrière, and a nephew of the philosopher Paul Janet—who made the remarkable discovery that Blanche, "a hysteric known by all and justifiably famous," had a "double personality."[136]

Janet's diagnosis of Blanche was not as medically bizarre in 1888 as it might at first appear. There had been several highly publicized cases of what was then called "double personality" in the news, among them Léonie, a patient of Pierre Janet's. The most famous case of double personality, however, was a hysteric from Bordeaux known as Félida X., whose case forms something of a framing narrative for Janet's diagnosis. Félida's case was followed for more than thirty years by a doctor named Eugène Azam, who first began to observe her in 1858, when she was thirty-two years old. According to Azam, Félida began exhibiting hysterical symptoms at puberty, symptoms that included severe headaches followed by spontaneous catalepsy, or a loss of consciousness. After these episodes, she would awaken in a second state in which she was happy and lively, utterly different from her usual somber self. In her normal or first state, Félida was a hardworking young dressmaker, serious to the point of being morose. She was in constant pain and so concerned with her health, so self-obsessed, that she was indifferent to anyone else. In her second state, she was kind and affectionate to her family, cheerful, carefree, and while she spent less time at her work, she did so with greater skill. Also, she suffered from none of the pain that usually plagued her. In her new state, she was completely aware of her other existence; however, the same did not hold true for her first self, which had no memory whatsoever of her second self. Over the years, the transition time between these two personalities became shorter and shorter, until it took a mere fraction of a second and was imperceptible to those around her. She therefore frequently found herself in baffling situations. Among the many episodes that Azam related is one in which she woke up to find herself riding in a coach, dressed in mourning and on her way to a funeral. She had become skilled at feigning understanding (Azam tells us that she was embarrassed by her condition and did her best to mask it), and she managed to piece together from her traveling companions' comments that her sister-in-law had died. In another episode, while in her second state, she was given a little dog that she adored and doted on, but once back in her first state, she pushed the animal away, thinking it was a stray that had mistakenly wandered into her home. Even more upsetting, her first self noticed that her abdomen had swelled and she initially refused to accept the doctor's claim that she was pregnant. She believed herself to be a virgin. In fact, she had had sexual relations with a man while in her second state, a man she eventually married after giving birth to his son. In the early years of her illness, her second state occupied only an hour or two of her day, but later it began to take up more and more of her time, a fact that made her home life increasingly pleasant, given the grim, painful reality of her first self. Eventually, she existed almost exclusively in her second state; her original self appeared only once in a while for brief periods.[137]

Azam interpreted Félida's second state as analogous to the state of somnambulism provoked by hypnosis, whereas her first state was her normal, awake state. Unlike the famous Félida, Blanche's second personality did not appear spontaneously. It was called forth under hypnosis. One day while hypnotizing Blanche, Janet, aware that "everyone knows in fact that it is Blanche Witt. who has served as the model for the study of the three hypnotic stages," decided to see what would happen if he went further than Charcot, and rather than following the usual progression from lethargy to somnambulism, placed her in an even deeper state of sleep. "Beginning with lethargy," he explains, "I try to go further. After several instants, Blanche becomes absolutely inert. I can no longer obtain in her any contracture from deep pressure on the muscles or nerves, and opening her eyes no longer brings about catalepsy. After several more passes, Blanche gives out several sighs. Soon her head stirs, she opens her eyes and sits up comfortably. She seems to have woken up and she answers all of my questions."[138]

Janet first believed that Blanche was in the classic somnambulic state; however, her behavior soon proved him wrong. First of all, she was remarkably happy and open, whereas her demeanor in ordinary somnambulism was quite somber. His suspicion that this was no ordinary somnambulic state was confirmed when he was unable to provoke hallucinations. The woman before him was in every aspect, except for her appearance, unlike the woman he had had before him only moments ago. As we know, Blanche in her wakeful state suffered many hysterical symptoms. When she first entered Janet's office, she was anesthetic on both sides of her body. Not only did she not feel pinpricks, but she was also completely unaware of the position her body was in once her eyes were closed. Her lack of sensation, however, was complicated by "hyper-anesthesia," that is, a morbid sensitivity, in both ovarian regions. Moreover, she was completely deaf in her left ear and had visual disturbances in her left eye: achromatopsy (color blindness) and a shortened visual field.

But in her new state, Blanche was able to feel and see and hear. She reacted to pinches and pokes, and responded correctly when asked to raise a specific finger with her eyes closed. She could see the full spectrum of colors with both eyes, and her visual field was completely normal. Moreover, she could hear perfectly well with both ears and her hysterogenic points disappeared. Janet devised a series of sensory examinations in order to put her remarkable recovery to the test, and she passed each one without difficulty. She was, in every aspect, a new woman. "The keenest observer," remarked Janet, "would not be able to distinguish Blanche Witt. from a normal, non-hysterical person. We no longer have a neuropath before us, an incomplete person, but a woman enjoying the full range of her nervous system."[139]

The only thing unusual presented by this new Blanche was what Janet referred to as her excessive "electivity," by which he meant that she showed a marked preference for him, one that was so extreme that she would ignore every other person in the room, unless Janet specifically requested that she engage in conversation with them. This electivity was extremely convenient, because another characteristic of her new state was that, unlike ordinary somnambulism, Blanche was not unwaveringly suggestible. "Blanche 2," wrote Janet, "can refuse to obey; she remains free."[140] However, given her extreme "electivity" for her physician, most of his requests were followed willingly.

This new Blanche, wrote Janet, had "a character, inclinations and properties so different" from the old Blanche, that it "is hard to believe that she is the same." In fact, this woman was so radically different from Blanche Wittmann in her waking state that Janet at first called her by a new name: "Louise." According to Janet, she readily accepted this shift in nomenclature. However, admitting that calling the new personality Louise might "lead to confusion," and perhaps realizing the hubris of such an act, Janet changed his mind, and chose to refer to the new healthy Blanche as "Blanche 2," and to the old, unhealthy version as Blanche 1.[141]

As Janet continued his research, he decided to focus on the relationship between the two personalities and discovered that, like Félida, Blanche in her sleep state (Blanche 2) was aware of the existence of Blanche 1, whereas Blanche 1 was ignorant of the existence of Blanche 2. "It is easy for me," wrote Janet, "when I am in the presence of Blanche 2, to verify that she knows perfectly well all of the details of the life of Blanche 1; to the contrary . . . Blanche 1 has no idea about the acts of Blanche 2, or even of her existence." Janet conducted many tests that led him to the conclusion that Blanche 2 was present as a kind of silent spectator in the life of Blanche 1. In order to prove his theory, he devised a simple sign language for Blanche 2. Raising her finger meant yes and raising her thumb meant no. He then summoned Blanche 1 and pricked her arm with a needle, asking her if she felt anything. She responded by telling him, "You know perfectly well that I can't feel a thing." However, as Blanche 1 was uttering these words, Blanche 2 had raised her finger, indicating that yes, indeed, she felt the prick. Janet conducted other experiments as well, and in each instance, Blanche 2, through the use of sign language, made her presence known by correctly seeing, hearing, or feeling sights and sounds and sensations that the compromised Blanche 1 was unable to identify. Moreover, added Janet, Blanche 1 had no idea of the movements her fingers were executing. "In short," he concluded, "Blanche 2 remains hidden behind Blanche 1 who covers her like a veil; she only appears in full light when this veil falls, the moment when Blanche 1 disappears."[142]

In his analysis of the relationship between these two personalities, Janet suggested an explanation for hysteria and for mental illness in general. Everyone, he claimed, is something of a double personality. However, with normal healthy subjects, these two personalities remain in balance, the second one asserts itself when the first personality is weakened—during sleep, for example; in a dream; or during a state of intoxication, when the second personality conducts uncontrolled and bizarre acts. In the case of a hysteric like Blanche, however, there is an imbalance of power between the two. The first one is "feeble, dwarfed and degraded," while the second personality is vigorous and strong, and has a natural tendency to take advantage of the first personality's weakness. Complicating matters, the two personalities, housed in the same body, have only one set of senses.

Wielding her power, Blanche 2 was particularly ruthless and played cruel tricks on the vulnerable Blanche 1. The abusive Blanche 2 came out while Blanche 1 was asleep and dragged her out to wander corridors and walk on rooftops (hysterics, including Blanche, often walked in their sleep). Blanche 2 would also brazenly appear "in broad daylight," and cause Blanche 1's hysterical attacks by "stunning the weak woman who walks before her and wrestling her to the ground in chaotic muscular gymnastics." There seemed to be no end to Blanche 2's mean streak. Out of pure spite, she deprived Blanche 1 of her mobility by "taking away her leg and in its place leaving, for all to see, her own leg. If she decides to leave it limp and without movement, we have paralysis; if, following her fantastic whims, she desires to contract it, we have a hysterical contracture." This, concluded Janet, means that the various disorders of hysteria stem from "the incomplete state of the first personality and the bad instincts of the second personality."[143]

Treating the disease then, became a matter of controlling the "bad instincts" of this second personality, who, when given free rein, "takes advantage of the debility of her companion in order to overwhelm her completely, or attack her part by part with her bad habits." The doctor must address not the first personality, but the second one: "It is she who is the cause of the evil; it is she, and she alone, who can fix it." Therefore, "in order to give the first personality a property that it lacks, it is necessary to take it from the second personality." Janet pointed out that Blanche 1 had lost all sensation, except for the small area underneath the gold bracelet she wore. He posed the question "Where does this sensation come from?" and answered not by pointing to the therapeutic qualities of certain metals but by explaining that "it comes from Blanche 2 who has temporarily lent it to Blanche 1."[144] He knew this because Blanche 2 had sensation all over her body, *except for the small area underneath the bracelet*. Moreover, when he asked that Blanche 2 give back to Blanche 1 the rest of her sense of touch, Blanche 2 agreed but then became entirely insensitive herself. "In short," wrote Janet, "we can fill in the gaps of the first personality with elements that we are sure to find in the second personality; we can transport the taints of the waking state to the hypnotic state and then suppress them for the patient." Janet was thus able to put an end to Blanche's frequent fits of contracture by summoning Blanche 2 and pleading with her "to stop this bad muscular joke." Given the "electivity" Blanche 2 felt for him, his request was promptly met: Blanche's contractures disappeared and did not reappear, at least not during the term of his study. Janet cured Blanche 1 of her chronic bouts of aphonia simply by asking Blanche 2 to stop stealing Blanche 1's voice, and "upon wakening, everything was back in order."[145] Janet attempted to transform the real hysteric into a latent hysteric, to make Blanche 1 stronger than Blanche 2 so that she would no longer allow herself to be bullied by her second personality.

However, Janet soon discovered that this new state was precarious and difficult to maintain for any length of time. At the slightest provocation, such as a heightened emotion or a sudden fright, Blanche 1 relinquished the elements that Blanche 2 had returned and reverted back to her old crippled self. This unreliable situation led Janet to try another approach—not unlike the one that occurred spontaneously with Félida—that of maintaining Blanche in her second state indefinitely. Janet ended his article here, promising the readers of the *Revue Scientifique* that he would keep them informed about his findings. However, no further articles about Blanche can be found in the following issues of the *Revue*. Janet, however, continued to publish reports of his experiments with double personality elsewhere. Almost one year to the day after his discovery of Blanche's second personality, he published a case of "another Félida" in the *Revue de l'Hypnotisme et de la psychologie physiologique*. As with Blanche, he put this patient, an unnamed hysteric, in a deep sleep and summoned her second personality to appear. "My patient," he wrote with Svengali-like power "is an artificial Félida whose two existences I regulate as I please."[146]

In an article published by Frederick W. H. Myers, a brief mention of what happened to Blanche 1 and 2 can be found. He reported that in a conversation with the French doctor "M. Janet tells me that last year he kept Blanche Witt- for months together in her second state, with much comfort to her; and that now, though he has ceased to attend her, he understands that her condition in the first state is much better than of old."[147]

The lasting therapeutic effects of Janet's experiment were less enduring than he had hoped. In 1891, Blanche, now back at the Salpêtrière, appears in two different articles, and Blanche 2 is nowhere to be found. In one, she is used as a subject in an experiment in sensory stimulation during hypnosis, conducted by Dr. Georges Guinon and a Dr. Sophie Woltke. No mention is made of any changes in her condition, and she is described exactly as she was before her stint at the Hôtel Dieu: a *"grande hystérique"* who suffers from the traditional three-phase attacks. Her visual field is narrowed, she has "dyschromatopsi," hemianesthesia, hysterogenic points—"all of the usual stigmata inherent to the disease." She continues to be highly hypnotizable, and, the doctors note, her name is linked to almost all of Charcot's work on hysteria and hypnosis as well as that of his students.[148] Blanche also appears in another study from 1891, and I believe it is her last published experiment. She is mentioned in an article by Dr. Gilbert Ballet, Charcot's first chief resident, in the *Gazette Hebdomadaire de Médecine et de Chirurgie*, which addresses, once again, the complicated issue of accountability when a crime is committed due to posthypnotic suggestion.[149] Blanche, the hypnotized subject, automatically carried out the orders of the doctor. In other words, in 1891, Blanche Wittmann was still a full-blown hysteric.

Endings

Eighteen ninety-three turned out to be a disastrous year for Gilles de la Tourette. Disliked by most of his colleagues but adored by Charcot, he was devastated by his mentor's death, both privately and professionally. Not only did he lose Charcot, but his young son Jean died of meningitis that same year, and then on December 6, he was shot by an ex-patient in his own home at 39, rue de l'Université. Of the three shots fired, one hit him in the back of the head, but the resulting wound was a superficial one, and the surgeon was able to easily remove the bullet. His assailant, Rose Kamper (née Lecoq), had been a patient at the Salpêtrière and she claimed her act was one of revenge. She accused Gilles de la Tourette of hypnotizing her against her will, from a distance no less, and claimed that he had ruined her life. She also accused Charcot and two other doctors of the same crime. After she fired the shot, she sat down and calmly waited for the police to arrive, all the while repeating: "I know that what I have done is wrong, but it was necessary, and now I am satisfied. At least one of them has paid for his crimes." When the police searched Kamper's apartment, they came up with little else than a stack of newspaper clippings about hysteria and hypnotism. Dr. Ballet, the one who used Blanche in the crime experiment, was appointed by the judge to examine Rose Kamper, and he determined that she was mentally ill. She was sent to Sainte-Anne, the same institution that housed Blanche's father, but after trying to stab a nurse with a fork, she was transferred to another asylum, from which she managed to escape. Since she had threatened to repeat her attack, Gilles de la Tourette was given police protection. However, she never followed through on her threat to come after him, and when the police found her, one year later, she was working as a seamstress and appeared to be stable. Rose Kamper was therefore allowed to continue living in freedom, which she did until her death in 1955 at the age of ninety-two.

Gilles de la Tourette did not have such a happy ending. His sanity began to deteriorate in the late 1890s, forcing him to leave his hospital post, where he worked in forensic medicine, in 1901. He had begun to behave erratically, and mean-spirited articles about the "deranged doctor" were beginning to appear in the press. Léon Daudet described a bizarre street encounter he had with the unstable physician during this period. Gilles de la Tourette, who had always and with good reason hated the writer, patted him affectionately on the back and with tears in his eyes told him how happy he was to see him. He then proceeded to follow Daudet around all afternoon. "I was unable to shake off his panting declarations of tenderness and devotion."[150] Charcot's widow tried, without success, to secure a pension for him and his family, and Charcot's son Jean-Baptiste, the future explorer but at that time still a physician, arranged for him to leave Paris and recuperate privately in Lucerne, Switzerland. While in Lucerne, his behavior became increasingly bizarre and included an episode in which he stole menus and toothpicks from the hotel restaurant. What then transpired is heartbreaking. In order to get the doctor admitted to a hospital, Jean-Baptiste Charcot told the once-illustrious neurologist that there was a "famous patient" waiting to see him at the local asylum. On May 28, 1901, Gilles de la Tourette arrived at the Cery Hospital to consult with the "famous patient" and was committed against his will. In a letter to the clinic, Charcot's son writes that Gilles de la Tourette had been suffering from "melancholia with suicidal tendencies" accompanied by "bouts of megalomania." At the hospital, he was diagnosed with paretic neurosyphilis, but he nevertheless continued to fight for his release. Only a few days after he was committed, the hospital records show that he became so agitated and so determined to flee the hospital that he was placed in a cell. Charcot's loyal disciple spent the rest of his life in that hospital, descending further and further into madness. Among his symptoms were convulsions, paralysis, and delirium. Georges Gilles de la Tourette died on May 22, 1904. He was forty-six years old.[151]

Blanche Wittmann, on the other hand, never experienced another convulsion, paralysis, or delirium following the death of Charcot. The Salpêtrière became a very different place without the great neurologist at the helm. With his disciples either unable or unwilling to carry on, the famous Salpêtrière School simply ceased to exist. As the living embodiment of that school, Blanche was essentially out of a job. The Salpêtrière no longer had any use for a Queen of Hysterics. She did not, however, leave the hospital, which had been her home for almost half her life.[152] She remained, not as a patient, but as an employee.

At first she worked as an assistant in the photography laboratory, surrounded by all the photographs she had once been the subject of—both the actual subject and the hallucinated one, as she had been in Londe's ludicrous donkey image. As an employee in the laboratory, she must have thought about the time she had spent there as a patient, the subject of so many photographs, and about the time she was caught by Londe "stealing" a plate. While the photography studio continued to be a functioning laboratory of the Salpêtrière, the photographs taken were never again as beautiful as those taken during Charcot and Blanche's reign.

She was later transferred to the radiology laboratory, where she worked as a technician. The unit, which employed the new science of radiology, first opened at the Salpêtrière at the beginning of the twentieth century, under the direction of Dr. Charles Infroit. During these early years, no one was aware of the carcinogenic effects of the rays, and not only were the radiologists exposed on a daily basis; they often tested the equipment on their own hands. The last information that exists concerning Blanche comes from an article by a doctor named Baudouin, written in 1925 as an homage to Charcot on the one hundredth anniversary of his birth. Baudouin first entered the Salpêtrière as an intern in 1905, in an atmosphere in which, he admits, "one didn't speak much about hysteria." He met Blanche, whom he knew by reputation, in the radiology laboratory. She was, he claims, still quite haughty, capricious, and moody, but she no longer suffered from hysterical attacks. As he explains, "she was one of those hysterics who had had their moment of fame," but when hysteria was no longer in fashion, "she had abruptly stopped having fits." Blanche, he relates, was very reluctant to talk about her life as a hysteric. "Like all of the hysterics from the *belle époque*, she seemed to deny her past, and when questioned about the slightest detail from that part of her life, she responded with a refusal tinged with anger."[153]

She did, however, open up just a bit to Baudouin sometime later, when she had nothing else to lose. Blanche Wittmann became one of the early victims of radiology-induced cancer and spent her last years suffering from the burns and serial amputations brought about by the disease. Dr. Infroit, the director of the radiology laboratory, died several years later in the same agonizing way. Blanche first had a finger removed, then another, then her hand, then her forearm and then her upper arm, before the same process began on the other side. Baudouin went often to visit Blanche in the surgery ward, and the two became friends. On her deathbed, Baudouin once again asked her what had really been going on in Charcot's famous hysteria ward.

Like us, Baudouin wanted to know the "truth." Had Blanche really been "played like a piano," mapped out with "hysterogenic" zones and hypnotized? Had she really been invested with supersensory powers, transformed into an automaton, a double personality? Or had it all been a farce, a medical scam? Blanche's moment in the limelight provides an extraordinary opportunity to look at the ways in which cultures and bodies collide to produce new sets of symptoms, which in turn produce new diseases. Because of it's short life span, Charcot's hysteria (as opposed to the ancient and ongoing hysteria) asserts itself as a self-contained object of study. It was born in the 1870s and died with Charcot, in 1893. Baudouin was old enough to know about Charcot and Blanche's reign as the King and Queen of Hysterics, but young enough to question the validity of their rule. History tends to dismiss these moments as embarrassing medical errors. All-knowing Science, in its continual advance forward, sheds its pure and objective light on the past, exposing fallacy and confirming truth. In this way, Charcot's work on multiple sclerosis has held up to the test of time; his work on hysteria has not. However, such a view completely ignores the reality of what occurred.

Like Baudouin, who had the opportunity to question Blanche about what was *really* happening, people have often asked me what I think these women were *really* suffering from, what did they actually have. They usually provide a variety of their own possible diagnoses: they were perhaps schizophrenics, or epileptics, or bipolar. If only they had been born later, they could have been properly diagnosed and benefited from the latest treatments and pharmaceuticals. Such reasoning, however, assumes that science exists outside of culture, that bodies live beyond thought. The symptoms suffered by Blanche and other hysterics are no longer an acceptable way to express illness. Paralysis, for example, was a widespread symptom in the nineteenth century. It was one of many in a long list of symptoms available in the mid to late nineteenth century.[154] Doctors' offices were filled with patients, hysterical and otherwise, who inexplicably could not move a limb or limbs. Usually, the paralysis would come and go, sometimes lasting for an hour or two, other times for weeks or months or years. Paralysis today is, for the most part, reserved for those who have suffered an accident or a disease of the spinal cord. We have our own "symptom pool" to draw from: fatigue, headaches, irritable bowel, depression, anxiety, to name just a few of the more common contemporary syndromes. Charcot himself clung to the idea that disease lived outside of the culture that produced it and tried to prove that his version of hysteria had always existed, that what was classified as demonic possession, for example, was merely misdiagnosed hysteria. Charcot's hysteria, however, as experienced by Blanche and thousands of others, did come to life at a given moment, and then it died.[155] Blanche really "had" hysteria. She lived during a period that allowed her to express her suffering in a particular way, through a particular set of symptoms, symptoms that are no longer an admissible way to express illness.

Diseases do not exist outside of diagnoses. As any American who has spent time outside of the country knows, different cultures experience bodies—their organs and bones and blood—in different ways. The French suffer from *mal au foie* or liver ache. The Japanese can be afflicted by *taijin kyofusho*, an intense fear that their body is offensive to others. In Malaysia, epidemics of *koro* have been reported. *Koro* produces symptoms of sudden and intense anxiety that one's sexual organs will recede into the body and cause death. Each of these disorders is recognized by their respective medical communities as a valid diagnosis. Every culture molds bodies; bodies adapt and respond with the appropriate symptoms.

Blanche experienced the life and the death of hysteria. Baudouin was curious and persistent enough to keep questioning her, and one day, when her illness was already quite advanced, he once again brought up the forbidden subject: "Listen, Blanche, I know that there are things you don't want to talk about, but you know me well enough to know that I would never mock you. I want you to explain something to me about your fits from before." She hesitated for a moment, but then responded, "Alright. What is it that you want to know?" Baudouin did not hold back: "Everyone's saying that all of those attacks were simulated, that the patients only pretended to be hypnotized, and that, during that entire episode they were simply making fools of the doctors. Is there any truth to that?" Blanche, quite literally on her deathbed responded: "There is no truth at all in that. Those are lies. If we were put to sleep, if we had fits, it was because it was impossible for us to do otherwise. Besides, it's not as though it was pleasant!" And then she added, "Simulation! Do you think that it would have been easy to fool Monsieur Charcot? Oh yes, there were certainly some jokers who tried! He would look them straight in the eye and say 'Be still.'"[156]

PART THREE

Augustine

The patient who came to be known as Augustine was not as famous as Blanche Wittmann during her stay at the Salpêtrière, yet over time she has become Charcot's most celebrated hysteric. Later generations have turned her into an icon: an object of desire, a victim of misogyny, or a feminist rebel, depending on who is claiming her for themselves. Artists, writers, choreographers, filmmakers, and cultural critics have adopted her as a kind of mascot and projected their own ideas and fantasies about femininity onto a teenager who spent several years at the Salpêtrière Hospital more than a century ago. Why Augustine?

I believe the answer can be found in the many photographs taken of her while she was in the hospital. The Salpêtrière used photography, a relatively new technology at the time, to document patients in various stages of the hysterical attack. Augustine was the most photographed hysteric in Charcot's ward, twenty-two images of her were included in Volumes 2 and 3 of the *Iconographie*. Not coincidentally, she was also extremely photogenic. As contemporary photographers have said about their most successful models, the camera loved her. Augustine was pretty, but not exceptionally so: in the literature from the period, it was Blanche who played the role of hospital beauty. Yet Augustine, not Blanche, became the "supermodel" of the clinic, the hysteric whose picture was taken again and again, and whose photographs fill the pages of the *Iconographie photographique de la Salpêtrière*.

The photographs in the *Iconographie* were ostensibly illustrations of Charcot's typology of hysteria. The camera was meant to turn Augustine into a series of isolated symptoms, and the perfectly flat and beautiful images that resulted were held up as evidence of Charcot's theories. But these photographs depict more than a set of symptoms. As Roland Barthes noted in his poignant reflections on photography, a photograph always carries its referent with it.[1] Unlike the other visual techniques employed at the hospital—the wax and plaster casts or the drawings, for example—photography conveyed more than the Salpêtrière doctors intended. While these pictures of Augustine were intended to illustrate specific neurological symptoms, they also inevitably depict the girl, and this ends up compromising their status as medical illustration. It's one thing to photograph a patient's contracted limb, isolated from the rest of her body, another thing to photograph a whole person. The *Iconographie* shows faces, and the moment someone's face appears, the image's objectivity is overwhelmed by subjectivity.

Theorists question whether or not photography is an objective document of reality and question its relationship to "the real." They point to the many ways a photographer intervenes to affect his subject matter: lighting, camera angles and backgrounds, to name just a few. And then there are many decisions to be made about how the image is developed and printed. We often lose sight of the fact that photographs are not simply bits of frozen reality. An anecdote about Picasso illustrates how readily we confuse the photograph with the photographed. While painting a portrait of a woman, Picasso noticed that her husband, in the room with them, was becoming distraught. He asked him what was wrong. The husband responded that the painting looked nothing like his wife. Picasso asked, "Tell me, what does your wife look like?" The man took a photograph out of his wallet and said,

"That's what my wife looks like." Picasso examined it carefully and said, "Oh, really! Small, isn't she?"[2]

Of course, photographs are not the same as the object they depict. But, like the flustered husband, I think we have to acknowledge that they occupy a more immediate relationship to the object they depict, than, say, a painting does. There is nothing uncanny about Brouillet's portrait of Blanche or Richer's sketches of the hysterics. They might be accurate, but they are not unsettling. When I look at Regnard's photographs of Augustine, I feel as though I am looking at the girl, as she was, where she was, at a particular moment in time. The same, of course, can be said about all of the photographs in the *Iconographie*, about all photographs anywhere. Photographs are like ghosts: they are not quite dead.

Augustine's images are more *beautiful* than the others. There are several photographs of Blanche taken while she was lying down with her eyes closed that are lovely, but in the ones in which she is awake and active, she looks stiff and matronly. Many of the photographs in the *Iconographie* suffer from too much ordinary humanity: crooked hair parts, unbuttoned dresses, double chins, and sagging skin. They are artifacts of unspeakable sadness but fail as medical illustration and even more so as objects of fantasy. Augustine's photographs, on the other hand, are unblemished. The symmetry of her features and the way the light hits her skin, combined with the photographer's careful composition and contrasts between light and dark, make her images more artistic than those of the other women and offer an idealized illusion of hysteria or an idealized illusion of pretty much anything the spectator might wish to project onto the picture. In this way, Augustine's photographs are not unlike those of movie stars; not the recent ones that focus on the ways in which celebrities are just like everyone else, but the studio shots of an earlier generation: George Hurrell's glamorous images that helped to turn actors into icons.

From the Wet Nurse to Convent School

Louise Augustine Gleizes was admitted to Charcot's service at the Salpêtrière on October 21, 1875. While Bourneville recorded in her case history that she was fifteen and a half years old at the time, she had in fact just turned fourteen; her birth certificate, as well as the hospital's own registry, records her date of birth as August 21, 1861. She came to the Salpêtrière after a stay at the L'Hôpital des Enfants-Malades, the world's first children's hospital, where she had been brought by her mother five months earlier because she was suffering from frequent convulsive attacks and a paralysis that had shifted from the left side of her body to the right. After she was released from the Children's Hospital, her symptoms returned and she was sent to the Salpêtrière.

Like Blanche, there is ambivalence in the literature about what to call her. In the nineteenth-century material about her, she is never called Augustine. She is either X. L., L., X., Gl., Louise, Louise Gl., Louise Gleiz., or Louise Glaiz., and sometimes just G. I came across the name "Augustine" in the medical literature only twice, and even then it was not used alone. In the first line of her case history in Volume 2 of the *Iconographie photographique de la Salpêtrière*, and in the first line of the supplement found in Volume 3, she is called "X. L. Augustine." Nonetheless, since in later references she became known as Augustine, this is the name I will use as well.

Augustine was a healthy, full-term baby, born in Paris. Her parents were in good physical health and worked as servants in the home of a man referred to as Mr. C. They didn't drink and, with the exception of the headaches they both suffered from—in her mother's case migraines that stopped after she married—had no nervous disorders. A baby boy was born one year after Augustine, followed by five more siblings who did not survive infancy.

Augustine was sent to a wet nurse for the first nine months of her life, a ubiquitous practice in France at the time. Having babies breast-fed by a woman who was not the biological mother had at one time been confined to the upper classes, but by the nineteenth century, as more and more women entered the workforce, the custom crossed economic lines.[3] The working classes joined the wealthy in hiring wet nurses. The rich, however, often employed nurses in their own homes, while poorer women sent their infants away to the country-side, where the conditions were often wretched. Historians have doc-umented the rise in the infant mortality rate as the numbers of babies sent to the countryside to be nursed increased. Poor families often neglected to pay the even poorer women they hired, and the infants suffered.[4] In Augustine's case history, Bourneville noted that her sister and two brothers died in their first fifteen months of life while they were living with a wet nurse: "we don't really know of what" he added. (*Iconographie photographique de la Salpêtrière*, vol. 2, p. 124.)

Although I am clearly influenced by my own culture's notions of familial and maternal bonding, I can't help wonder what it must have meant for both baby and mother to spend the first year or years apart. Even if one dismisses the sexist tirades against working moth-ers that have given rise to a relatively new "hysteria" that demonizes both working mothers and the caregivers they hire (nanny cams and the false accusations of sexual and satanic ritual abuse against day-care centers come to mind), I believe it is important to acknowledge that at the very least this prolonged separation must have altered the attachment formed between a mother and her baby. There were many nineteenth-century critics of the practice as well, both within the medical profession and outside of it. In the 1860s, Dr. Alexandre Mayer launched a campaign to end the practice: "We are going to conduct a crusade against an inconceivable, absurd, and barbaric custom, the custom which has prevailed of abandoning, a few hours after its birth, a cherished being to a coarse peasant woman whom one has never seen, whose character and morality one does not know, and who goes off, bearing our treasure, to an unknown corner of the provinces whose name is sometimes not even marked on the map of France. The whole thing is so revolting to good sense and morality that in twenty years people will refuse to believe it ever happened."[5] Mayer's campaign and others like it were successful in bringing reform to the wet-nursing business in France. By the time Augustine entered the Salpêtrière in 1875, the French government had stepped in to regulate the practice, guaranteeing salaries and providing a degree of supervision that significantly reduced the infant mortality rate. Mayer's hope to abolish the practice altogether went unrealized for another fifty years. Wet-nursing continued in France well into the twentieth century.

Augustine's separation from her family continued even after she left the wet nurse. Once weaned, she was sent to live with relatives in Bordeaux, and other than the fact that she walked and talked quite late and suffered from several eye infections, we know nothing about her early years. When she was six and a half, Augustine was sent to a convent school in La Ferté-sous-Jouarre, a small town about forty miles east of Paris, where she remained until she turned thirteen. By her own account, she was a mischievous student. Easily bored in school, especially by the required reading of *Lives of the Saints*, she found other, less pious diversions, including teasing the nuns and masturbating. When she and two other little girls were found touching themselves, the sisters tied the children's hands down at night. Other punishments included isolation in a cell and slapping. When their discipline did little to curb the irreverent behavior of their young pupil, the nuns, suspecting demonic possession, turned to a higher power. They threw holy water in the girl's face and once, during a religious retreat, had her exorcised by a priest.

Despite her unruliness, Augustine enjoyed a degree of freedom while at school. She took walks in the countryside and was known to let the local boys kiss her in exchange for candy. While out on these excursions, she would sometimes stop in to visit an older friend, a woman who was unhappily married to a housepainter named Jules. Here Augustine witnessed violent arguments between the two: Jules beat his wife and dragged her about by the hair. One day he turned his attentions to the ten-year-old girl and tried to sexually assault her.[6] Later on, when she was a patient at the Salpêtrière, Augustine would revisit this brutal scene again and again during her hysterical attacks.

She spent her school vacations with her family in Paris. Because her parents worked during the day, she and her brother, Antoine, were left to their own devices. Although a year younger than his sister, he knew more about "the ways of the world" and among other things, told her about sex. It was during one of these vacations that Augustine first met her parents' employer, Mr. C., whom her mother insisted she call "father."

Mr. C.

When Augustine turned thirteen, she left school and moved to Paris, where her mother arranged for her to live in the household of Mr. C. Augustine was told that she would learn to sing and sew side by side with C.'s own children. It soon became clear, however, that her situation was not as her mother had presented it. Her bedroom turned out to be nothing more than a small closet, and her benefactor, a sexual predator. When his wife was away on a trip, Mr. C. tried to seduce the thirteen-year-old girl. When his overtures failed, he insisted that she move out of her closet and sleep in his room, where he renewed his seductions, promising to buy her pretty dresses if only she would give in to his wishes. Once again, he was rebuffed. The next night Mr. C. came armed: he threatened Augustine with a razor and, taking advantage of her ensuing terror, forced her to drink liquor. He then undressed her, threw her on the bed, and raped her.

The following day, she was unable to walk and stayed in bed. The day after that, she managed to come to the table, where her pallor and refusal to greet Mr. C. with the customary kiss made Mrs. C., who had returned from her travels, suspicious. During the meal, C. took every opportunity to send the girl threatening glances in order to keep her quiet. C., who must have been anxious to get Augustine out of the house before she told his wife about the assault, sent her back to her parents. Because she complained of pain and had severe abdominal cramps and episodes of vomiting, her mother summoned a physician. Without even examining her, the doctor diagnosed her condition as her first menstrual period rather than the traumatic injuries of rape.

A few days later, Augustine became terrified as she looked into the green eyes of a cat, and suffered her first hysterical convulsions. For the next six weeks, she had an attack every day. Scarified cupping glasses were applied to her spinal column, a form of bloodletting that was used as a common cure-all remedy at the time, but were of no help. A short time later, while running an errand, Augustine bumped into her rapist, who cornered her and grabbed her by the hair. She managed to escape, but that night she had another attack, more violent than any of the others.

Despite her traumatized condition, her parents found Augustine work as a chambermaid for an elderly woman. She continued to have attacks, but they occurred less frequently and were milder than before. During this period, the thirteen-year-old began to lead what Bourneville called "a somewhat adventuresome life." She spent her free time with her brother and two of his friends, Émile and Georges. Augustine liked both boys, especially Émile, and she became sexually active. She had sex with Georges at least once and with Émile on a regular basis. When Émile found out about Georges, he was furious.

When her parents found out about Émile and Georges, they too were furious.

The scenes that erupted in her household following the news of her sexual activity became the catalyst for the revelation of other family secrets. Augustine discovered that her father was convinced her brother was not his son, which explained why he had always treated him so badly, and that her mother was Mr. C.'s lover. While it is not mentioned in the text, this revelation raises the real possibility that her brother is her rapist's son. Augustine also finds out that her mother had sold her daughter to Mr. C. as a sexual favor. Augustine's father was not directly involved in the sordid transaction, but he was of little help to his daughter. He chose a passive role and chose to forgive his wife. Bourneville does not tell the reader whether or not the parents continued to work for Mr. C., but following these family dramas, Augustine's hysterical fits became more frequent and more debilitating. Her mother brought her to the Children's Hospital (she was, after all, a child), and then later to the Salpêtrière.

Photography at the Salpêtrière: Antecedents

Augustine arrived at the Salpêtrière the same year photography did, in 1875. The nature of photography—its claim to truth and its status as science and as art—has been debated since its inception. While ephemeral camera images have been around since the Renaissance— Leonardo da Vinci's drawing of a camera obscura is from 1516—the photograph as a permanent object was a nineteenth-century invention. The first photograph came into being roughly the same year as Charcot—1825—when a French inventor with the alliterative name Nicéphore Niépce successfully fixed a camera image to coated metal plates.[7] A few years after this first photograph, Niépce entered into a partnership with the Parisian set painter Louis-Jacques-Mandé Daguerre, who was also experimenting with the photographic process. Niépce died only a few years into their ten-year contract, leaving Daguerre to continue alone. In 1837 he invented the "daguerrotype." Daguerre's eponymous discovery created sharply detailed images with a full range of tones, but they could not be reproduced. In 1841 the English inventor William Henry Fox Talbot patented a technique that made multiple prints possible: the calotype. Calotypes, however, were more distorted than daguerrotypes, revealing the flaws in the paper they were printed on. The collodion process, discovered by another Englishman, the sculptor Frederick Scott Archer, combined the best of both techniques. The photographs it produced retained the sharp detail of the daguerrotype but were reproducible, like the calotype.[8] In the 1850s, the Parisian photographer André-Adolphe-Eugène Disdéri patented his photographic *carte de visite*, a mass-produced paper photograph, 2½ by 4 inches in size, that was pasted to the back of a printed visiting card. The *carte de visite*, which could be reproduced in large quantity at little expense, was enormously successful and launched a popular fad that democratized portraiture.[9]

While much has been made of Charcot's innovative use of photography, photography had in fact been used for medical purposes for over twenty years when he first took charge of his service at the Salpêtrière in 1862. The French physician Alfred Donné had worked with an apparatus called a microscope-daguerrotype to photograph cells and sections of bones and teeth as early as 1841. And in 1851, Dr. Jules-Gabriel-François Baillarger photographed cretins at the famous Charenton Asylum, home to the Marquis de Sade during his final years. At around the same time in England, Dr. Hugh Welch Diamond was taking pictures of mental patients at the Surrey County Asylum.[10] When the first volume of the *Iconographie photographique de la Salpêtrière* was published in 1876, medical photography was no longer in its infancy. Nor was Charcot, as some have claimed, the first to install a photography studio in a hospital. Bellevue Hospital in New York City had a full photography department in 1868 under the direction of Oscar G. Mason. Photography was in the air and, given Charcot's emphasis on the visual reproduction of neurological symptoms, it made sense that he would include it as a tool at the Salpêtrière.

Duchenne de Boulogne

Guillaume-Benjamin-Amand Duchenne de Boulogne undoubtedly influenced Charcot's decision to photograph his patients. He was the same man who had introduced another technology to the hospital, electrical stimulation, that animated the facial muscles of Blanche and other patients in order to trigger corresponding gestures. Duchenne was something of an outsider in the Parisian medical scene, a shy man unaffiliated with any institution. Born in 1909 in Boulogne-sur-Mer, he studied medicine in Paris, but due to less-than-outstanding work on his thesis, he failed to obtain an academic post. Without a position in Paris, he decided to return to his hometown in northern France, where he fell in love and married a local girl. Duchenne opened a private practice that was just beginning to flourish when his beloved wife died in childbirth. After his mother-in-law publicly and wrongly blamed him for the death of her daughter, his patients stopped coming, his practice dwindled, and the grief-stricken doctor floundered. His infant son was raised by his dead wife's family, and they prevented Duchenne from having any contact with the boy, a separation that continued for more than thirty years. Following a brief and unhappy second marriage, he returned to Paris alone to pursue medical research.

Without institutional affiliation or private funds, conducting research was difficult. Duchenne practiced general medicine during the day and spent his evenings in the public hospital wards, observing patients and pioneering studies on the electrical stimulation of muscles. Undeterred by the mean-spirited mockery he endured from hospital doctors who ridiculed him as a provincial and penniless outsider (Duchenne referred to them as "monarchs"), he carried on, combing the wards for cases of neuromuscular disorders. He invented a device for local faradization, a technique that stimulated an individual muscle without piercing the skin, the same apparatus the Salpêtrière doctors would later use on Blanche. If the doctors were less than welcoming, the patients enjoyed his company: "When the women at la Salpêtrière," wrote a physician many years later, "saw Duchenne coming along, always carrying a sort of small barrel organ, which was in fact a mahogany case with a handle that contained his famous battery and induction coil, they whispered with a sense of secrecy: *here comes the little old man with his mischief box*. But none of them had the intention of mocking Duchenne. Quite the contrary, they all requested the favor of being electrified by him."[11] He also invented an electrical needle that he called "Duchenne's histological harpoon," an unnecessarily violent name for what was essentially a forerunner to today's needle biopsy. His meticulous research and electrical inventions led to his accurate descriptions of many forms of neuromuscular disorders, including a disease that still bears his name: Duchenne muscular dystrophy.

Duchenne's desire to have a permanent record of the facial muscle faradizations he was conducting first led him to photography. "From 1852 onwards," he wrote, "I had the idea of illustrating, with the help of this wonderful procedure, the specific action of individual muscles through electrical faradization. . . . This convinced me to learn and study the art of photography from the point of view of its application to physiology and pathology."[12] He learned the collodion process from Adrien Tournachon, the younger brother of the famous photographer Nadar. The resulting book, *The Mechanism of Human Facial*

Expression, or an Electro-physiological Analysis of the Expression of the Passions Applicable to the Practice of the Fine Arts, published the same year that Charcot took over the direction of the Salpêtrière, hoped to document nothing less than the complete "orthography of facial expression in movement."[13] The eighty-four photographs included in the book depict a variety of subjects, from a beautiful child to an old toothless man. The latter is photographed extensively: he suffered from facial anesthesia, a condition that enabled Duchenne to use his electrical apparatus at full throttle. The images show him in various stages of distorted scowls and wide-mouthed howls, his face turned into a series of abject masks. (See Figure 13.) Aware that the expressions created by his machine were not those of genuine feeling, Duchenne cast one of his subjects as Lady Macbeth, the perfect character, he believed, to express dissimulated emotion. His model is shown clutching her breast with one hand and a dagger in the other, a "false smile" on her lips, as she goes to meet King Duncan.[14] Duchenne puts the viewer into a kind of vertigo of detached signifiers: his apparatus created meaningless facial expressions on a model playing the role of Lady Macbeth during a scene in which she dissembles for another character in the play, a performance which is then reproduced in a photograph.

Unlike the "monarchs" before him, Charcot, from the moment he took over the service at the Salpêtrière, was drawn to Duchenne, deeply impressed by his application of three of the nineteenth century's most significant sciences: electricity, photography, and physiology. The younger doctor (Duchenne was nineteen years older than Charcot) admired Duchenne's methodology, which like his own process, involved clinical observation and classification, distinguishing between symptoms that looked alike but belonged to separate diseases. With his orthography, Duchenne had isolated the precise movements that make up facial expressions, detached from any genuine feeling. His photographs attempted to document expressions created by elec-

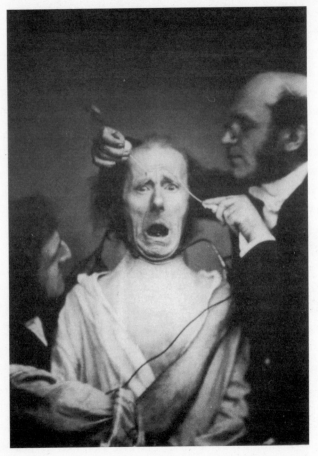

Figure 13. This photograph of the old man by Duchenne de Boulogne was
used to demonstrate how the electrical stimulation of the m. *corrugator*
supercilii and the m. *platysma* produces an expression of "terror mixed with
extreme pain." Duchenne appears on the right, an unidentified assistant on
the left. Duchenne de Boulogne, *Méchanisme de la physionomie humaine ou*
analyse electro-physiologique de l'expression des passions applicable à la pratique
des arts plastiques, Paris: Jules Renouard, 1862. École Nationale Supérieure
des Beaux-Arts, Paris. Photographed by Jean-Michel Lapelerie.

trical stimulation, not by emotions. As Charcot confronted hysteria, with its surplus of signs that pointed in wrong directions, its simulation of symptoms, Duchenne's meticulous classification and his efforts to divorce the mechanism of expression from the motivation appealed to him. Charcot learned much from Duchenne about how to approach neuromuscular symptoms and identify the clinical features that define and separate neurological disorders. Influenced by Duchenne's orthography, Charcot created his own lexicon for hysteria. And influenced by Duchenne's work in photography, Charcot brought photography to the Salpêtrière. He repeatedly acknowledged Duchenne in his lectures and writings, calling him "that great figure in French neurology" and referring to his clinical descriptions as "vivid and remarkable (. . .) rightfully considered a masterpiece."[15] Over the years, their professional relationship developed into a friendship. When Duchenne died from a cerebral hemorrhage on his sixty-ninth birthday, Charcot was with him. He had been sleeping in his friend's room for several days.[16] The year was 1875, the same year that photography and the clinic's iconic model arrived at the Salpêtrière.

Désiré-Magloire Bourneville

If Duchenne inspired Charcot to include photography in his repertoire of visual techniques, Désiré-Magloire Bourneville was the man who made photography at the Salpêtrière possible. Bourneville, born in 1840, was from Garencières, a village in Normandy that was also the hometown of Louis-Jean-François Delasiauve, a prominent alienist, and a family friend of the Bournevilles. Delasiauve had wards at both the Salpêtrière and Bicêtre hospitals, and he encouraged the young Bourneville to pursue a career in medicine. Bourneville took his advice and trained to become an alienist. The term "alienist," no longer current in English, is usually replaced by the word "psychiatrist." This substitution, however, isn't entirely accurate. While alienists were doctors who specialized in mental illness, they were not primarily concerned with the psyche but with heredity. Nineteenth-century science viewed mental illness as an inherited condition, one that might mutate into a different form in the next generation. A parent suffering from alcoholism, for example, could pass a weakness down to his or her children, in whom it might appear as hysteria, epilepsy, or madness. Alienists in the second half of the nineteenth century were trained in the theory of degeneration. Not only was mental illness genetic, it worsened with each generation.[17] They specialized in physiognomy, the science of physical appearance and were trained to search for physical signs of hereditary taints: ears, eyelids, and foreheads were scrutinized for the stigmata of insanity. Some alienists worked to reform conditions for patients institutionalized in asylums. Delasiauve, for example, was an advocate for educating the mentally retarded, and Bourneville became active in hospital reform and patients' rights. But there was a dark side to nineteenth-century alienists as well: degeneration theory bolstered social hygienists who argued for isolation and sterilization of those it deemed tainted.

In 1868, Charcot made the somewhat surprising decision to select Bourneville as one of his interns, even though he did not fit the usual criteria. Bourneville, like his mentor Delasiauve, was an alienist, and Charcot was not interested in mental illness. He classified hysteria as a neurological disorder, not madness. In fact, in the thousands of pages Charcot published, only one article addressed mental illness, and it was coauthored—some argue largely written—by a colleague who was an alienist.[18] Furthermore, Bourneville was not an exceptional student. He had ranked in the bottom half of his class. Charcot's other interns had all finished at the top of their classes. If Charcot did not select Bourneville for his academic skills or his medical focus, why was he chosen?

Bourneville offered Charcot something his other interns couldn't, something that became hugely beneficial to both the neurologist and the Salpêtrière: he was a journalist. When he became an intern in 1868, the twenty-eight-year-old Bourneville had already embarked on what would become an important and prolific career in journalism. He had published articles in a variety of medical journals and had founded not one, but two of his own: *Le Mouvement Médical*, and *La Réforme Médicale*. Bourneville was engaged in republican politics; both his journals promoted left-wing ideas and, as the title of the second one suggests, medical reform, a cause Bourneville would champion for the rest of his life. Charcot's choice of Bourneville proved to be providential: long after his internship ended, he continued to promote his mentor. Not only did he become Charcot's spokesperson, the primary publicist for the Salpêtrière School, he went on to create the most successful French medical journal of the nineteenth century, the weekly *Le Progrès Médical*. Bourneville's journal promoted many radical causes, such as the secularization of hospitals and the admission of female candidates to medical schools, but it was also the main organ for the dissemination of the Salpêtrière School's ideas. The lead article in the first issue was a lecture by Charcot, which set the tone for years to come. Nearly every week, the neurologist was published, reviewed, or mentioned in its pages. Charcot's name appeared so often that some insinuated that he owned the journal.[19] While this is patently false, Bourneville's promotion undeniably raised Charcot's profile. Not only did *Le Progrès Médical* regularly publish his work, it ran rave reviews of his books and, in its weekly announcement of upcoming lectures, it printed his name in a larger typeface than the others.[20]

While Charcot had no way of knowing it when he first took him on as an intern, Bourneville would later become a politician as well as a journalist and a physician, a position he used to promote a republican agenda and medical reform, and more specifically, to intervene on behalf of Charcot and his hospital. He started out as a member of the city council for the 5th arrondissement in Paris and was later elected a deputy to the French parliament. Bourneville was also a member of the Committee for Public Hygiene, on the supervisory board for state-run sanitariums, and, most important for the Salpêtrière, the budget commissioner for the Assistance Publique. He used all of these roles to improve patient care and promote patient rights. He became indispensable in the execution of Charcot's ambitious plans for the Salpêtrière. Because of Bourneville's commitment, connections, and influence, the hospital received the necessary funds to install not only the large amphitheater where Charcot delivered his lectures and displayed the hysterics, but also a research laboratory, an art studio for plaster and wax models, an electrotherapy room, a museum of pathological anatomy, and a large photography studio.

Among Bourneville's many contributions to journalism was his collaboration on the *Revue photographique des hôpitaux de Paris*, first published in 1869. Its stated aim was to bring together the "most interesting cases" found in the hospitals of Paris and illustrate them with photography, a medium "whose veracity," wrote Bourneville, "is superior to all other genres of iconography."[21] The volumes of the journal are filled with photographs of medical monsters: men, women, and children suffering from extreme cases of myriad diseases. It was while working on the journal that the idea of photographing Charcot's patients first occurred to Bourneville. "During my collaboration on the *Revue photographique des hôpitaux*," he wrote in the preface to the first volume of the *Iconographie*, "I had the idea to take photographs of the epileptic and hysterical patients that my regular visits to the special wards of the Salpêtrière allowed me to observe while they were in the throes of an attack. Because we were obliged to bring in a photographer from outside of the clinic, our first efforts were not very fruitful: often, by the time the photographer arrived, the fit was over. In order to bring about the goal that we were pursuing, we needed a man who knew photography close at hand, inside the

Salpêtrière even, and was dedicated enough to be ready, each time that the circumstances required, to respond to our call. The dedicated and skilled man that we needed, we were lucky enough to find in our friend, Mr. P. Regnard." (*Iconographie photographique de la Salpêtrière,* preface, vol. 1, pp. iii–iv.)

While Albert Londe is often credited as Augustine's photographer, it was in fact the "dedicated and skilled" Paul Regnard who took her pictures, as well as all of the photographs included in the volumes of the *Iconographie photographique de la Salpêtrière.* Londe entered the Salpêtrière as a chemist in 1882, two years after Augustine had left. He became director of the photography studio and was also the photographer for a later journal, entitled *Nouvelle iconographie de la Salpêtrière,* which ran from 1888 until 1918. Regnard began taking photographs of Charcot's patients during the first year of his internship, and he continued to do so until he left the Salpêtrière in the late 1870s, to work with the physiologist Paul Bert at the Sorbonne. As far as I know, his career as a medical photographer did not continue after that.

The Photographic Iconography of the Salpêtrière

The first volume of the *Iconographie,* published in 1875, is an album of photographs. The only words that accompany the images are chapter headings that divide the book into hysterical patients, epileptic patients, and "varia," a section of miscellaneous photographs. There are no case histories, names, or captions to tell the viewer what we are supposed to be seeing. The first image is of a hysteric: she is sitting calmly, her hands in her lap. The next image is a close-up of someone's lower legs, one foot pointed, the other one flexed. One photograph appears after another, fifty-one hysterics followed by thirty-one epileptics. The pictures in the "varia" section depict an old, stooped woman, and the bizarre coda to the entire album is a photograph of a human brain, propped up theatrically on some drapery. Did the disembodied brain belong to the old woman? Did Bourneville include it in order to emphasize Charcot's insistence that all of the women in the photographs, the hysterics as well as the epileptics, were suffering from a disorder of the brain? Without labels, these pictures are baffling and raise more questions than they answer. For example, there is an image of a woman asleep in the courtyard, her head positioned comfortably on a pillow: how did she end up prostrate on the cobblestones, with her pillow no less? Other images are striking only for their banality and decided lack of anything that might suggest illness, much less the chaotic violence of an "attack." There are photographs of women in their beds, asleep and awake, seated in chairs and standing up, indoors and outdoors, in street clothes and in hospital gowns. With the exception of one woman's terrified expression, and another who appears to have fainted into the arms of two nurses, the pictures do not seem to signify much of anything at all. If these photographs are supposed to serve as an index for disease, they fall short. The viewer can spend hours searching for signs of symptoms, but like the final photograph of the brain, these images reveal little that seems pathological. If anything, this first volume of the *Iconographie* defies Bourneville's faith in the superiority of the photographic image.

The *Iconographie photographique de la Salpêtrière* might never have developed any further if Charcot, perhaps aware of the conceptual vacuum these photographs created, hadn't encouraged Bourneville to publish his case histories and use the photographs to illustrate them, a suggestion Bourneville took and then assembled the next three issues. The *Iconographie photographique de la Salpêtrière*, therefore, came about in a somewhat haphazard fashion. Bourneville had already written the case histories and Regnard had already taken the photographs. Under Charcot's direction, Bourneville edited the volumes, selected the images, and inserted them as he saw fit. He included photographic plate numbers in parentheses in the text that instruct the reader when to look at the corresponding illustration. There is an odd disconnection between Bourneville's text and Regnard's images. While a book such as *Études cliniques sur l'hystéro-épilepsie ou grande hystérie* (Clinical Studies on Hystero-Epilepsy or Major Hysteria), written and illustrated by Richer, flows seamlessly (his drawings really do illustrate the text and serve to elucidate his subject), the photographs in the *Iconographie* interrupt the text in a jarring way. Although this is partly due to the fact that it was assembled after the fact, it is also due to the very nature of photography. While the text might instruct us to look at a contracted limb, we inevitably look at the person attached to the limb. Richer was able to control the content of his drawings, and include only what was needed to visualize his point. The photographs in the *Iconographie* haunt its pages, the ghosts of women who refuse to be reduced to medical illustrations.

Some of the photographs from the initial volume are reprinted in the three following volumes, so we now know that the woman with the terrified expression was not frightened but was suffering from a persistent "hysterical contracture of her face" and that the woman who appears to be doing nothing other than sitting calmly in a chair, posing for the camera, is in fact exhibiting the "onset of an attack." Unfortunately, the startling image of the patient asleep in the courtyard, the one with the pillow under her head, is not in any of the later volumes, so we have no story to attach to her peculiar circumstances. At the same time, as viewers, we also need to be somewhat wary of the words that accompany these pictures. For example, is that woman in the photograph said to be experiencing the beginning of an attack really feeling its early signs? If so, why does she look so peaceful? While the photographs taken for the *Revue photographique des hôpitaux de Paris* are successful as documents of individuals with

Figure 14. "Hystero-Epilepsy: Normal State." Photograph of Augustine Gleizes by Paul Regnard from Désiré-Magloire Bourneville and Paul Regnard, *Iconographie photographique de la Salpêtrière*, Volume 2, Paris: Aux Bureaux du Progrès Médical, Delahaye & Lecrosnier, 1878, Plate 14. Yale University, Harvey Cushing/John Hay Whitney Medical Library.

visible medical conditions, their bodies ravaged by disease and birth defects, many of the photographs of hysterics only add to the disease's elusive character.

Augustine in Pictures and in Print

Augustine's images were not included in the first, wordless album. They appeared later, in the 1878 and 1879 issues of the *Iconographie*. Her first photograph, "Normal State," was probably taken when she first arrived. Augustine is seated in her street clothes, her head cocked to one side, propped up by her left hand. Her right hand rests in her lap, showing no sign of the paralysis that crippled it. (See Figure 14.) Augustine was clearly posing: she appears to be a girl who had had her picture taken before. She looks as though she might be sitting for a *carte de visite* rather than for a hospital photographer. Photographers in Paris took advantage of the *carte de visite* vogue by setting up sidewalk booths and selling snapshots for as little as one franc a piece. Augustine may very well have been one of the multitudes who had sat for such a portrait, and even if she hadn't, the cards were so ubiquitous she would have been aware of the conventions of posing for them.

The description provided by Bourneville on the page opposite this photograph informs the reader that Augustine was tall and blond, traits her portrait does not show. He also wrote that she "is active, intelligent, affectionate, impressionable, and capricious. She loves being the center of attention. She is coquettish and spends much on her appearance and in fixing her hair, which is full and long, sometimes in one style, sometimes in another. Brightly colored ribbons make her happy." (*Iconographie photographique de la Salpêtrière*, 1878, vol. 2, pp. 127–128.)

If we look again at her picture, we can see that she was indeed neatly dressed and coiffed. More striking, however, than her pretty

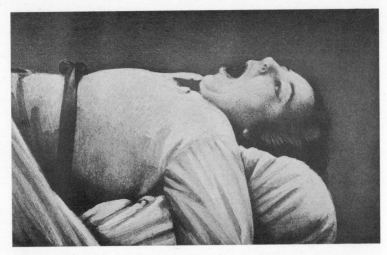

Figure 15. "Onset of the Attack: Cry." Photograph of Augustine Gleizes by Paul Regnard from Désiré-Magloire Bourneville and Paul Regnard, *Iconographie photographique de la Salpêtrière*, Volume 2, Paris: Aux Bureaux du Progrès Médical, Delahaye & Lecrosnier, 1878, Plate 15. Yale University, Harvey Cushing/John Hay Whitney Medical Library.

hairstyle is her expression. Unlike the other hysterics, who in their "normal state" portraits glance modestly to the side or stare vacantly ahead, Augustine looks directly at the camera, a slight smile on her lips. Her gaze meets the viewer's and she looks unashamed. No doubt this is the attitude that made Bourneville remark several pages earlier that she was "too brazen for her age." (*Iconographie photographique de la Salpêtrière*, vol. 2, p. 125.) But Augustine, in spite of this "normal state" photograph, was not normal. The next photograph of her appears eighteen pages of clinical notes later, pages that record twenty-one months of her life in the hospital, and they are filled with alarmingly abnormal reports. She is shown in a hospital gown, lying down in profile, her mouth wide open and her lips curled over her teeth, in the manner of children pretending to be toothless. But there's nothing playful about the image. Her visible arm is held at an odd angle to her body, thrust down and bent under her back. What looks like a leather strap encircles her waist. The label reads "Onset of the Attack: Cry." (See Figure 15.) Bourneville explained that sometimes when Augustine was about to have an attack, she would gape and let out a series of muffled "Ahs!" (*Iconographie photographique de la Salpêtrière*, vol. 2, p. 146.)

The text that separates this disturbing image from the first one of Augustine, as she might have appeared on the day she arrived at the hospital with her elaborately styled hair, chronicles the multiple symptoms of her disease. Even before the doctors had the opportunity to witness an attack, they determined she was a hysteric. "Everything in her," wrote Bourneville, "announces the hysteric. The care that she takes in her toilette; the styling of her hair, the ribbons she likes to adorn herself with." (*Iconographie photographique de la Salpêtrière*, vol. 2, p. 168.) Nevertheless, a diagnosis of hysteria based on a fourteen-year-old girl's interest in pretty ribbons and hairdos, was not sufficient. The doctors conducted a series of medical tests. They pulled her hair, tickled, pinched, and pricked her; they examined the mucous membranes of her eyelids, nostrils, mouth, tongue, and vulva; they tested her hearing, vision, taste, and sense of smell. In every instance, they determined that her right side was compromised: she could not smell even the most potent odors or tastes on that half of her body, and her right eye had a loss of peripheral vision and was color-blind, or "dyschromatopic": she confused red and blue, orange and green. Her right arm had lost all tactile sensitivity. Charcot, during one of his demonstrations, pierced her hand from one side to the other.[22] Besides hemianesthesia, Augustine suffered from intermittent cramps, trembling, muscle contractions, and paralysis of her right leg, which made it impossible for her to move it or feel it at all.

She also suffered from periodic bouts of "hysterical rhythmic chorea," named by Charcot to describe an involuntary movement of her head, torso, right arm and leg. Her muscles flexed and extended repeatedly, causing Augustine to execute something that resembled ongoing sit-ups. Her doctors counted as many as thirty or forty of these movements every minute all day long. Excited by her condition, Charcot brought her to one of his lectures on a day when she was suffering from it. "One of the patients in our service, afflicted with hystero-epilepsy," he announced, "has developed a rare pathological condition that as such is worthy of being placed before your eyes. It is by nature essentially unstable and mobile, as is the sex it prefers to afflict."[23] Charcot's introduction to Augustine for his class (sexist remark aside) reduced her to her symptoms. It was her rhythmic chorea that was the focus, not the girl afflicted with the disorder. Anyone who has spent time in a hospital is aware of the way doctors tend to treat the disease, perhaps out of necessity, not the patient. Unlike Charcot, Bourneville had not entirely mastered that skill. Early on in his lecture, Charcot promised his audience that he would discuss the "main episodes" in her life. I imagine his listeners believed he would talk about the traumatic events that had landed her in the hospital. But by "main episodes," Charcot meant *medical* episodes, and his lecture never veered from a discussion of her symptoms. Bourneville, who edited Charcot's collected works, seemed aware of the implied but unfulfilled promise of his mentor's words and added a footnote, referring the reader to his case history of Augustine, where the "main episodes" of her life are indeed discussed.

Augustine had her first hysterical attack at the Salpêtrière on December 10, a little less than two months after she was admitted. By the following spring, she was afflicted with attacks so frequently that Bourneville did not bother to record the details, only the numbers: "This morning," he wrote, "she was overcome at 7 o'clock, and by 10 o'clock we had counted 21 attacks." The next day, "Her attacks came back this morning at 4. By 11, she had already had 26." Three weeks later, the number increased: "Between 7 in the morning and noon, 52 attacks." (*Iconographie photographique de la Salpêtrière*, vol. 2, pp. 131–132.) One day the following winter, Augustine suffered a shocking *154* attacks. During this unrelenting series of fits, she was once again brought to Charcot's class as a case study of the various phases of hysteroepilepsy.

Before an attack, Augustine experienced an aura that began with psychic disturbances and ended with somatic sensations. Richer wrote more extensively than Bourneville about her aura, or prodrome, as he preferred to call it. She also heard voices. Sometimes a single voice called to her, but often she heard several familiar voices chatting away about ordinary things. The voices were frequently followed by the sensation of someone embracing her, lifting her off the ground, and kissing her. "A curious fact worth noting," remarked Richer, "she only feels the kiss on the right cheek."[24] She also had visual hallucinations, but unlike the later hysterical stages of the passionate poses and final delirium, she was aware her mind was playing tricks on her. Window-panes might appear tinted with various colors, like the stained glass windows in a church. The illusion was so lifelike she would see these colors reflected on the ground or on other people in the room. She had frightening visions of "very black and very dirty rats" and a black, hairy man, covered in sweat sitting in the corner of her room, who rolled his big black eyes at her. The man terrified her, even though she knew he wasn't real: "She is gripped with fear, all the while being aware of the illusion that her senses are the object of. Therefore she summons up her courage, gets out of bed, and walks up to the phantom. She holds out her hand to him, but he has already disappeared. She has barely returned to her bed, when the frightening vision comes back in the same place."[25] Augustine also saw scenes from novels she had read played out before her eyes in which she became the heroine. Unfortunately, Richer did not elaborate any further on her literary

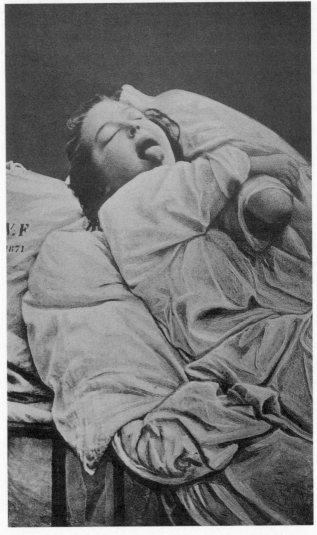

Figure 16. "Onset of an Attack: Cry." Photograph of Augustine Gleizes
by Paul Regnard from Désiré-Magloire Bourneville and Paul Regnard,
Iconographie photographique de la Salpêtrière, Volume 2, Paris: Aux Bureaux
du Progrès Médical, Delahaye & Lecrosnier, 1878, Plate 28. Yale
University, Harvey Cushing/John Hay Whitney Medical Library.

tastes or heroic fantasies. These sensory, auditory, and visual hallucinations would come and go rapidly during the day—short bursts of
psychic disturbance—but at night they happened slowly, becoming "a
long scene in which the patient played her part."[26]

As her attack approached, Augustine felt intense pain in her right
ovary that radiated down her leg. Her right ovary was also the origin for her "*boule hystérique*," which rose through her digestive tract,
reached her throat and caused a suffocating sensation. "The patient
feels something like a small apple at the base of her neck," Richer
explained.[27] The "boule" was followed by ringing in her ears, pressure
on her eyes, violent heart palpitations, and the sensation of a hammer
pounding on her temples. Sometimes her tongue became immobile
and contracted, its tip curled back, or thrust out of her mouth. (See
Figure 16.) Then, just before she lost consciousness, her vision grew
foggy, her head turned to the right, and she felt her hands painfully
clench. (See Figure 17.)

The epileptoid phase of the attack, composed of tonic and clonic
seizures, came next. The Salpêtrière doctors all acknowledged that it
was difficult to distinguish between real epilepsy and hysteroepilepsy
by observation alone. The epileptoid stages of the hysterical attack
were often superficially identical to those caused by epilepsy, but they
were separate disease entities. Epileptic seizures, according to Charcot, often caused life-threatening spikes in body temperature, while
hysteria did not. As she lost consciousness, Augustine emitted a cry
classically associated with epilepsy, not hysteria. Charcot, however,
noted the difference between her muffled "ahs" and a true epileptic
scream. There was an easier method to differentiate between hysteria and epilepsy. If a patient's seizures were arrested by pressing on
her hysterogenic zones, she was a hysteric, because true epilepsy did
not respond to this intervention.[28] Augustine often suffered from this
phase of the attack alone and, perhaps anticipating that his readers
might conclude that she had been misdiagnosed, Bourneville stressed

Figure 17. "Contraction." Photograph of Augustine Gleizes by Paul
Regnard from Désiré-Magloire Bourneville and Paul Regnard, *Iconographie
photographique de la Salpêtrière*, Volume 2, Paris: Aux Bureaux du Progrès
Médical, Delahaye & Lecrosnier, 1878, Plate 16. Yale University, Harvey
Cushing/John Hay Whitney Medical Library.

that she only *appeared* to be an epileptic, that "epilepsy is there only
on the surface and not at the foundation," since ovarian compression
stopped her seizures. (*Iconographie photographique de la Salpêtrière*, vol.
2, p. 169.)

For Augustine, the next stage of the attack, the grand movements
or "clownism," often took the form of repeatedly sitting up and slam-
ming herself back down again on her bed. She might then execute the
"circular arch" in which she did a kind of back bend, supported by the
top of her head on one side and her feet on the other. Richer referred
to this phase of the attack as a "tour de force" because it required so
much muscular energy.[29] Unlike Blanche, who presented these phases
with remarkable regularity, what the doctors referred to as "mechanical precision," Augustine was not always consistent. Sometimes she
regained consciousness between seizures and other times she didn't.

She also experienced incomplete attacks during which she skipped one of the phases. Like the other hysterics in Charcot's ward, she was treated with ether, ethyl valerate, chloroform, morphine, ovarian compression, electrical stimulation, and amyl nitrate. She was also what Charcot called "polymetallic": a variety of metals temporarily restored sensibility to her right side.

While the epileptoid and grand movement phases of Augustine's attack were not exceptional, she distinguished herself from the other hysterics in her execution of the next phase: the *attitudes passionnelles*, or passionate poses. This is the third phase of the hysterical attack, and, strangely, Bourneville did not use the term "passionate poses" in her case history but instead called it the fourth phase: delirium. He did label ten of her photographs "passionate poses," even though the stage in the text the photographs illustrate is delirium. The gap between the photographs and the narration emphasizes a disjunction that already exists between the images and the text.

Augustine's Passionate Poses

This series of photographs became famous and, looking at them, it is easy to understand why. Regnard's images are undeniably beautiful. Augustine's pictures were taken in the hospital's photography studio, so there are no distracting details. The background is a black screen and Augustine is luminous. And unlike the picture of Augustine in her "normal state," in which her dress and hairstyle locate her in the period, these images are timeless. Her hair is loose and her white hospital gown could be from any era. The folds of the bedding and gown have an almost sculptural appearance and her poses are theatrical. (See Figures 18–25.) Some of the hallucinations that this series illustrates were erotic, yet the images seem remarkably chaste. In "Amorous Supplication" (Figure 20), Augustine looks as if she is

Figure 18. "Passionate Attitudes: Auditory Hallucinations." Photograph of
Augustine Gleizes by Paul Regnard from Désiré-Magloire Bourneville and
Paul Regnard, *Iconographie photographique de la Salpêtrière*, Volume 2, Paris:
Aux Bureaux du Progrès Médical, Delahaye & Lecrosnier, 1878, Plate 24.
Yale University, Harvey Cushing/John Hay Whitney Medical Library.

Figure 19. "Passionate Attitudes: Call." Photograph of Augustine Gleizes by Paul Regnard from Désiré-Magloire Bourneville and Paul Regnard, *Iconographie photographique de la Salpêtrière*, Volume 2, Paris: Aux Bureaux du Progrès Médical, Delahaye & Lecrosnier, 1878, Plate 19. Yale University, Harvey Cushing/John Hay Whitney Medical Library.

Figure 20. "Passionate Attitudes: Amorous Supplication." Photograph of Augustine Gleizes by Paul Regnard from Désiré-Magloire Bourneville and Paul Regnard, *Iconographie photographique de la Salpêtrière*, Volume 2, Paris: Aux Bureaux du Progrès Médical, Delahaye & Lecrosnier, 1878, Plate 20. Yale University, Harvey Cushing/John Hay Whitney Medical Library.

praying rather than pleading with her lover "for more," and "Ecstasy" (Figures 21 and 23) exudes spiritual, not carnal, bliss. In "Eroticism" (Figure 22) she appears positively virginal.

Like Duchenne's actress playing Lady Macbeth, Augustine acted out a drama—her passionate poses—while she was photographed. Bourneville did not discuss the specifics of how this transpired. We know that Regnard provided the Salpêtrière with an on-site photographer, but he was not roaming the wards with a camera. The hysterics were brought to him in the fully equipped studio, with its bed, screens, lamps and darkroom. Regnard used a wet collodion process that has an exposure time of two to three seconds. While much shorter than earlier photographic techniques, this nonetheless means that Augustine had to be still while her picture was taken. In some photos where she was lying down, there was no problem. But many of the images suggest movement. In the photographs "Menace" (Figure 24) and "Mockery" (Figure 25), for example, Augustine would have had to have held her position for several seconds in order for Regnard to achieve such clear prints. "Mockery" implies rapid movement and shows her in the act of rubbing one index finger against the other. In the photograph, Augustine's nose is precisely centered on the page; her body framed horizontally by the bars of the bed at the bottom and the black background above her head have a deliberate staged quality.

Many of the images of the other hysterics in these volumes were taken while they were lying down on the studio bed, after they had

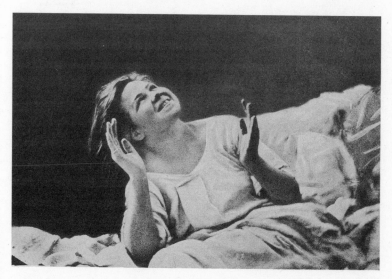

Figure 21. "Passionate Attitudes: Ecstasy, 1876." Photograph of Augustine Gleizes by Paul Regnard from Désiré-Magloire Bourneville and Paul Regnard, *Iconographie photographique de la Salpêtrière*, Volume 2, Paris: Aux Bureaux du Progrès Médical, Delahaye & Lecrosnier, 1878, Plate 22. Yale University, Harvey Cushing/John Hay Whitney Medical Library.

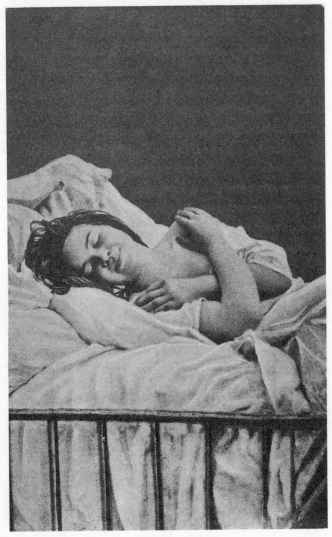

Figure 22. "Passionate Attitudes: Eroticism." Photograph of Augustine
Gleizes by Paul Regnard from Désiré-Magloire Bourneville and Paul
Regnard, *Iconographie photographique de la Salpêtrière*, Volume 2, Paris: Aux
Bureaux du Progrès Médical, Delahaye & Lecrosnier, 1878, Plate 21. Yale
University, Harvey Cushing/John Hay Whitney Medical Library.

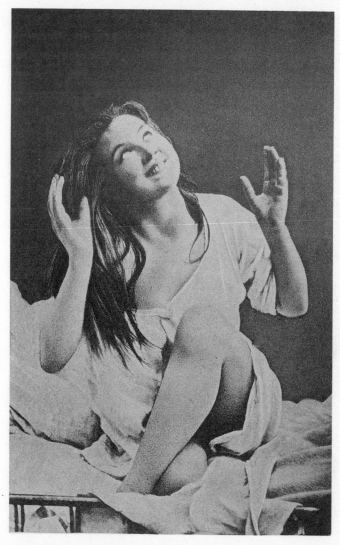

Figure 23. "Passionate Attitudes: Ecstasy, 1878." Photograph of Augustine Gleizes by Paul Regnard from Désiré-Magloire Bourneville and Paul Regnard, *Iconographie photographique de la Salpêtrière*, Volume 2, Paris: Aux Bureaux du Progrès Médical, Delahaye & Lecrosnier, 1878, 23. Yale University, Harvey Cushing/John Hay Whitney Medical Library.

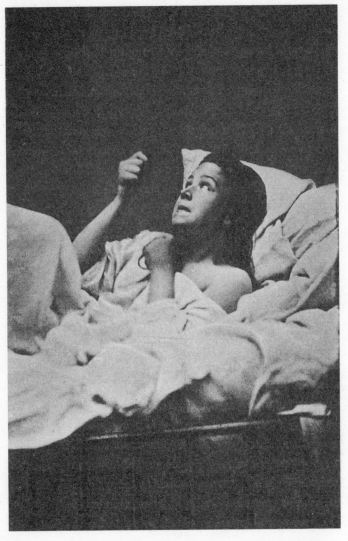

Figure 24. "Passionate Attitudes: Menace." Photograph of Augustine
Gleizes by Paul Regnard from Désiré-Magloire Bourneville and Paul
Regnard, *Iconographie photographique de la Salpêtrière*, Volume 2, Paris: Aux
Bureaux du Progrès Médical, Delahaye & Lecrosnier, 1878, Plate 27. Yale
University, Harvey Cushing/John Hay Whitney Medical Library.

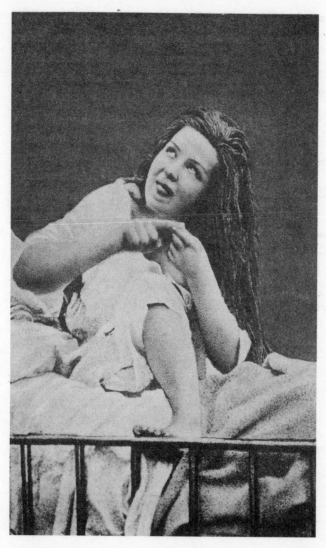

Figure 25. "Passionate Attitudes: Mockery." Photograph of Augustine Gleizes by Paul Regnard from Désiré-Magloire Bourneville and Paul Regnard, *Iconographie photographique de la Salpêtrière*, Volume 2, Paris: Aux Bureaux du Progrès Médical, Delahaye & Lecrosnier, 1878, Plate 26. Yale University, Harvey Cushing/John Hay Whitney Medical Library.

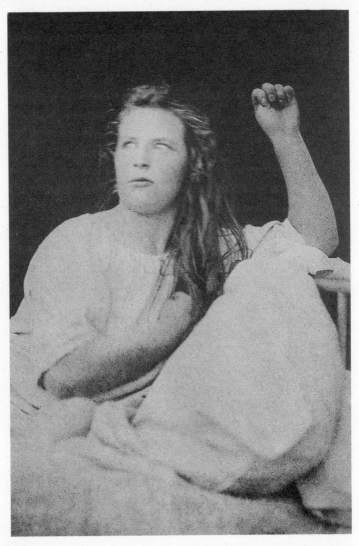

Figure 26. "Hystero-Epileptic Attack: Delirium." Photograph of Blanche Wittmann by Paul Regnard from Désiré-Magloire Bourneville and Paul Regnard, *Iconographie photographique de la Salpêtrière*, Volume 3, Paris: Aux Bureaux du Progrès Médical, Delahaye & Lecrosnier, 1879–1880, Plate 4. Yale University, Harvey Cushing/John Hay Whitney Medical Library.

been hypnotized and therefore immobilized or while they were sitting for their "normal state" portraits. Those that attempt to catch them during a moving stage are often blurry, the photograph of Blanche entitled "Delirium," for example. (See Figure 26.)

Augustine, then, was not only the most photogenic model but she was also the most gifted. Whether she deliberately froze her movements to allow Regnard a great shot is impossible to know. But the end result of what happened in that studio are the extraordinary portraits we have today.

After Regnard left the Salpêtrière for the Sorbonne and Bourneville left for Bicêtre, the photography studio was not used as often, and fewer photographs from the hospital were published until the *Nouvelle iconographie de la Salpêtrière* was founded in 1888. I believe that Charcot was more ambivalent about photography than is usually acknowledged. He wrote very little about it, and when he did, his words are not an unqualified endorsement. Charcot's statement "But in truth I am only there as a photographer; I inscribe what I see," is often quoted and held up as an example of his unwavering faith in the accuracy of the camera.[30] But it seems to me that he was instead articulating a faith in his own powers of observation, to fend off criticism that he invented hysterical symptoms. The photographer Alfred Londe was hired as a chemist in 1882 and became director of the photography studio in 1884, and one of the editors of the *Nouvelle iconographie de la Salpêtrière*.[31] Significantly, the word "photographique" was dropped from the new journal, and Richer, whose drawings were able to consolidate tendencies in a way that photographs could not, was also one of the editors. After Londe dedicated *La photographie médicale* to him, Charcot responded graciously. He noted that photography was destined to make important contributions to medical science, and while he wished Londe success with his book, he was not especially effusive in his praise of the medium. Charcot preferred art to photography and wrote about a sketch by Rubens as "the most faithful *photograph* of the contortions of an attack of hysteria."[32] Charcot's scientific method sought to locate the common and empirical features of a disease, while photography, despite or maybe because of its status as an objective medium, tends to tug in the opposite direction. Rather than seeing the clinical features Charcot had worked so hard to isolate, the viewer of these photographs is overwhelmed by an individual's idiosyncrasies. Photographs were too alive, too inflected with personality.

Reminiscences

While Bourneville glossed over the convulsing stages of Augustine's attacks, he devoted an enormous amount of time to the next phase: her vivid hallucinations and reenactments of episodes from her life. He conveyed much of this by transcribing what she said. He gave her a more developed voice than he was willing to give his other patients. Augustine's hallucinations were visual, tactile, and auditory and they lasted a long time. Initially, Bourneville made certain generalizations about this stage, as he had for the epileptoid stage. He noted that the housepainter Jules who had attacked her would often appear, sometimes with a knife clenched in his teeth, as would a dog that bit her brother and ran off with a piece of his flesh in its mouth. She also saw enormous rats with long tails. Another recurring hallucination was "the chariot of death," a cart pulled by six black beasts with long flat ears, loaded with emaciated corpses whose terrible eyes glowed. A dozen men with flames shooting from their mouths, surrounded by ravens, and draped in the tricolor flag, called her. The image is both hackneyed and rather comical. It might have been a cartoon from one of the many reactionary Catholic dailies of the time, the symbol of the Republic hauled off to Hell. This vision, noted Bourneville, had tormented Augustine ever since a nun at the Children's Hospital told her that she had seen the chariot of death and that one of the men in the parade had reached out and given her a slap. (*Iconographie photographique de la Salpêtrière*, vol. 2, p. 132.)

At the beginning of 1877, Bourneville abandoned this impulse to summarize and began to record Augustine's hallucinations at length, and he did so in her own voice, quoting long passages verbatim. As Bourneville noted, Augustine's delirium was "more expansive" than those of his other patients. In fact, it was so expansive that he allocated over eight pages of text to it, printed in a smaller typeface than the rest of his clinical notes. I must wonder how he accomplished this feat. As she spoke, carried on conversations with imaginary beings, fought off and gave into the sexual demands of her hallucinated boyfriends, reenacted the rape by Mr. C. and the scenes that had erupted in her family, Bourneville was ostensibly in the room writing it all down. This was before the invention of phonographs. Did he take shorthand, and then later transcribe his notes? Did she repeat herself so often that he was able to fill in the sections he might have missed from memory? In any case, he must have devoted a lot of time to her case history, because he wrote down what she said and interspersed her long quotations with comments that serve as stage directions to provide the reader with a sense of what was happening physically during the reenactment. For example, in the following hallucination of Émile, who had apparently come to visit her at the Salpêtrière, Bourneville filled in the blanks of her monologue for the reader. The italics and the ellipses are Bourneville's:

But Georges is never like that . . . He behaves at the Salpêtrière . . . I should never have given in to you . . . I don't understand why it means so much to you . . . Me, I can control myself . . . not completely . . . , but partly . . . You did a good job, you will not kiss me . . . This is the second time that you come and you absolutely want . . . but there is not a place for that at the

Salpêtrière . . . unless we do what the young girl I was talking
about earlier did . . . (*She struggles because Émile does not want
to listen to reason*) . . . I don't feel anything? . . . Well, I didn't
feel anything . . . but I feel now, I made sure of it myself. (She is
unhappy; Émile does not believe her; she struggles, cries, shakes,
clenches her teeth.) You will not make it happen . . . I don't
want that kind of thing . . . Ah! true, you make me . . . Again!
again! Gestures, pleads: You don't want any more . . . I'm getting up. (one would say that her lover is on top of her, rolls off
next to her, gets up, etc.) X. sits, sticks out her tongue, moves
her left foot, places her elbows together; her physiognomy is
mocking. (*Iconographie photographique de la Salpêtrière*, vol. 2,
p. 154.)

What is surprising about Bourneville's remarks is that not only does
he observe Augustine's actions, but he visualizes what her invisible
lover, Émile, was doing. How did he know that Émile did "not want
to listen to reason"? I think it's fair to say that Charcot never would
have made this comment. But then Charcot would not have bothered
to pay close attention to what she was saying.

Charcot was famously uninterested in his patients' words. When
he listened, he listened for physiological indicators and noted impairments such as stutters and aphasia. He considered the hysterics' utterances to be vocalization, not communication, a clinical feature that
helped to differentiate hysteria from diseases it resembled, such as epilepsy. During one of his Tuesday lectures, Charcot presented a young
hysteric in order to demonstrate the different phases of the hysterical
attack. The patient had just presented epileptoid tonic and clonic
seizures when Charcot had an intern press on a hysterogenic point,
which triggered the passionate poses. The patient screamed, "Mama,
I'm scared," and a moment later cried out again, "Oh, Mama!" Charcot remarked to his audience: "You see how hysterics scream. One

could say that it is a lot of noise about nothing. Epilepsy," he continued, "is more serious and much more silent."[33]

During another class, Charcot provoked "an artificial contraction"
of Augustine's tongue and larynx muscles that effectively silenced the
talkative girl. Unfortunately, he was unable to make the contraction
go away and Augustine was sent back to the ward mute. Bourneville
managed to loosen the contraction of her tongue, but not her larynx.
Augustine was aphonic and had painful cramps in her neck. Her doctors applied a powerful magnet, but this cure only resulted in making her deaf as well as mute. They then tried electrical stimulation,
hypnotism, ether, and the ovarian compressor. Finally, six days after
Charcot's demonstration had gone awry, following a hysterical attack
and an inhalation of amyl nitrate, the girl's voice returned.

Bourneville, however, did not dismiss Augustine's words as "noise
about nothing." Maybe it was the social activist in him, the man
committed to a political agenda that advanced individual liberty
and patients' rights that prompted him to pay such close attention
to his patients' stories. Especially with Augustine, Bourneville's clinical distance was often punctured by more than a touch of tenderness and human outrage at the behavior of the adults in her life.
"X.'s background," he wrote, "reveals how much she was neglected
in childhood. The conduct of her mother and the relationships her
brother established between his sister and his friends, in part explain
the . . . loose behavior of our patient. She's a good person at heart; she
has even preserved, in spite of everything, a certain naivety, and, in
reality, she is more reserved, less licentious than her life and her talk
would make one believe at first glance." (*Iconographie photographique
de la Salpêtrière*, vol. 2, pp. 167–168.) His republican commitment to
social issues and reform inflect his language, and he strayed from
the strict parameters of the Salpêtrière platform. When Augustine
first arrived at the hospital, Bourneville wrote that her mother provided the information he had about her. However, as her case his-

tory unfolds, it becomes clear that he discovered the most significant pieces of her short life from her delirious utterances. Augustine, a traumatized fourteen-year-old, was perhaps unable to speak about the gruesome events that had happened. But during her hysterical attacks, she could not stop talking about them. It's important to note that Bourneville never doubted the truthfulness of what she was saying and included both the rape and her mother's culpability in her case history.

Augustine had frequent hallucinatory conversations with her brother and his friends, detailing an adolescent love life in which she was the victim of the boys, but was by no means defenseless.

> Émile, don't get involved, I beg you . . . (. . .) You believe that boy more than me? I swear to you, that that boy never laid a hand on me. Oh! Are you serious or just teasing me? . . . Enough . . . and what day? Give me all the details . . . He kissed me, then he tickled me . . . I put him in his place. I didn't respond to his caresses . . . We were in a field . . . I swear that I didn't want to . . . (. . .) Antonio, you are going to repeat what he told you . . . that he touched me . . . But I didn't want to . . . Antonio, you're lying! . . . It's true, he had a snake in his pants, he wanted to put it in my belly, but he didn't even undress me . . . You kissed me more than a thousand times . . . Me, I'm crazy? . . . Antonio, you're laughing. I'm going to slap you. (She struggles). (. . .) Georges, you're such a pig. You like girls for one thing only. I don't love you enough for that. Why did you tell my brother? He repeats everything . . . Émile wouldn't go and tell Antonio; he'd keep the secret to himself. You're so funny, all three of you! You look stupid! (. . .) Georges, you complain that I like Émile more than you . . . Well, look and see if he's not more discreet than you are . . . (. . .) if you knew everything Georges had gone and told my brother! . . . What,

you too? . . . You refuse to believe that I would be faithful to you. (*bis*) But don't cry over it. (*bis*) I promise you that it's not so. He's such a gossip monger, that Georges! (*Iconographie photographique de la Salpêtrière*, vol. 2, p. 149.)

Far more disturbing than these adolescent troubles were Augustine's hallucinations of being raped and the circumstances that had allowed it to occur. Again and again during this phase of her attack, Augustine would reenact the rape, screaming and making movements with her body: "Pig! pig! . . . I'll tell papa . . . Pig! you're so heavy! . . . You're hurting me." (*Iconographie photographique de la Salpêtrière*, vol. 2, p. 139.) She repeated that he had "put rats in my behind," and expressed rage at her parents, especially her mother: " 'You are a despicable mother! And my father forgave you! . . . You are a filthy woman, a woman of vice.' (She cries, covering her face with her hands.) 'If one was allowed to beat one's mother, I would beat you.' (. . .) 'He put rats in my behind.' " (*Iconographie photographique de la Salpêtrière*, vol. 2, p. 47.) Her hallucinations reveal that her mother had visited her at the hospital, but she came to try and keep her daughter from going to the police. "I behaved like an innocent, that's what papa says, (. . .) you don't want me to tell you the truth . . . Each day you come, you cry . . . So you've changed for the better, have you? Well now it's too late . . . You say that I spoil the household . . . I disown you as my mother! . . ." (*Iconographie photographique de la Salpêtrière*, vol. 2, p. 147.)

Augustine also talked about her traumas when the doctors drugged her: "Mr. C. told me he would kill me . . . He spread my legs . . . I did not know that it was a beast that was going to bite me . . . He told me he would kill me . . . He hurt me . . . He told me that later it would be good for me . . . it's a sin . . . (. . .) That's how little children are made . . . ! A baby! If Mr. C. makes me make a baby . . . And mama who claimed she was putting me in a safe house! . . ." (*Iconographie photographique de la Salpêtrière*, vol. 2, p. 161.)

Richer also wrote about Augustine's hallucinations during the third phase of her attack. He quoted her less extensively than Bourneville, but revealed additional details. We discover that Mr. C. bound her legs and arms and beat her. In both Richer's and Bourneville's quotations, Augustine spoke as if she were aware that she had an audience. For example, while reliving the trauma, she screamed, fought off her rapist, and addressed him: "Leave me alone!" "I won't give in!" "Please, you're hurting me!" But she also interspersed these examples of direct speech with comments that rupture the flashback, and seem uttered in order to make sure her doctors knew what was happening: "He's tying me down!" and "I'm worried that I won't be able to take my first communion."[34] These remarkably lucid repeated scenes became a way to tell her doctors that she had been brutally beaten and raped.

Augustine revealed during her delirium that Mr. C. had come to see her at the Salpêtrière. The man had actually sat in on Charcot's classes in the hope of catching a glimpse of the girl he had assaulted. On two separate occasions he watched her from the audience. "A man like you, a forty-year-old man . . . What do you know about medicine . . . ," she demanded. "You will not see me in the class . . . I have decided to tell . . . On two Sundays. (Expression of anger, agitation) . . . Why did I hide my face in class? . . . Because of you . . ." (*Iconographie photographique de la Salpêtrière* vol. 2, p. 160.) Several days later, when she was not hallucinating, Augustine told Bourneville that the second time he came, she had spoken to him and threatened to denounce him if he ever returned.

Bourneville also included Augustine's dreams. Her entire case history was used to support one of Charcot's clinical departures from previous criteria for hysteria: that it was prevalent only in women during their childbearing years, that it began with the onset of menstruation and ended with menopause. Bourneville introduced her *observation* with the words "We usually imagine hysteria as being linked in an intimate way with menstruation, or, in other words, it only appears in women who have gone through puberty and disappears with meno-pause. (. . .) Besides other particularities, the following observation will show that major hysteria can develop in a girl long before she menstruates." (*Iconographie photographique de la Salpêtrière*, vol. 2, p. 124.) Although she looked like a girl who had been through puberty, with developed breasts and pubic hair, Augustine had not yet men-struated when she arrived at the Salpêtrière. While the "other partic-ularities" of her case dominate, Bourneville recorded her first period. It came nine months after she entered the hospital and was preceded by a dream. On July 4, Augustine felt pain in her lower abdomen, dif-ferent from the ovarian pain with which she was all too familiar, and that night she "dreamt that she was in a slaughterhouse, seeing the animals killed, the blood run. When she awoke, she had her *period for the first time.*" (*Iconographie photographique de la Salpêtrière*, vol. 2, p. 132.) Augustine's nightmares included one in which she went to the theater and saw a play about a revolution. Negroes with red eyes and blue teeth attacked one another with fiery weapons and the blood flowed. (*Iconographie photographique de la Salpêtrière*, vol. 2, p. 190.) Bourneville frequently mentioned Augustine's dreams. Besides bloody revolutions and slaughterhouses, she dreamed she was robbed, that someone was trying to kill her, and that she was suffocating between the mattresses. Sometimes her dreams were too horrible to repeat. While Bourneville provided no interpretation of Augustine's dreams—this was twenty some years before Freud's *Interpretation of Dreams*—he nonetheless felt that they were important enough to include in her case history.

Bourneville lavished so much attention on her stories that he was

obliged to defend himself. Toward the end of her case history, he
remarked, "If we enter into the minute details of the childhoods of the
patients we are observing, *into the circumstances that produced convulsive hysteria*, it is certainly not with the aim of excessively developing
facts that are sufficiently interesting to prune them of all that is super-
fluous." (*Iconographie photographique de la Salpêtrière*, vol. 2, p. 167,
emphasis mine.) Bourneville did not elaborate on what many contemporary readers find obvious—traumatic childhood events might
lead to illness. In the mid 1870s, this was not a commonplace observation. Charcot would later pave the way for a psychogenic model
of hysteria, but for the time being, the Salpêtrière School promoted
a purely somatic understanding of the disease. Bourneville justified
himself by pointing out that he included a great deal of information
about his patient's life "so that our readers can clearly appreciate the
links that exist between real life events and the different phases of
the delirium phase of the attack." (*Iconographie photographique de la
Salpêtrière*, vol. 2, p. 167.) In his case history of Geneviève, he wrote:
"In their delirium, hysterics have reminiscences of past events from
their lives, physical pains as well as emotions they experienced, and
most especially, perhaps, of the events that were the cause of their
attacks." (*Iconographie photographique de la Salpêtrière*, vol. 1, p. 97.)
This was sixteen years before Freud and Breuer published their famous
words: "Hysterics suffer mainly from reminiscences."[35]

    While Bourneville's inclusion of his patients' memories was pre-
scient, his anxieties were not without foundation. When the second
volume of the *Iconographie* was published in 1878, the reviewer for
the *British Medical Journal* lamented, "We must say that we regret
that a work of such great scientific interest should be to English readers rendered somewhat unsavoury reading by the introduction of
long pages of the obscene ravings of delirious hysterical girls, and
descriptions of events in their sexual history. Such events, and the

impressions they made on the minds of these unfortunate girls, who were in some cases brutally subjected to rape and seduction at a very early age, have, of course, a most important bearing on their medical history, and as such should be duly chronicled; but, if described in the loose words of the patient when delirious and completely under the influence of a hystero-epileptic attack, such description may be interesting to the inquisitive student of diseased and degraded human nature, but is actually, in the words of the law-courts, 'matter unfit for publication.'"[36]

Recovery

About a week after Augustine recovered her voice, she got well. Her compromised limbs and sensory impairments, her bouts of rhythmic chorea, convulsing seizures, and hallucinations disappeared. "Sensibility completely restored," noted Bourneville. On New Year's Eve, she was doing so well that she replaced one of the nurses on Charcot's service. Bourneville specifically used the word "nurse," but according to the employment records of the hospital, she was actually hired as a *fille de service*, or ward girl. "Will this amelioration last?" he asked. "We will find out later." (*Iconographie photographique de la Salpêtrière*, vol. 2, p. 166.)

Because the third volume of the *Iconographie*, published in 1879–1880, includes a supplemental section about Augustine, we do find out. From that day in December 1878 when her symptoms precipitously vanished until the spring of 1880, Augustine remained healthy. In 1877 alone, Bourneville had counted an astounding 1,296 attacks, so hers was indeed a remarkable recovery. Augustine was released from the hospital on February 18, 1879, but she continued to live at the Salpêtrière as an employee and worked as a ward girl. Her wages were 15 francs a month when she started and gradually increased to 20 francs. With the exception of a one-time unnamed infraction on August 6, 1880, for which she had her wages docked, all went smoothly, or as Bourneville paternalistically noted, she "behaved well." Throughout this period, even though she was no longer a patient, she was a frequent object of Charcot's experiments in hypnotism. Even though she was not symptomatic, Augustine was still a hysteric and, by the criteria of the Salpêtrière, therefore capable of being hypnotized. The photographs that accompany these pages depict her in various stages of trance, as photogenic as ever, her hair stylishly arranged under her white nurse's cap.

Although Augustine no longer suffered from hysterical contractions, her doctors created artificial versions through hypnosis, and just as easily made them disappear. (See Figure 27.) In countless experiments, Augustine, like Blanche and so many others, was subject to provoked or "artificial" hallucinations in which she found herself in various scenarios: she stamped the ground at suggested snakes, sniffed starch as though it were perfume, ate paper when told it was a potato, and spit it out in disgust once informed it had been in the garbage. She listened to music that wasn't there and waltzed with her invisible lover. The doctors also "imprinted" gestures on her that triggered the corresponding facial expressions. When her hands were put in the position of an angry person, her face expressed anger. And when the doctors placed her index and middle fingers to her lips, as though she were in the act of blowing a kiss, a look of "amorous pleasure" appeared on her face. (See Figure 28.)

According to Richer, Augustine lent herself readily to these experiments, and could be "cataleptisized" very easily. If, on her way out the door once a session was over, someone banged the gong, she would be instantly transfixed in whatever position she happened to be in. There are many accounts of inadvertent hypnotisms at the Salpêtrière. Richer mentioned that during the annual Corpus Christi parade that

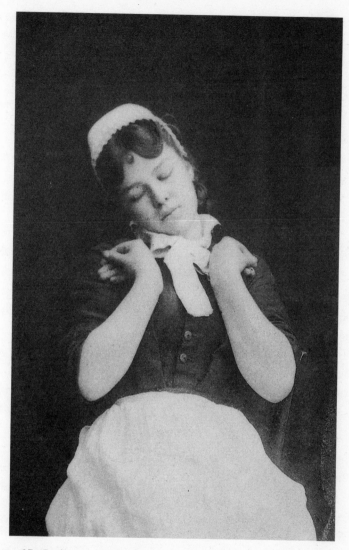

Figure 27. "Lethargy: Artificial Contracture." Photograph of Augustine Gleizes by Paul Regnard from Désiré-Magloire Bourneville and Paul Regnard, *Iconographie photographique de la Salpêtrière*, Volume 3, Paris: Aux Bureaux du Progrès Médical, Delahaye & Lecrosnier, 1879–1880, Plate 13. Yale University, Harvey Cushing/John Hay Whitney Medical Library.

Figure 28. "Catalepsy: Suggestion." Photograph of Augustine Gleizes
by Paul Regnard from Désiré-Magloire Bourneville and Paul Regnard,
Iconographie photographique de la Salpêtrière, Volume 3, Paris: Aux Bureaux
du Progrès Médical, Delahaye & Lecrosnier, 1879–1880, Plate 18. Yale
University, Harvey Cushing/John Hay Whitney Medical Library.

passed through the hospital, several hysterics were plunged into a cataleptic state by the clash of cymbals. On another occasion, a patient
from the hospital had received a day pass to attend a concert. While
listening to the music, she became cataleptic three times. "The person
who accompanied her to this event," wrote Richer, "knew the most
simple way to bring her out of this kind of catalepsy: she had only to
blow in her face to bring her back to normal life and the concert."[37]
For most of the Salpêtrière hysterics, the sound had to be unexpected
to bring on catalepsy. Any sudden loud noises—a dropped object, a
dog barking in the courtyard—could stop hysterics in their tracks.
Augustine, on the other hand, could be hypnotized by an expected
noise. One day the doctors asked her to strike the gong herself: "She
had barely given it a bang," Richer wrote, "when she leans back on
the wall next to her, still holding the two parts of the instrument,
her arms almost horizontal, and she remains thus immobilized."[38] A
sudden bright light could also trigger a cataleptic state. Augustine
and other hysterics were hypnotized by the flash of the camera. (See
Figure 29.) Photography in this case was not a neutral and passive
technique used to document a patient's hysterical symptoms, but an
active technique to create hysterical symptoms. When the flash went
off, Augustine was frozen in catalepsy, rendered immobile even before
the exposure was completed.

Once she was transfixed in catalepsy, Augustine's body became
pliable and could be molded into any position, natural and unnatural. Regnard photographed her in a bizarre pose. She is bent over
backward, her legs obscured by her skirt and apron, but it appears
as though they are straight. If her head were facing down, or if her
hands were supporting her on the ground in a back bend, there would
be nothing odd about the photograph. But as is, she looks like a doll
whose articulated joints have been twisted in the wrong direction.
(See Figure 30.)

Augustine was also subject to a spectacular stunt borrowed from

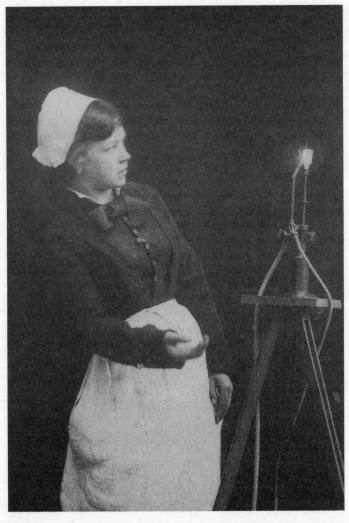

Figure 29. "Catalepsy Provoked by a Bright Light." Photograph of
Augustine Gleizes by Paul Regnard from Désiré-Magloire Bourneville and
Paul Regnard, *Iconographie photographique de la Salpêtrière*, Volume 3, Paris:
Aux Bureaux du Progrès Médical, Delahaye & Lecrosnier, 1879–1880,
Plate 17. Yale University, Harvey Cushing/John Hay Whitney Medical
Library.

Figure 30. "Catalepsy." Photograph of Augustine Gleizes by Paul Regnard from Désiré-Magloire Bourneville and Paul Regnard, *Iconographie photographique de la Salpêtrière*, Volume 3, Paris: Aux Bureaux du Progrès Médical, Delahaye & Lecrosnier, 1879–1880, Plate 15. Yale University, Harvey Cushing/John Hay Whitney Medical Library.

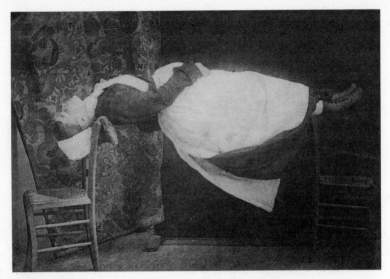

Figure 31. "Lethargy: Muscular Hyper-excitability." Photograph of
Augustine Gleizes by Paul Regnard from Désiré-Magloire Bourneville and
Paul Regnard, *Iconographie photographique de la Salpêtrière*, Volume 3, Paris:
Aux Bureaux du Progrès Médical, Delahaye & Lecrosnier, 1879–1880,
Plate 14. Yale University, Harvey Cushing/John Hay Whitney Medical
Library.

entertainment hypnotists. During the period of lethargy, her doctors
induced a muscle contraction of her whole body, from neck to ankles.
She became an inflexible object. (See Figure 31.) "We place her head
on the back of a chair," explained Bourneville, "and then we rub
the muscles of her back, thighs and legs, and we place her feet on a
second chair: her body, completely rigid, remains in this position for
quite a long time (we have never prolonged this experiment for more
than four or five minutes); it is even possible to place a weight of 88
pounds on her stomach without bending her body." (*Iconographie photographique de la Salpêtrière*, vol. 3, p. 192.)[39]

Augustine volunteered for these hypnotic experiments and mostly they proceeded without a hitch, with one important exception. As Bourneville told it, her doctors' carelessness nearly killed her.

> One day, we inadvertently left X. asleep. The nurse put her to bed. We tried to wake her several times but we were unable to do so. The intern on call tried splashing her with cold water, ovarian compression, faradization—nothing worked. The next morning, after 22 hours of deep sleep, Mr. Charcot observed her. Her body was limp; her pulse was 28–32; her breathing had slowed to three to six breaths per minute; her temperature was below 36 degrees Celsius; her face was cyanotic. In a word, we were confronted with an extremely dangerous situation. (*Iconographie photographique de la Salpêtrière*, vol. 3, pp. 192–193.)

Where the intern had failed, however, Charcot succeeded. He was able to bring her back to consciousness by pressing on her hysterogenic zones. Augustine was in a stupor but alive. Their unfortunate error had one felicitous consequence for science: the Salpêtrière doctors had accidently discovered "an attack of artificial sleep." Bourneville remarked that her artificial sleep mimicked one caused by narcotics, in which the person appears to be dead.

On another occasion, Augustine inhaled suggested "ether." Like Blanche, she had developed more than a little fondness for the drug, which caused a kind of erotic euphoria. Bourneville included a statement, written by Augustine at his request, that described the sensations and explained, he noted, why she requested it so often. She wrote about her intensely pleasurable feelings, romantic and erotic, during which she focused on her "beloved" but refused to reveal his identity. "I will not name this person, for I do not think that is necessary for you to know." And then she added, "Besides, I wouldn't dare," suggestive that the object of her affection was perhaps illicit. Instead of a name, she adopted the current medical practice and referred to him with an initial: "M."

I was always with my dear beloved M.; my thoughts were only of him. Everywhere that I'd go, it seemed to me that I would see him, hear him calling to me. The moment I was alone, I would try to figure out what I could do in order to . . . love him and possess him like I wanted to. Then I would cover my face in my hands, and at that moment I would feel a great happiness and I would ask him: "Do you love me?" It seemed to me that he answered "Yes" and I was overcome with joy. I believed that I felt him kiss me and press me to his heart. Sometimes I heard him ask me and I always answered him "Yes." (But unfortunately, it was only a dream.) (. . .) When bedtime came, it got even worse. I could feel him in bed with me, intertwining me in his arms, hugging me to his heart while telling me to go to sleep. I wanted to, but I would have preferred it if he had first made me completely happy and proved that he loved me. But he seemed to say "No." So I remained confused and angry over this response. I felt a discomfort that I want you to know about: I had sudden chills, my heart was pounding, a cold sweat passed over my face. I wanted to get up, but I couldn't move my arms or my head. This would last for four or five minutes. Then, in the end, I felt a pleasure that I do not dare explain to you. I would feel this each time I felt him press against my breasts. I felt him kiss me on my chest, and I asked him for something that he did not want to do. Then I would feel that discomfort again and I had a hard time falling asleep, even after I chased away these kinds of thoughts. (. . .) Each time I have had the opportunity to see this charming person, he always makes me want to kiss him, yet when he's in front of me, I am intimidated, and I try as hard as I can to not show him that I love him." (*Iconographie photographique de la Salpêtrière*, vol. 3, pp. 188–189.)

Despite Augustine's reluctance, Bourneville insisted she write about her experience. She gave in only after he had repeated the request. Augustine was no longer officially a patient, but she remained a ward of the Salpêtrière, near the bottom of the hospital hierarchy, a notch above a hysteric in the ward but, to continue the metaphor, miles beneath Bourneville. She complied with his request, but as in her opening refusal to name the object of her desire ("I do not think that is necessary for you to know"), she ended with the foreboding postscript: "P.S. I am through telling you everything that you asked me to and then some. I would speak more openly if I dared: but I am scared that this will be read by everyone." (*Iconographie photographique de la Salpêtrière*, vol. 3, pp. 188–189.)

Sex, wanted and unwanted, was the subject of most of the hallucinations Bourneville recorded. However, unlike the quotations from her earlier hallucinations, Augustine had become less conflicted about her desires. She wanted to have sex with M., and his refusal made her angry and confused. As in the extensive quotations from Volume 2, Bourneville gave Augustine space to record her own thoughts, to publish openly an account of her sexual pleasure. I believe this should be understood as a gesture made out of humanitarian impulses rather than purely medical ones. Unlike Charcot, who dismissed his patients' words as noise, Bourneville paid attention. At the same time, he didn't know quite what to do with the material he had taken the time to record. These passages, especially in the context of the *Iconographie*, have a theoretically gratuitous feeling and Bourneville's liberal use of quotation marks may also be construed as a way to include erotic material without the responsibility of authorship. Given Augustine's postscript, the reader can't help but feel like a Peeping Tom.

In the hypnotic experiment, Augustine inhaled the suggested ether and experienced sensations similar to what she had described in her written account: "He is coming to kiss me . . . We will sleep together before the end of the year . . . I will escape for sure . . . It has been a long time since I kissed him." (*Iconographie photographique de la Salpêtrière*, vol. 3, p. 196.) Bourneville never used the term "placebo," and I have never come across it in any of the medical literature I read from the period, but these experiments with ether that had been suggested hypnotically function as precursors to current controlled studies using placebos.[40] While the purpose of these tests, to determine a drug's effectiveness, is different from the experiments at the Salpêtrière, the results are similar: placebos work. They bring about actual, measurable changes in the physiological functions of many subjects.[41] Placebos, like the symptoms produced by hysteria and hypnotism, frustrate biomedical objectivity and blur the categories of real and unreal.

Relapse

During the sixteen months Augustine worked at the hospital, she continued to be an experimental subject, hypnotic and otherwise. Bourneville wrote that while she no longer suffered from spontaneous attacks, her doctors could still provoke them. Why they did so when they had a ward full of women who erupted into hysterical fits quite independently is not addressed. And then, just as suddenly as she had improved, Augustine relapsed and returned to Charcot's service as a patient. She suffered great bouts of agitation, including a violent outburst during which she broke windows and tore her straitjacket. For the first time, Augustine was put in a cell.

Throughout this section of the supplement, Bourneville's tone is much colder than before. His fondness for the girl seemed to diminish as she aged and as her condition improved. And once she relapsed, there was no change. He might have been disappointed in his patient. Augustine was no longer the vulnerable girl who had arrived at the hospital in desperate need, but a nineteen-year-old young woman who no longer wanted to be at the Salpêtrière. Another possible explanation might be that someone other than Bourneville wrote this section of her case history. Bourneville had received an appointment at the Bicêtre Hospital in 1879, so he would no longer have been in the wards of the Salpêtrière on a daily basis. We know that he edited the volume, which is dated 1879–1880, but it might have been another doctor who recorded the last parts of her case history. There was a collective mentality among Charcot and his disciples, one that is jarring for today's reader. It is not unusual to read a work by one Salpêtrière doctor, and suddenly stumble upon the work of another. There are long passages from the *Iconographie*, for example, in Richer's book on hysteria. This was not a case of plagiarism, but rather evidence of a communal spirit. In any case, whether these pages were written by a Bourneville who had hardened toward his patient or by another doctor who had never felt any fondness for her to begin with, the language is devoid of empathy.

After two months in her cell, Augustine managed to rip the brackets from the casement window and escape. The next day she was found sitting in a cold bath and was returned to the ward, but not to her cell. Charcot tried to hypnotize her, but his efforts were in vain. The girl who had been so easily hypnotized, who could hypnotize herself, could not be put under by the master himself. In July of that year, she took advantage of a concert at the Salpêtrière to escape again. Bourneville, or his dispassionate ghostwriter, wrote that she was caught "in the nick of time" just as she was about to step into a carriage stopped on the boulevard in front of the hospital. No mention is made about who was waiting for her inside the coach, but it is not difficult to speculate or fantasize that the mysterious M. was inside.

As Augustine was escorted back into the hospital, she fell on the stairs and cut her right knee, and then, once in her room, she injured herself again. To watch the people who had gathered for the concert, she climbed on a chair and fell, fracturing her right kneecap. For a month, all hope of flight was dashed by her injury. Augustine suffered agitation (including a bout that left her with a sprained thumb) and hysterical fits. Her symptoms were listed in a detached and clinical manner, with no elaboration. If she hallucinated, it wasn't recorded, nor were any treatments: no chloroform, no ovarian compression, no amyl nitrate, no ether. The last dated entry reads: "On September 9, Augustine escaped from the Salpêtrière, disguised as a man."[42]

And this time she was not caught. Augustine's disguise was more than a clever ruse. During an era in which female roles were rigidly defined, dressing in drag was not only a transgression; it was against the law. Augustine had not conformed to the narrow dictates of her convent school. But at the Salpêtrière, she complied and became a medical pinup girl. That role, too, became oppressive, and in the end, Augustine rebelled. The model of the Salpêtrière became, if only for a moment, a man. And as a man, she enjoyed what she had never experienced before—freedom. A footnote elaborates that since her escape it had been discovered that she was living with her lover, whom she had met at the Salpêtrière. It also notes that she had been admitted to La Charité Hospital for a phlegmon of the large ligament (not hysteria), and after she was released, she had returned to live with her lover. No doubt it was Bourneville who added the footnote. Not only was he the author and editor of the volume; he was the single physician who would have bothered to find out what had happened to her.

Bourneville remained close to Charcot even after he left the Salpêtrière. He continued to publish and promote his mentor's work in Le Progrès Médical, and in 1880 he became the editor of the Archives de Neurologie, a journal that Charcot had started. At Bicêtre,

Bourneville created a special pediatric unit for epileptic and mentally retarded children that focused on humane treatment and education. The center included a pathological museum modeled after the one at the Salpêtrière, a library, and a school that taught the children a range of skills, from chewing and swallowing food for the most severely impaired patients, to job training for the least impaired. The pediatric unit reflected Bourneville's commitment to social causes— improving the lives of a previously neglected patient population—as well as to medical research. He remained at the center of Paris's medical nobility with the full backing of Charcot. But when Charcot died in 1893, Bourneville lost his biggest supporter. Bourneville was not among the many of Charcot's coterie who turned on their mentor and scrambled to disassociate themselves from the Salpêtrière School, and he suffered for it. *Le Progrès Médical*, once so influential, fell into financial difficulty, and in 1898, Bourneville abandoned it altogether. His center at Bicêtre was attacked as too costly, and Alfred Binet, for one, contemptuously mocked Bourneville's work with pediatric patients in the press. In 1909, at the age of sixty-nine, Bourneville died in poverty.[43] Bourneville continues to be acknowledged today for his contributions to neurology, in particular for the disorders that bear his name: Bourneville syndrome and Bourneville-Pringle disease.

I do not know what happened to Augustine after she escaped from the Salpêtrière. I was able to confirm that she had in fact spent six days at La Charité Hospital after she escaped from the Salpêtrière. The admission registry lists her address as 19, rue du Sommerard, in the 5th Arrondissement. I'm not sure what I thought I might discover as I stood in front of that building, but of course it offered no information about Augustine whatsoever.

Asti Hustvedt

Reincarnations

I do know, however, what happened to her photographs and to her story. Augustine was brought back into the world by André Breton and Louis Aragon in 1928. They reprinted six of her photographs in *La Révolution Surréaliste*, in order to commemorate "the fiftieth anniversary of hysteria." The "delicious Augustine" was held up as the "perfect hysteric." I believe that this was the first time since their publication in 1878 that Augustine's images were reproduced. The adolescent girl was exposed to a new generation of artists, writers, and viewers. In 1928, she would have been sixty-seven years old. I don't know if she was aware Breton and Aragon had published her photographs, if she knew about the Surrealists, or whether or not she was even alive. Charcot's work on hysteria was no longer medically relevant at the time, but Breton, who had trained to become a doctor and had studied under Joseph Babinski, the handsome doctor holding Blanche in Brouillet's painting, was a fan of Charcot's work.[44] Even after he left medicine, he remained fascinated with psychiatry and embraced Charcot's hysteria as "the greatest poetic discovery of the late nineteenth century."[45] Breton and Aragon were also, no doubt, the ones responsible for her becoming known as Augustine rather than Louise.

Since that resurrection in 1928, Augustine's story and her photographs have been an inspiration to historians, playwrights, choreographers, visual artists, performance artists, and filmmakers. For Elaine Showalter, Georges Didi-Huberman, Lisa Appignanesi, and other historians and writers, Augustine, not Blanche, is the iconic Salpêtrière hysteric.[46] The feminist artist Mary Kelly borrowed Regnard's photographs of Augustine, replaced her images with women's clothing and accessories, but kept the French titles of the passionate poses. For example, "Appel" (Call) shows a leather bag on its side open

as if it were a mouth in the act of calling out. In the end, her inanimate objects are more literal depictions of the titles than are Regnard's photographs. The philosopher Jean-Claude Monod and writer
Jean-Christophe Valtat directed a short film called *Augustine* (2003),
a faithful account of the material included in her case history. The
artist Zoe Beloff also made a short film called *Charming Augustine*
(2005), which is more imaginative than accurate. Shot in a stereo-
scopic format, she attempts to link Augustine to early cinema, how
to her mind Augustine "supplied the psychic drive that would come
to flower in the works of D. W. Griffith." Augustine has also inspired
choreographers, who interpret hysterical seizures as expressive body
language. Fleur Darkin (*Augustine*, 2007) and Narelle Banjamin (*I
Dream of Augustine*, 2004) have created dance pieces that appropriate
hysterical contortions and poses. Dianne Hunter wrote and choreo-
graphed a dance theater performance called *Dr. Charcot's Hysteria
Shows*, in which she imagines that Augustine traveled to Chile to
become a cabaret performer and impresario. Anna Furse's play *Augustine (Big Hysteria)* (1991), has Augustine's time at the Salpêtrière overlap with Freud's. It ends with Augustine's escape in men's clothing,
but the garments belong to both Charcot and Freud.[47] These are only
a few of the works that Augustine inspired. In the end, not one of
them, no matter how much poetic license they take, outperforms the
true story of a sexually exploited girl who became Charcot's most
photographed hysteric and then, after years of submission, fled the
hospital and male medical authority, dressed as a man.

PART FOUR

Geneviève

U nlike Blanche Wittmann, my next subject would never perfectly incarnate the entire spectrum of hysterical symptoms. And unlike Augustine, she was not exceptionally photogenic. Instead, Geneviève Basile Legrand found a career in a particular niche of Charcot's theory: she became a living example of his conviction that demons and saints, from the past as well as the present, were hysterics. Throughout the medical literature about Geneviève, she is compared to women possessed by spirits, holy and otherwise. Charcot and his disciples diagnosed saints and witches as hysterics who suffered from "hallucinations" and presented "epileptiform" seizures and contractures, while Geneviève and other women hospitalized at the Salpêtrière, experienced visitations from Heaven and Hell and displayed "crucifixion poses," "stigmata," "ecstasies," and "demonic attacks." In a creative manipulation, her doctors interpreted cases of divine and demonic possession through Geneviève's behavior, rather than the other way around, transforming demons and saints into hysterics, and their hysteric Geneviève into something of a saint and something of a witch. How she came to occupy this position begins with her birth in Loudun and in a story that blends science and religion, articulates the complicated battle between doctors and priests for control of women's bodies.

Jeanne des Anges: Charcot's Seventeenth-Century Hysteric

Geneviève's story begins with another story, one that took place more than two hundred years before she would take her first breath. It is, however, a narrative that profoundly marked her life, one into which she became inextricably written through the accident of her birth in a village named Loudun, a small town that has the dubious honor of being home to the most famous demonic possession in French history.

Legend has it that on one September night in 1632, Jeanne des Anges, mother superior of the village convent, spotted a handsome ghost lurking in her private chambers. A short while later, she fell writhing on the floor, shouting obscenities and making lewd gestures. Other nuns in the convent soon fell prey to the same forces, until seventeen in all were similarly afflicted. Church authorities, doctors, and town officials called in to manage the chaos, all reached the same conclusion: they were in the presence of the devil.

News of Satan's presence in Loudun spread quickly, and people from the region, and indeed from all over France, flocked to the village to witness the infernal spectacle. The possessed women were displayed in the public square and exorcised before crowds of medical men, religious leaders, and the merely curious. It soon became apparent that the Devil was not acting alone but had an entire host of demons working with him, among them Behemoth, Leviathan, and Isacaaron. Moreover, according to Leviathan, who spoke through the mouth of Jeanne des Anges, a well-known local priest named Urbain Grandier had been acting as Satan's accomplice.

Grandier, a powerful, eloquent, and handsome man, was also known to be quite the libertine, rumored to have enjoyed the favors of many—according to some accounts, most—of Loudun's women. His list of conquests included grieving widows, unhappy wives, and local maidens. Indeed, legend had it that the only women in town who had not been seduced by the less-than-priestly priest were the "old ones and the ugly ones."[1] Moreover, Grandier was an outspoken critic of Cardinal Richelieu and could therefore add the politically powerful to his list of enemies, a list that already included jealous husbands, outraged fathers, and jilted women.

So, when Jeanne des Anges testified that it was Grandier's spectral figure that had appeared in the convent that September night, "seducing her with caresses that were as insolent as they were impure," and taking from her "that which she had vowed to keep for her heavenly husband Jesus Christ," Grandier found himself without much support.[2] The most damning evidence against him came during one of the many exorcisms the mother superior underwent. Once again it was Leviathan who testified via Jeanne des Anges to the existence of a pact signed in blood between Satan and Grandier. And in case this verbal testimony wasn't proof enough, a document stating as much miraculously appeared at the exorcist's feet. On August 18, 1634, Urbain Grandier was found guilty of sorcery and sentenced to death. He was tortured by Spanish boots, a device that crushed his legs to a bloody pulp, and then burned at the stake in the town square.

Grandier's execution did not, however, fully exorcise the prioress's demons. Isacaaron, the demon of lust, was particularly tenacious, and caused her to utter coarser obscenities and make lewder gestures than any of the other possessed women. Isacaaron also informed her that she was carrying his child, and sure enough Jeanne des Anges proceeded to manifest the various symptoms of pregnancy: she stopped menstruating, she felt queasy and vomited, her abdomen swelled, and she exuded "a white liquid from her breasts." In a desperate attempt to outwit the devil, she planned to cut open her own belly, remove the demon child, and quickly baptize it, before ending both of their lives. Her plan, however, was foiled by a fit of convulsions. The priests then came up with a scheme of their own to kill the demon child growing in her womb: during an exorcism, they ordered Isacaaron himself to destroy what he had created. Yielding to the priests' higher power, the demon was forced to oblige, and Jeanne des Anges expelled the child in a great vomiting of blood.

Several years later, on February 7, 1637, while recuperating from a particularly grueling exorcism, Jeanne des Anges experienced a possession of a different sort. Saint Joseph appeared before her and cured a crippling pain on her side with a sacred ointment, some of which rubbed off onto her chemise and exuded an exquisite odor. News of the divine visit from Saint Joseph traveled, and her garment, on which five heavenly drops remained, drew pilgrims who believed that it had healing powers.

Eight months later, the mother superior experienced another miracle. When the very last demon, Behemoth, was finally exorcised from her body, he inscribed the names of his conquerors—JESUS, MARY, JOSEPH, and SAINT FRANÇOIS DE SALES in blood on her left hand. Long after the blood had dried, the names written by the demon remained, permanently etched into her flesh. As the living embodiment of demonic and divine intervention, Jeanne des Anges toured France with her sacred chemise and her diabolically inscribed hand, drawing thousands of pilgrims wherever she went.

When the initial furor died down, she went back to her convent in Loudun where she continued to enjoy success as a living relic for almost a decade. One visitor, however, concluded that Jeanne des Anges was nothing but a fraud. As he tells it, when he reached for the hand supposedly "sculpted by the devil," his fingernail caught on the letter M of Mary and managed to remove it. Nonetheless, Jeanne des Anges continued to draw pilgrims, albeit fewer than before. When she died, on January 29, 1665, the nuns reported that her corpse gave off a saintly aroma. They placed her head in an elaborate reliquary. The convent also commissioned a large tapestry depicting her final exorcism. The explicit tapestry with its sensational images brought in visitors and their contributions for more than a century, until a church official, outraged by the lurid representation, demanded it be removed. The nuns, anxious to be obedient but reluctant to give up an important source of income, appeased the priest by hanging an even larger portrait of Christ next to the offending tapestry. Nonetheless, the convent entered into a period of decline, and the bishop of Poitiers, anxious to put an end once and for all to the struggling nunnery's unsavory past, shut it down, selling off the furniture and distributing the remaining Ursulines to neighboring convents. Unfortunately, no one knows what happened to the devilish tapestry, the miraculous chemise, or Jeanne des Anges's decapitated head.

The Orphan from Loudun

Some two hundred years after these events, Geneviève, an orphan from Loudun, was cast by her doctors at the Salpêtrière as their very own version of Jeanne des Anges. Geneviève's birth in Loudun is so emphasized in the medical writings that I became suspicious that it might have been a convenient fabrication by her physicians. For Geneviève—a woman possessed demonically, divinely, hysterically— to have been born in Loudun seemed all too fitting, a detail more at home in fiction than fact. Moreover, her case history clearly states that she was a ward of the state in Poitiers—not Loudun. And while Loudun is not far from Poitiers, I couldn't help wondering how a woman who had just given birth would have been able to abandon her newborn in a city that is nonetheless more than thirty miles away. The more I thought about it, the more I became convinced that the doctors had misrepresented the place of her birth to suit their own purposes. The only way to confirm my suspicions was to track down her birth certificate. I contacted the Departmental Archives of Vienne, the department that encompasses both Loudun and Poitiers, and was told that if her birth certificate still existed, they would have it. I was warned, however, that there were deficits in the collection, and that there was no guarantee that any records pertaining to my subject would be found. My trip to the archives in Poitiers was both successful and humbling. As it turns out, Geneviève was indeed born in Loudun, and I have a copy of her birth certificate to prove it. I should have known that Charcot, the great positivist, would not have stooped to fiddling with facts.

Yet, while Geneviève's physicians did not doctor her birthplace, they never considered the possibility that it may have influenced her behavior, or if they did, they never acknowledged it in writing. According to Charcot, suggestibility was one of the major symptoms of hysteria. Hysterics were so suggestible that they were capable of simulating all sorts of medical conditions, among the more common, pregnancy, epilepsy, and syphilis. Even a case of hysterical gangrene was documented. The fact that Geneviève was born in Loudun and came to believe herself to be possessed by spirits holy and unholy is not unlike a scenario in which a girl born in Salem, Massachusetts, might believe herself to be a witch. In both cases, the girls would have grown up steeped in the lore of their towns, listening to stories of the devil possessing young women, young women who in turn became powerful characters in highly dramatic events. And while Geneviève's birthplace is emphasized, it is discussed as a bizarre coincidence, not an active influence on her behavior.

The drama of Geneviève's birth does not end with its locale. Like the beginning of so many nineteenth-century novels, she was left on a doorstep. We will never know who her parents were, but it would not be unreasonable to assume that her mother was poor and unmarried. As the visible sign of sexual transgression, illegitimacy during the mid nineteenth century was so scandalous that the lives of babies born out of wedlock were often at risk. In fact, the establishment of public orphanages, or "foundling hospices," as they were called, was a direct response by the Empire to the large number of infanticides committed each year. Adoption was not practiced in France at the time, and each year thousands of babies born out of wedlock, or to married parents too poor to care for them, were simply abandoned.[3]

What to do with their unwanted children is a problem most societies have to contend with. Unlike England or the United States at that time, France did not set up state-run orphanages. Rather, it established foundling hospices that served as centralized centers that distributed the orphans to foster families, mostly in the countryside. The government was anxious to keep these children out of public view and considered the family the ideal institution for raising them. Foundlings, most of them illegitimate children, were socially stigmatized. Given the prevailing medical theory that degenerative traits were inherited just like physical characteristics, foundlings were thought to be at risk for developing deviant disorders. Raising these children within a family, as opposed to an orphanage, was thought to be the best way to produce good French citizens. Moreover, by placing these children with rural families, the government could both hide their existence and remove them from what it considered to be unhealthy urban environments, settings that would only exacerbate the foundlings' supposed natural tendencies toward immoral behavior. Sending these orphans to the countryside was also part of a state plan to counter the dwindling populations in rural areas caused by the large numbers of people moving to cities to work in factories. Paying foster parents to take them in also proved to be the most economical way to raise these children and it provided peasants with an extra pair of hands to help out on the farm. This was the system in place when Geneviève entered the world.

On January 2, 1843, at eight o'clock in the evening, a newborn girl wrapped in filthy rags was discovered on the doorstep of the Loudun hospital by one of its employees, named Marie Coindreau. Two days later, this woman brought the baby to the town hall, where she became the first entry of the year in the town's registry. Coindreau was a witness to these proceedings, along with the mayor, a cobbler, and a tailor.[4] The baby was given the name Geneviève Basile. These handwritten documents, preserved in the regional archives, reveal dates, names, and the fact that she was "wrapped in filthy rags." About everything else, however, we can only speculate. Had the cobbler and tailor already been at the town hall for other business when they were called upon to act as witnesses, or had the mayor sought them out specifically? Was the little group moved by the baby girl no one wanted, honored to have been chosen to be part of this civil ceremony, or were they merely performing a duty, anxious to return to their interrupted lunches? Had Marie Coindreau already named the baby before coming to the town hall, or did the group ponder the decision together? In any case, her name was not a random choice: as was customary in France at the time, the Roman Catholic Calendar of Saints was consulted. Geneviève and Basile (the feminine form of Basil) are the saints for those first days of January.

The very next day, on January 5, Geneviève was entered as an *"enfant trouvé,"* or a foundling, at the hospice in Poitiers, which was a section of the local Hôtel-Dieu Hospital. A handwritten document in the Archives reveals the reason for her transfer from Loudun to Poitiers: during the mid nineteenth century, the government was implementing a plan to centralize state institutions, and Poitiers became the only center allowed to accept abandoned children in the region of Vienne.[5] By 1843, the year Geneviève was born, the July Monarchy had begun attempts to give the state more control over the increasing numbers of abandoned children. Among them was the establishment of regional centers where all abandoned babies and orphans from that area were sent.

These centers were equipped with special depositories called *"tours"* built to facilitate abandonment and thereby prevent infanticide. When I first arrived in Poitiers, I made the mistake of looking for a tower (the French word *tour* translates to "tower") at the huge hospital complex that still stands. When I didn't see one, I assumed it had been torn down in one of the many renovations over the past 150 years. Further research revealed that the "*tour*" was never a tower at all, but a "turner," a kind of cubbyhole built into the wall of the hospice, with a revolving platform that could be swiveled and opened up onto the outside as well as the inside. The system was designed to assure the anonymity of those who abandoned their babies. Once the infant had been placed in the "*tour*" and the platform had been revolved, the mother, or person leaving the child, would close the door and ring a bell, and a nurse would respond by opening a door on the inside, from which she would retrieve the infant.

These regional institutions were highly regulated and subject to yearly inspections by the central government. A reading of the evaluations of the Poitiers Hospice from the period reveals a severely overtaxed system.[6] In 1843 alone, almost two hundred children were abandoned. One of the recommendations put forward by the government inspector to reduce this number, was to make the dimensions of the "*tour*" smaller so that only the youngest babies could fit. "As it is now," he argued, "children as old as ten are able to crouch down inside." The necessary alterations were made but did not reduce the number of foundlings. Nor did it reduce the plight of these babies once they were abandoned. Of the 181 babies registered in Poitiers in 1843, the year that Geneviève arrived, more than half did not survive childhood, and out of these, most died before their first birthday.

It is here, at the Poitiers Hospice, that the name Legrand is attached to Geneviève for the first time. Perhaps the person responsible for registering the infant assumed that Basile was a middle name, or simply thought the common Legrand would be a more suitable surname.[7] Whatever the reason, this additional name begins what will be a lifetime of confusion in civil records and hospital registries, a confusion, I might add, that makes the researcher's job that much more difficult.

Throughout the various archives, she is sometimes listed as Geneviève Basile, sometimes as Geneviève Legrand, sometimes as Geneviève Basile Legrand, and sometimes as Geneviève Basile, *"dite"* (or
known as) Legrand. Moreover, there is much inconsistency regarding
her date of birth. In the "Register of Hospice Entries," her birthday is
listed as January 3, 1843, not January 2, which is what appears on her
birth certificate. Even the year of her birth is sometimes recorded as
1842 or 1844, not 1843. This uncertainty surrounding her name and
birthday seem to mirror a disordered self.

In Geneviève's case, a foster home was found for her the very day
she arrived in Poitiers. On January 5, 1843, she was sent to live with
a family named Garreau in Marçay, a rural village about eleven miles
southwest of Poitiers. While doing research for this book, I visited
the tiny Marçay, population 454, with its single church and single
café surrounded by sunflower fields and farms. By all appearances,
it hasn't changed much since the time Geneviève lived there. With
nothing more specific in the hospice registers than the name of the
village and the family, I had no way of finding the house she lived in,
even if it is still standing. There is no longer anyone with the name
Garreau listed in the current telephone directory; however, I did find
the name in the local cemetery.

From the records I saw, placing infants, obviously incapable of
farmwork, was easier than placing older children, which at first glance
seemed counterintuitive. This can in part be explained by the fact
that the monthly allowances given to foster parents decreased as the
children grew older. Indeed, by the time a child was six or seven, the
state subsidies were barely large enough to cover their basic necessi-
ties. The allowance for a baby less than one year old was 84 francs
per year. By the time a child turned nine, that allowance was reduced
to only 30 francs a year.[8] The brutal implication of the sliding fee
chart is that very young children were expected to work to earn their

keep, transforming the French system of foster care into a kind of indentured-servant system for cast-off babies.

Geneviève remained with the Garreaus in Marçay for almost eight years, when on October 18, 1850, she was sent back to the hospice. No reason is offered for her return; however, given her age at the time, it may have been motivated by the impending decrease in financial compensation that her foster parents would receive had they kept her. No matter what the reason, it seems reasonable to assume that any attachment the Garreau family may have had toward the little girl they had raised from birth was not strong enough for them to keep her. Geneviève would later tell her doctors that she remembered little about her first foster family. She did not accuse these people of cruelty or even indifference. Rather, she believed that their rejection of her was her own fault, describing herself during that period as a scatter-brained and difficult child, subject to fits of violent anger. Whatever the reason for this second abandonment, she was sent, only a few days later, to live with a woman referred to as "the Widow Brossard," who, uncharacteristically, had a home in the center of Poitiers. Less than a year later, on June 25, 1851, she was once again sent back to the hospice and was placed in another home in the rural village of Beaumont, some ten miles north of Poitiers. She remained with this new family, the Suires, for a little over a year, when, on October 24, 1852, she was returned, once again, to the center in Poitiers.

This time she remained at the hospice for almost seven months before a new foster family was found. Placing older children in foster families tended to be more difficult since they brought in lower monthly allowances. However, a short handwritten note I came across in the regional archives provides another, more sinister, explanation for Geneviève's prolonged stay at the hospice. Written by a government official during his yearly inspection, the letter accuses the nuns who staffed the Poitiers hospice of abusing their power by using the children in their care to turn a profit. "It appears," the inspector wrote, "that the Mother Superior secretly encourages the return of these children in order to increase the number of hands for the manufacturing of sheets done by the Hospice of Poitiers." A nun from the hospice, contacted years later by the Salpêtrière staff, made no mention of Geneviève's sheet-making skills, but did remember her as "a crazy little girl" with a "mania for bouncing off the walls." (*Iconographie photographique de la Salpêtrière*, vol. 1, p. 50.) She added that she was in frequent need of punishment and that they were often "obliged to tie her up." Whatever the reason for her seven-month stay, it must have been a relief for everyone involved when, on May 22, 1853, a new foster family, named Dubois, was found in Vendeuvre-du-Poitou, a rural community less than three miles from Beaumont. Like Marçay and Beaumont, Vendeuvre-du-Poitou is a small, picturesque, and well-preserved village that has resisted the changes of modern life.

Her new foster parents, who had no children of their own, put her to work on the farm and did not send her to school. According to what she told her doctors years later, she was an unruly child, prone to fits of rage that became more pronounced as she grew older. And while she recounted that twice she was whipped with stinging nettles, once for tearing her dress, in general she spoke about this period of her life as quite pleasant and insisted that her foster parents loved her and let her do as she pleased. Moreover, she claimed to have felt no pain whatsoever from these brutal chastisements, a fact that her doctors, ever on the lookout for data to refute the accusation that hysteria was something manufactured by Charcot at the Salpêtrière, interpreted as abnormal insensitivity, a symptom of their patient's hysteria that predated her entry to the Salpêtrière by more than a decade. Another interpretation of her insistence that she felt no pain might be a stubborn and heroic refusal on her part to succumb to this abuse of power, a form of dissociation not uncommon in brutalized children.

Camille

It was during her stay with the Duboises that an event occurred that would become a driving force in her life, an overwhelming passion, or according to her doctors years later, an obsessive mania: she fell in love with a boy named Camille. The two became engaged when she was only fourteen years old, but their romance ended tragically when Camille died of a "cerebral fever." Her foster father, fearing that his young charge would make a scene at the funeral, forbade her to attend the service. Furthermore, not trusting her to obey his orders, he locked her in her room. Geneviève, in what would be the first of many escapes from forced confinement, managed to slip out through the window and make her way to the cemetery. There, calling out to her beloved, the distraught girl tried to throw herself into the boy's grave. Prevented from doing so by the other mourners, she collapsed and was carried back home, where she remained unconscious for twenty-four hours, "like a corpse," according to the doctor who was summoned to her bedside.

This sad episode is recorded in her case history, and while the doctors questioned much of what their hysterical patients said, they never doubted the truth of this event. In fact, Bourneville, the author of the *Iconographie*, frequently interjected assurances as to the veracity of his account when he feared his reader might be growing skeptical. "Is the story of Geneviève we have provided the truth?" he asked. "We are very inclined to believe that it is." (*Iconographie photographique de la Salpêtrière*, vol. 1, p. 90.) Bourneville went on to support her version of events by stating that no matter how many times he interrogated her, sometimes with long intervals of time in between, she always repeated the same version of events. And in case the reader is still doubtful, he had corroboration in the form of letters from a nun at the hospice and the director of the ward for the insane in Poitiers. When he had nothing but the word of Geneviève to rely on, he chose, at least in this instance, to believe her.

While in Poitiers, I combed the archives for any information I could find pertaining to Camille. Without a last name, I thought the work would amount to the proverbial search for a needle in a haystack. I consulted the decennial tables of Vendeuvre-du-Poitou, as well as those from the neighboring Beaumont, for deaths in the area between the years 1850 and 1860, and found no one who might have been the Camille in question. I then consulted the registers from all of the neighboring villages within a twenty-mile radius of Vendeuvre, and I found no death on record of a young male named Camille—or for that matter of a young man of any name—between the ages of twelve and thirty. This was not a particularly difficult task, even without a last name, given the tiny populations of these rural communities.[9] Not trusting the regional records, I set out to visit Vendeuvre and search the cemetery itself. There I found one Camille—a baby who died at twenty months. I also searched the cemetery for any young man who died between the years of 1856 and 1858, and found no matches. There may well be a logical explanation for this absence: Geneviève's beloved may have come from some other place, or may have died in a hospital far from these villages. However, according to her case history, the cemetery would have been within walking distance of her foster home in Vendeuvre. Another possibility must be addressed: perhaps Camille never existed. Perhaps the seminal event in her life, the event that would continue to haunt her decades later, was a phantom she conjured up to give body to the repeated abandonments she had already suffered. Or perhaps, as Geneviève herself came to believe later on, Camille faked his own death and changed his identity in order to escape from her.

An Attack of Nerves

In any case, Camille's death, whether imagined by a delusional girl, feigned by a fiancé with cold feet, or real, had a profound impact on the fourteen-year-old girl. Geneviève, who had been abandoned at birth and rejected by four different foster families, had now lost her fiancé. She reacted to this loss with increasingly erratic behavior: she spent days on end in profound sadness, refusing to speak or eat, and when she did finally break her silence, it was only to burst into rages. Then, when it seemed as though life couldn't get any worse for the young mourner, her foster mother became terminally ill and died. Unable to care for a teenage girl on his own, especially an unstable one, her foster father brought her back to the hospice in Poitiers.

She was transferred to the Hôtel-Dieu Hospital, where she would remain for almost a year. Her prolonged silences and outbursts of anger continued, and her doctors responded with "hydrotherapy," a combination of cold showers and prolonged baths. Hydrotherapy was common medical practice at the time, and while ostensibly "thera-peutic," it was more often used as a punishment to control difficult patients. Prolonged baths could last anywhere from six to eight hours, and the "showers" were large hoses that sprayed forceful jets of water directly at the patient. Jacques Joseph Moreau de Tours, a leading physician at the time, once tried hydrotherapy and found it, quite simply, "unbearable."[10]

In spite of these "treatments," Geneviève's condition improved enough to leave the hospital. She had now reached an age where she was no longer eligible for foster care and was sent out to work in town. She was placed briefly with a laundress named Courtaud, before going to work as a servant in the home of a Mr. Levrault. Working as a maid in nineteenth-century France was notoriously difficult and fraught with danger. Female servants, often unmarried young women, were vulnerable to unwanted sexual advances by their employers, and it is not surprising that domestic servants made up the largest percentage of women who gave birth out of wedlock. Moreover, the work of a maid was physically grueling and typically included hauling loads of wood, coal, and food; boiling clothing, diapers, and bed linens before washing them; cleaning cooking pots, dishes, fireplaces, and stoves, as well as emptying and washing out chamber pots. The young Geneviève, however, was no stranger to hard work, and she spoke of herself during this period with a certain contentment and pride. She was aware of the fact that she was pretty, an opinion that the hospital records corroborate, noting that "her young body was perfectly developed." Her physical charms did not go unnoticed by her employer, who, on several occasions succeeded in kissing her, even though she had forbidden him to do so. "I was very pious," she explained, "and I had misgivings about those kinds of things." She did admit, however, that she enjoyed the attention, and thought of "nothing but that man." (*Iconographie photographique de la Salpêtrière*, vol. 1, pp. 51–52.)

It was during this period that she suffered from what the Salpêtrière doctors would later diagnose as her first major attack of hysteria. It happened in the middle of the night, and as she screamed and flailed about, her employer ran for help. When he returned with the doctor, the two men found her unconscious. Geneviève later claimed to have no memory of what had taken place; she only knew that when she regained consciousness, she was tired and bruised. The physician who had been summoned declared that she was suffering from "an attack of nerves" and readmitted her to the Hôtel-Dieu Hospital in Poitiers.

For the next five or six months, Geneviève had a similar attack every day. Her abdomen became increasingly swollen and the nuns who nursed her concluded that she was pregnant. Their assumption was not unreasonable: along with her growing belly, her appetite was unpredictable and she vomited frequently. And Geneviève certainly fit the profile of an unwed mother to be: a poor young woman who had been working as a servant. Moreover, as a foundling, the nuns would have assumed that she had inherited her mother's immoral character; an assumption supported by the current scientific understanding of heredity, which believed that "degenerative" traits were genetic. Instead of caring for their charge, the women responded viciously. Indeed, her case history states bluntly that they "persecuted" their young patient. When she convulsed and flailed around the room, banging her head against the wall, they accused her of trying to murder her unborn child. When the time came, Geneviève was transferred to the maternity ward, where a simple physical examination revealed that she was not expecting a child. Not knowing what else to do with the disturbed but decidedly not pregnant teenager, they transferred her to the lunatic ward.

Like Blanche at the Salpêtrière, Geneviève must have dreaded this section of the hospital, not only because of the mad patients housed there, but because the little freedom she had earlier enjoyed was now taken away. Nineteenth-century insane asylums had terrifying reputations, and for good reason. People were rumored to enter sane and exit mad; even doctors who worked there were said to lose their minds.[11] Once confined in this ward, the doctors administered belladonna, a powerful narcotic. However, instead of taking her medicine, Geneviève secretly hoarded her pills, and when she had saved up a lethal dose, took ten at once. In small amounts, belladonna acts as a sedative. In large doses, however, it can cause agitation, delirium, and death. Geneviève, her vision blurred, ran through the ward, hallucinating. She managed to take ten more pills before she was caught and had an emetic administered with an esophageal probe. Oddly, her doctors do not refer to this episode as a suicide attempt. It is cited as "unruly behavior" rather than a carefully planned and executed attempt on her own life, one that she had every reason to believe was without hope.

Self-Mutilation

Only a few days later, she embarked on yet another desperate act: a horrific self-mutilation. Her case history unceremoniously states: "Without
being able to explain why, she used a scissors to completely cut off the
nipple of her left breast." (*Iconographie photographique de la Salpêtrière*,
vol. 1, p. 52.) The Salpêtrière physicians make no attempt to explain
this brutal event; rather, they focus on the fact that she claimed she felt
no pain. Like the lack of feeling during the punishments she suffered as
a child, the Salpêtrière doctors interpret this as evidence of Geneviève
suffering from "hemi-anesthesia," a classic symptom of hysteria, one that
in her case existed before she had ever set foot in their hospital in Paris.
Her doctors, sensitive to criticism that Charcot's clinic manufactured
hysteria, were always on the lookout for evidence of symptoms that predated a patient's entry into the Salpêtrière. Perhaps, like many patients,
Geneviève was eager to provide her doctors with what they were looking for. Or, maybe, she really did not experience any physical pain.

The Escape Artist

Following her suicide attempt and her self-mutilation at the hospital
in Poitiers, Geneviève managed to escape and flee to the home of an
acquaintance, a laundress. While her case history does not say so, this
woman was probably Madame Courtaud, the laundress who had briefly
served as a foster mother and who lived on the rue de l'Hôpital, the
street that runs directly in front of the hospital. In any case, whoever
this person was, she refused to shelter the girl and quickly informed
the authorities of the fugitive's whereabouts. The next morning, when
Geneviève awoke, she found herself surrounded by two nurses and

the director of the hospice, who lost no time in escorting her back to the institution. Back in the hospital, Geneviève continued to suffer from attacks, including a contracture of the left side of the neck that was so pronounced her chin touched her shoulder and so prolonged it lasted six weeks. Once again, she refused to eat, and for a period of three months, she was force-fed with a tube.

Geneviève had turned seventeen. She had not been in the hospital for long before she escaped again, this time with the help of a boyfriend, a medical intern at the hospital. Interestingly, Bourneville did not comment on this turn of events. Her case history merely states: "the couple fled to Paris together." In Paris, the two lovers lived together, and while she continued to have attacks, they were less violent than the one that had landed her in the hospital. After three months in Paris, the young couple returned to Poitiers, where she had an attack while out on the street alone. The police brought her back to the dreaded Hôtel-Dieu Hospital, where once again she was committed to the ward for the insane. No further mention is made of the intern.

Geneviève had become a master of escape. This time she fled on her own to Tours, a city sixty-four miles from Poitiers. She hid for three or four days before the police commissioner found her and sent her back to the asylum in Poitiers, where she remained until she was released a year later. Now nineteen, Geneviève returned to Paris and found work as a chambermaid. Not long after she arrived, she had another attack and was admitted to the Hôtel-Dieu Hospital in Paris, and from there she was transferred to Necker, another clinic. At Necker, she was a difficult patient. She refused to eat, had no feeling on the left side of her body, suffered from "ischuria"—she did not urinate—which meant that a catheter was needed, and she sprained her right wrist during an attack. Necker was not equipped to handle her case, so she was transferred to the hospital where women in her

Figure 32. Geneviève Basile Legrand. Photograph of Geneviève Basile Legrand by Paul Regnard from Désiré-Magloire Bourneville and Paul Regnard, *Iconographie photographique de la Salpêtrière*, Volume 1, Paris: Aux Bureaux du Progrès Médical, Delahaye & Lecrosnier, 1877, Plate 15. Yale University, Harvey Cushing/John Hay Whitney Medical Library.

situation often ended up: the Salpêtrière. The date was December 6, 1864. Her first photographs would not be taken until photography entered the Salpêtrière more than ten years later. (See Figure 32.)

Bourneville's Campaign Against the Church

When Geneviève was first admitted to the Salpêtrière, the medical faculty in Paris was under constant surveillance by the Catholic-dominated government of the Second Empire (1852–1870). The Church was threatened by medical science, in particular by neurology and psychiatry, new disciplines that undermined many of its teachings and openly accused religion of being backward and of standing in the way of progress. Much of what the Church believed was divine or diabolical, medicine considered pathology. Not only did medicine recategorize religious behavior as illness, but Charcot and his school were radical reinterpreters of human behavior. Sins committed by sinners were recast as the involuntary symptoms of morbid conditions, deserving medical treatment and sympathy, not punishment. The late nineteenth century witnessed an explosion of new disorders and diseases, setting in motion questions of moral responsibility and legal liability, questions that continue to be asked today. For the first time, thieves were thought of as "kleptomaniacs"; drunkards, "alcoholics"; and promiscuous women, "nymphomaniacs." Doctors made frequent appearances in court, where they testified as experts on behalf of the accused. The sentence against one woman convicted of stealing was overturned when a doctor confirmed that she was suffering from kleptomania.[12] Even murderers, as I discussed earlier, could be found not guilty if doctors testified that they were hysterics who had been exploited by manipulative hypnotists.

The Church responded to this attack on its authority with a vengeance. The battle between medicine and religion escalated to the

point that during the early years of the Third Republic, between
1873 and 1876, the prefect of police in Paris sent a spy named Cujas
into the University Medical School to infiltrate classes and report
back to the government on the state of the anti-Catholic climate in
academia. Jean-Martin Charcot and his students figured prominently
in these reports. Lectures deemed too scientific were canceled and
degrees were withheld from candidates whose theses were branded
atheist. The pro-Church faction, however, began to lose ground in
the early 1880s when a new government that supported the separation of Church and State took over. When Jules Ferry was appointed
minister of education, the universities were freed from the grip of the
Catholicism. Secular schooling was mandated and religious instruc-
tion was banned from public schools. In an enormous blow to the
Church, the clergy were expelled from university boards and lost the
right to award degrees.[13]

Bourneville was one of the Church's most vocal critics. While
Charcot tended to keep his religious and political leanings somewhat
private, Bourneville was openly hostile to religion and ran a very public and ultimately successful campaign to laicize the nursing staff of
the public hospitals, which, like the rest of the state system of health
care, relied on the inexpensive labor provided by the Church. Nuns,
Bourneville argued, were not only medically untrained, but they
exercised undue influence on patients, especially when it came to
highly suggestible hysterics. While Charcot remained diplomatically
in the background of Bourneville's efforts to oust the Church and
its nuns from the city hospitals, it would never have been a success
had it not had the director's full support. Under Charcot, Bourneville established the first professional nursing school in France at the
Salpêtrière, one that replaced nuns with medically trained nurses
and, in the process, an exclusively female nursing staff was usurped
by mostly male nurses. By 1883, patients were no longer required to

attend church services, and the hospital wards were renamed after scientists instead of religious figures.

This was the climate of the Salpêtrière when in walked Geneviève: a crucifix-clutching, demonically writhing, flesh-scourging young woman who, on top of everything else, was born in Loudun. Bourneville in particular must have felt grateful for the fortuitous timing: Geneviève arrived at the very moment when the clinic was fighting to claim territory that belonged to the Church and provided her doctors with a living example of Charcot's theory that extraordinary behavior understood by the Church to be divine or diabolic was the medical symptom of a neurological disease.

Mortification of the Flesh: Geneviève and the Saints

Geneviève was deeply religious. While she had never received formal schooling, she learned to read from religious texts, and her doctors complained that she always had her nose buried in a well-worn copy of *Lives of the Saints*, a book they blamed for exacerbating her hysteria. At the very least, it provided her with a litany of female saints who were experts at mortifying their flesh. Blessed Clare of Rimini had herself bound and whipped; Catherine of Siena practiced self-flagellation three times a day and scalded herself with sulfuric water; Christina of Spoleto had her body torn by iron hooks and pounded a nail through her foot; and Mary Magdalene de' Pazzi, who took as her motto "to suffer or die," wore a crown of thorns and a corset onto which she had attached piercing nails. She also walked barefoot through the snow, dripped hot wax onto her body, and licked the wounds of the diseased, including those afflicted with leprosy. Besides these self-inflicted agonies, female saints suffered at the hands of others, were sick with multiple, agonizing diseases, pain they relished and transformed into sacred acts of self-abnegation. Saint Agatha was tortured by having her breasts cut off. Others were flayed, scourged, and burned at the stake. Saint Lydwine of Schiedam suffered from every disease known to man. In his hagiography, the famous decadent writer, J. K. Huysmans, a contemporary of Geneviève and her doctors, described the saint's festering body in excruciating detail, with its fantastic vermin and suppurating wounds.[14]

In a fascinating footnote to Geneviève's horrific nipple amputation, Bourneville noted, "This mutilation recalls the one that the Skoptzy execute on their followers." (*Iconographie photographique de la Salpêtrière*, vol. 1, pp. 52–53.) No explanation is given as to who or what the Skoptzy are, indicating the reference would have been familiar to contemporary readers. More than a hundred years later, however, the term is no longer a household word, and I had to look it up in order to discover that the Skoptzy are a fanatical Christian sect from Russia who practice castration on the men and amputation of the nipples (and sometimes the entire breast) on the women as an initiation rite. These religious practices were making headlines in nineteenth-century France, and Geneviève had very likely heard of them. Bourneville strategically incorporated contemporary and past religious practice, albeit extreme religious practice, into the medical narrative of hysteria.

While Geneviève's amputation of her nipple was her most extreme act of self-mutilation, it would not be her last. After she arrived at the Salpêtrière, she repeatedly hurt herself. At times she would use sharp objects to cut her arms, and when none were available, she would use her own teeth. Bourneville recorded these incidents with a ho-hum detachment, listing her self-injury side by side with her temperature, her menstrual cycle, and muscular contractures: "G. bled herself on the right arm: the blood came out in spurts." Or "G. made herself bleed from her right arm using a scissors. In order to reach her goal, she cut herself three times: the blood flowed abundantly." (*Iconogra-*

phie photographique de la Salpêtrière, vol. 1, pp. 58, 59.) On another occasion, she "bit herself on her right arm with an extreme violence." The nurses were only able to get her to let go by "vigorously pinching her nose." (*Iconographie photographique de la Salpêtrière*, vol. 1, p. 83.) Geneviève also mentions her self-injury in a manner that suggests how regularly it was happening. Speaking of a stint she spent in the epileptic ward under the care of the head nurse, Madame Delsinne, she claims that she was so closely guarded there that "I was never able to hurt myself on my arms." (*Iconographie photographique de la Salpêtrière*, vol. 1, p. 76.)

Anorexia

Not only did Geneviève mortify her flesh by cutting her arms and amputating her nipple, she also starved herself. The doctors note that she would go through phases when she refused to eat, often accompanied by a refusal to speak. Shortly after she arrived at the Salpêtrière, she went through a bout of starvation and mutism. Bourneville did his best to persuade his patient to talk and take some nourishment. "The first day," he wrote, "I was satisfied to simply encourage her to take some food. Having no success, and being told by the nurse how sensitive she was, I limited myself that night to simply remarking that it was an advantage to have a patient that didn't talk, since the others talked too much, and I recommended that she be shown the mechanism that was used for force-feeding. All of this having failed, I tried once again the next morning to use persuasion, but in vain. At the end of my visit, I mocked her, declaring that her refusal to eat made no difference to us, that hysterics could go a long time without eating and that if she kept it up, she would save the administration money." Geneviève still refused to eat. When she persisted in not opening her mouth for either food or speech, Bourneville's coaxing turned to punishment: "All of these speeches had no effect, and it was then that I made her take a very strong mustard bath, an experience she would not forget. She was in the bath for only a few minutes when she recovered her speech and consented to take some food." (*Iconographie photographique de la Salpêtrière,* vol. 1, p. 54, n. 1.) There were times, however, when the punitive and painful baths did not work to break her vow of silence or abstinence from food. Her doctors then force-fed Geneviève through a feeding tube.

After another long period of refusing nourishment, Charcot tried a different tactic to overcome her anorexia, one that had often been used by the church doctors to determine whether or not a claim of going without food for a long time was a miracle or a hoax: he recommended constant surveillance. In the entry for March 19, 1874, Bourneville recorded, "Mr. Charcot wakes up Geneviève with an ovarian compression. She then recounts her visions. Our master recommends exercising a meticulous surveillance in order to insure that no one is secretly giving her anything to eat, in order to find out how long a hysteric is able to go without food. Charcot had not yet crossed the threshold out of her room when Geneviève, sitting on her bed in a rage, imperiously demanded something to eat: in quick succession she finished off several bowls of bouillon, some wine, soup, etc." (*Iconographie photographique de la Salpêtrière,* vol. 1, p. 66.)

Much has been written on the history of anorexia nervosa, locating its origins in the fasting saints of medieval Europe and tracing its development up to the current epidemic in the United States.[15] Saint Catherine of Siena, for example, subsisted on a few herbs, and would make herself vomit by forcing sticks down her throat when she was forced to eat. She ultimately died of self-starvation. Geneviève would also make herself vomit after she had been fed with a feeding tube. Saint Veronica supposedly ate nothing except for five orange seeds every Friday. Louise Lateau, the Belgian stigmatic discussed below, allegedly subsisted for years on nothing but a daily communion wafer and a few sips of water. Within a religious context, prolonged fasting by women was a sign of female holiness, an asceticism that brought them closer to Christ. Pain and suffering became for these religious women a transcendental experience that yielded significant rewards: they gained power in a culture that otherwise denied it to them.

The Salpêtrière regarded self-starvation and self-mutilation as medical symptoms of hysteria, rather than a form of sacrifice and penance. In *La Possession de Jeanne Fery*, a book that Bourneville reprinted and annotated about the diabolical possession of a sixteenth-century nun, he noted that Jeanne Fery's ability to go without eating was encountered regularly in his patients at the Salpêtrière, in Geneviève, for example, "one of the most famous hysterics at the Salpêtrière."[16] And like Jeanne Fery, Geneviève "deserved special mention for the severity of her self-inflicted bites, scratches and wounds."[17]

In much of the current literature that exists on self-harm, either through mutilation or starvation, one of the themes reiterated by the mostly young women who engage in these practices, is that they experience their cutting and food deprivation in a positive way. They report feeling "in control" and, like Geneviève, they often claim they feel no pain. I don't want to make the same mistake Charcot and his disciples made by simply transposing the psychiatric theories of today onto a patient who lived more than a century ago, yet the analogy seems useful. By inflicting pain on herself, by refusing to eat, Geneviève tried to transform her suffering into an act she controlled rather than one inflicted on her.

Moreover, Geneviève explicitly framed her suffering and degradation as something that made her more Christ-like. On her knees, clasping and kissing her crucifix, she lamented: "Poor Geneviève! , , , poor foster mother! . . . You used to beat me. . . . You thought it would do me good . . . I loved you anyway. . . . Our Lord was whipped. . . ." (*Iconographie photographique de la Salpêtrière*, vol. 1, p. 69.) And later, following one of her many escapes from forced confinement in an asylum, she compared her need to beg for food to Christ who also "asked for alms." Geneviève, a poor orphan who occupied the lowest social level of society, framed her misery as active imitation of Christ, and thereby reinvented it as noble.

Bourneville accused the Church of taking advantage of weak women to perpetrate its superstitions and maintain its power. Highly suggestible girls raised to believe in saints and demons were all the more likely, he argued, to engage in ascetic forms of worship or become demonically possessed—in other words, to succumb to hysteria. What he never acknowledged was that these same girls might have been just as easily manipulated by medical authority. The Church and the clinic were both patriarchal institutions that sought to control women. They both shaped female experience with expectations for their behavior, and they both rewarded girls and women who best embodied those expectations.

Geneviève, however, was not a docile worshiper of either the Church or the clinic. Her relationship with the nuns she encountered was frequently stormy. Her case history emphasizes the abuse she had suffered at the hands of these women. Not only had she been taunted, she had been beaten and bound with ropes, relentlessly "persecuted" (in Bourneville's admittedly biased language) by the good sisters who were assigned to care for her. It is Bourneville's voice that is heard throughout Geneviève's case history, reminding the reader of the nefarious influence of nuns on his patient. If ever a sister took Christian pity on the unfortunate girl, Bourneville did not record it. We read only of the unmitigated cruelty and medical mishaps she suffered at the hands of the religious women entrusted with her well-being. Bourneville's nuns were at best superstitious ninnies, at worst sadistic brutes. Geneviève, looking back on the miserable time she spent at the hospital in Poitiers, agreed: "In the hospitals, the nuns mistreat hysterics." (*Iconographie photographique de la Salpêtrière*, vol. 1, p. 83.) Later, during one of her many leaves from the Salpêtrière, she found work at another hospital, in the maternity ward at Saint-Antoine. After two or three months, she got into a heated argument with a nun and, no longer a helpless girl, Geneviève assaulted her. Not surprisingly, she lost her job and ended up back at the Salpêtrière.

Geneviève's contentious relationship with the Church and its nuns was not all that unusual. The history of Catholicism is populated with nuns who became possessed by demons and by female saints who were rebellious girls. Many canonized women were initially labeled troublesome and headstrong, marginalized by their mother superiors and Church leaders. Moreover, the line that separated divine inspiration from demonic possession was fragile. Women were particularly vulnerable to possession by outside forces, from Heaven or from Hell. Many of the signs of possession—trances, ecstasies, and convulsions—were the same for those possessed by Satan and those possessed by God, and many female saints struggled with demonic forces before they were consumed by the divine. The Church often had difficulty figuring out who was a saint and who was a witch. The ecstasies of Saint Teresa of Ávila were suspected of having a demonic origin, and Saint Veronica was possessed by a demon who slapped, bit, and kicked her, knocked her off ladders, and showed her the fires of Hell.

Bourneville meticulously catalogued Geneviève's actions and compared them point by point, gesture by gesture, with the historical descriptions of religious excess from the past and the present. Jeanne des Anges, Jeanne Fery, the convulsionists of Saint-Médard, Marguerite-Marie Alacoque, Madeleine Bavent, Louise Lateau, and a long list of other saints and witches were diagnosed as hysterics who presented symptoms identical to Geneviève's. And, like these women, Geneviève repeatedly engaged in mortification of her flesh and had patches of anesthesia, which in traditional Christian doctrine is proof that a human has consorted with the devil. She twitched and trembled and flailed with a demonic fury rarely seen, even at the Salpêtrière. She starved herself and made herself vomit when force-fed. She had bursts of extraordinary strength when she could scale walls and rooftops and even tear straitjackets to shreds. Geneviève was also sporadically mute, which, as Bourneville pointed out, the Church considered a sign of making a pact with the devil. "However," he added, "while the exorcists were powerless to break the silence, we have our ways to undo the pact: *ovarian compression*." (*Iconographie photographique de la Salpêtrière*, vol. 1, p. 103.) Like Jeanne des Anges, Geneviève could withstand freezing temperatures stark naked or lightly clothed: "Geneviève will walk in the courtyard in her chemise under a downpour, she will walk on the rooftops and spend the night in the frigid cold, she will sit on a bench outdoors, her chemise under her arm, recalling point by point a famous possessed woman, the mother superior of the Ursulines of Loudun." (*Iconographie photographique de la Salpêtrière*, vol. 1, p. 91.) Even a posture that seems a bit peculiar but not particularly demonic—Geneviève balanced on her bed on one foot—is related to the seventeenth-century possessed woman who also stood in such a position. (*Iconographie photographique de la Salpêtrière*, vol. 1, p. 96.)

For young women like Geneviève, extreme religious behaviors, whether construed as demonic or divine, became a way to access power in a society that oppressed them. It makes perfect sense that Geneviève would identify with Jeanne des Anges. I don't mean that her identification was calculated, or even conscious. However, her options were so limited that the path to glory through self-mortification must have been at least as appealing as her other options. As a route to escape her situation, religious excess was perhaps the only one available to her. Geneviève was powerless, and to be possessed by God or Satan was to be invested with power.

Bourneville compared Geneviève's symptoms to the convulsionists of Saint-Médard, a group of fanatical girls who went into convulsions when they visited the grave of François de Paris, a priest who died in 1727 of self-starvation and was buried in the cemetery of the Saint-

Médard Church in Paris. His tomb became the site of reported miracle healings, and the mostly young female pilgrims lay on the grave and ate the dirt that covered it, upon which they would erupt into ecstatic trances and convulsions that were startlingly erotic. The girls touched themselves suggestively and mimicked sexual intercourse. At first there were only a few, but soon there were hundreds of girls, and instead of simply eating dirt, they found increasingly horrible ways to degrade themselves: they had themselves squashed under paving stones, they pierced their tongues, they raked their bodies with hot irons and had themselves hung up by their ankles and beaten with sticks.[18] The convulsionists were so disruptive to the neighborhood that in 1732 the cemetery was sealed by royal decree. Louis XV exercised his supreme sovereignty with the following mandate: "By order of the King, God is hereby forbidden from working any miracles in this spot."[19] While God complied, the girls proved more difficult to manage and continued their convulsing and increasingly more flamboyant and excruciating forms of self-torture: some swallowed live coals and others had themselves nailed to a cross. A year after the cemetery was closed, a law was passed forbidding the convulsionists from practicing in public. Needless to say, the threat of punishment and prison was not particularly effective on this group of girls.

Shortly after the cemetery of Saint-Médard was sealed, another vexing problem arose. Nuns at a nearby convent erupted in a chorus of meowing. They would begin at the same time each day and meow for several hours. Once again, the beleaguered neighbors complained and the royal guard was called in to quiet the feline women. Nor was this kind of vocal transvestitism limited to Paris and to cats. Elsewhere in France, there were outbreaks of women barking. The most famous incident occurred in Josselin, a small village in Brittany. The story about the "*aboyeuses*," or the barking women of Josselin, made it across the Atlantic and appeared in the February 26, 1882, issue of the *New York Times*:

In Brittany, it seems, women and young girls are sometimes addicted to barking. This is the result of the rudeness of their ancestresses in ancient times. The Virgin Mary passed one day, under the guise of a beggar woman, near a spot where some Breton women were washing linen. Being attacked by a dog they had with them, she appealed to them to restrain it; but they only encouraged it to bark more fiercely at the holy passer by. Thereupon they were informed that, as a punishment for their evil behavior, they and their female posterity should be occasionally afflicted by an irresistible desire to bark like dogs. Since that time, their female descendants have been liable to temporary fits of barking. They can be cured only by being taken to the statue of the Virgin at Josselin, near Auray, and compelled to kiss its feet.[20]

The story of the barking women has grown into something of a legend and is still repeated. The municipal Web site of Josselin recounts the story with only a slight variation. It refers to the "*aboyeuses*" as suffering from "barking epilepsy" and claims the afflicted were miraculously cured by merely touching the statue, not kissing its feet.

Geneviève's Demonic Behavior

According to Charcot and the Salpêtrière School, religious excess and the extraordinary behavior it could produce in mostly young women was classic hysteria. They had Geneviève, their own version of a possessed woman, to prove it. Paul Richer, who recorded Charcot's stages of hysteria and sketched Geneviève on many occasions, found himself challenged by the violence and chaos of her demonic contortions and seizures. Richer's book on anatomy is still in print. In fact, it was recently cited as "not only the most complete but the most accurate" work on artistic anatomy.[21] Yet Geneviève proved difficult to sketch for even the gifted Richer because her body, he wrote, obeyed no law "other than the law of the strange and the impossible."[22] Indeed, when faced with her frantic movements, he felt obliged to "put down the quill and take up the pencil," because even in his skilled hands, ink was too permanent to capture her abruptly shifting seizures and "the most terrifying expressions" of her face. "Her eyes are wide open and her pupils sometimes converge in a frightening strabismus or are completely hidden under her eyelids. Her eyebrows contract, her mouth gapes and her tongue sticks out. Her features, pulled in opposite directions, make her face asymmetrical. *It is the image of one possessed by the devil.*"[23] (See Figure 33.)

Less than three centuries ago, remarked Bourneville, Geneviève would have been considered possessed, "because the mark of the devil is blatantly apparent in her." And those "unfortunate women from the olden days were hysterics just like Geneviève is: we are speaking of the demonically possessed, in particular, the possessed women of Loudun, the birthplace of our patient." (*Iconographie photographique de la Salpêtrière*, vol. 1, p. 95.) Had Geneviève lived in that era, he added, she would no doubt have been burnt at the stake.

While Geneviève proved to be a perfect model for her doctors' theories about extreme religious behavior, her demonic behavior did not make for a particularly docile patient. She was belligerent and difficult. One morning when Charcot visited her room, she chased him, screaming "Just wait until I get my hands on you!" (*Iconographie photographique de la Salpêtrière*, vol. 1, p. 62.) Besides threatening the director of the hospital, she stole chloroform and wine, smashed windows and furniture, brawled with other patients, and she loved hiding, often choosing the hospital rooftops. With her endowed abilities to scale walls and withstand inclement weather, she made it hard for the hospital staff to find her. Once, she hid in the courtyard under a manhole cover. The nurses looked for her for hours, focusing their search on the roofs. When she revealed herself, she laughed. "Aren't they stupid, to look for me up in the air when I'm down here on the ground." (*Iconographie photographique de la Salpêtrière*, vol. 1, p. 76.) Sometimes when escaped, she drank. On several occasions, Bourneville noted that she managed to get hold of "large quantities of wine" and would return to the ward intoxicated.

Figure 33. *Demonic Attack*. Drawing by Paul Richer from *Études cliniques sur l'hystéro-épilepsie ou grande hystérie*, Paris: Adrien Delahaye et Émile Lecrosnier, 1881.

Her case history includes innumerable flights from the ward and sometimes from the hospital grounds altogether. One day she had been given permission to leave the hospital in order to go into town with a nurse. She snuck off and ran to a lover's house. On another occasion, she fled with a fellow patient and stayed out all night. The following day, "at two in the afternoon," wrote Bourneville, not without humor, "we were visited by the two fugitives, accompanied by a little black dog that they had found only who knows where." (*Iconographie photographique de la Salpêtrière*, vol. 1, p. 88.) She also found her way onto a train and ended up at the station in Saint-Leu, a town north of Paris, where she tore posters off the wall and fell to the ground in a fit. She was arrested and brought to the insane asylum in Clermont, where she was held for six months.

Bourneville wrote that during the Siege of Paris, which lasted from September 1870 until January 1871 and finalized the humiliating defeat of France in the Franco-Prussian War, Geneviève left the hospital "on a whim," which probably means yet another escape, and somehow wound up at a military post near Saint-Denis on the outskirts of Paris. Because she refused to answer questions ("hysterical mutism" according to Bourneville), she was taken for a spy and arrested. In this particular instance, her frequent brushes with the law served her well because when she was brought to the prefecture of police, she was immediately recognized and all charges were dropped.

Geneviève had an uncanny ability to slip out of straitjackets. In the spring of 1874, on one of her many unauthorized excursions outside the ward, she made it as far as the general infirmary when she was stopped by an attack. Charcot managed to end her seizures with an ovarian compression and bring her back to her room, but she managed to sneak off again and climbed to the roof. "It is only with great difficulty," remarked Bourneville, "that we succeed in getting her down and putting her in a straitjacket." (*Iconographie photographique de la Salpêtrière*, vol. 1, p. 64.) Satisfied that these measures would keep their patient in her room, the doctors left her in bed, bound in the hospital "*camisole*," a word that sounds nicer in French than the English translation: straitjacket. At one in the morning she was found in the courtyard of the general infirmary, sitting on a bench, stark naked, no *camisole* in sight. Richer also commented on Geneviève's talents as an escape artist. "The straitjacket cannot contain her," he wrote, "she soon rips it to pieces with her teeth."[24]

The doctors officially released Geneviève from the Salpêtrière seven different times over a period of fourteen years. Altogether she spent more than eight years at the Salpêtrière; her longest unbroken stay was three years and nine months. In December of 1866, during one of these periods, she ended up in the insane asylum in Toulouse. Her case history does not explain how or why she found herself in Toulouse, only that she was there for several months, managed to gain the confidence of the nun-nurses, was given permission to move about the hospital with relative freedom, and she took advantage of the situation to escape. She then *walked* from Toulouse to Paris, more than four hundred miles. Dressed in the uniform of the asylum, a hospital gown and wooden shoes, she slept in the woods and bathed in ponds and rivers. Along the way, she asked for food from farmers and begged for money only when her hunger pushed her to do so, rationalizing "that the Lord our God asked for alms," and she "could do likewise." (*Iconographie photographique de la Salpêtrière*, vol. 1, p. 55.) Her voyage lasted almost three months. Bourneville, anticipating that his readers might balk at the credibility of such a story, noted that he had a letter from the director of the insane asylum in Toulouse, a Monsieur Marchant, that corroborated Geneviève's version of events. (*Iconographie photographique de la Salpêtrière*, vol. 1, p. 90.) I could not find any record of Geneviève's stay in Toulouse. Unfortunately, old hospital records, like so much else, are sometimes misplaced or accidentally destroyed.

Désirée

On August 31, 1867, Geneviève was back at the Salpêtrière after a year of living away from the hospital, a year that included her walk across much of France. This time her swollen abdomen was the result of a real pregnancy, and in February 1868 she gave birth to a healthy baby girl. Bourneville's account is brutally short: "The birth presented no complications. She wanted to breast-feed but circumstances necessitated placing the infant at the hospice of rue d'Enfer. She had an abscess of the left breast—the one whose nipple she had previously cut off." (*Iconographie photographique de la Salpêtrière*, vol. 1, pp. 55–56.) I found the baby's birth certificate in the municipal archives of Paris, and the cruel irony of her situation became more apparent. The unwanted child from Loudun who grew up to become the possessed woman of the Salpêtrière, gave birth out of wedlock to a baby she poignantly named Désirée, which in French means "desired one." The baby was sent to a state institution on the rue d'Enfer, or Street of Hell (which now goes by the less sinister sounding avenue Denfert-Rochereau). Désirée, listed in the hospice's records as "Abandonée #24,641" spent the first three weeks of her life on the Street of Hell and then, in a pattern that repeated her mother's life, was sent to live with a foster family in the countryside outside of Paris. The same records describe Geneviève was an "*aliénée*," or an insane woman, an error that would no doubt have injured the hysteric's pride.

Geneviève spoke often about Désirée and made many plans to reunite with her. Bourneville mentioned that when she was not in the throes of multiple attacks, Geneviève was a hardworking seamstress in the Salpêtrière workshops, "sewing with much activity in order to earn money to decently support her daughter. She is a very skilled worker." (*Iconographie photographique de la Salpêtrière*, vol. 1, p. 75, n. 1.) We know nothing of the baby's father, and other than a brief mention during one of her hysterical attacks, he remained unnamed and, apparently, unloved. The following passage, recorded by Bourneville is full of bitter pathos. More than eight years after Geneviève gave birth, Bourneville noted: "G. is reclining on her bed, propped up on pillows. Her head is upright; her gaze is fixed; her expression is marked with a sort of resigned sadness. (See Figure 34.) She speaks of her mother, of her first lover, Camille, a true love, if we are to believe her. She talks about her second lover, the father of her daughter, about her daughter herself, etc.

> "Poor Geneviève! . . . Your existence is so sad . . . oh! my girl! . . . Your father, I never loved him . . . oh! the traitor! . . ." She weeps, then takes up where she left off: "No, I never loved him . . . Oh! my Camille, where are you? . . . My fiancé! . . . Well, I would never betray him . . . If I wasn't good, it wasn't my fault. . . . The traitor, he laid traps for me . . . He told me I would be cured. . . . Oh, Mary, Mother of God, take pity on me! . . . Oh! my daughter . . . my joy . . . You are a sad memory for me, but I love you . . . Without you, my dear girl, I would have killed myself. . . . For you, I will work night and day. . . . I will not be like my mother, I will not abandon you . . . I am thinking of you, my girl . . . Why would I want to destroy myself? . . . God did not let me take my life . . . I have a friendly smile from no one. . . ." (*Iconographie photographique de la Salpêtrière*, vol. 1, pp. 68–69.)

Other than noting that in the delirium phase of the hysterical attack patients frequently ranted about events in their own lives, Bourneville did not comment any further on Geneviève's grief. The reader is left to wonder if "the traitor" she mentioned, Désirée's father, had seduced her with the promise that she would be cured if she gave in to his advances. Geneviève's reference to killing herself was not

Figure 34. "Terminal Period: Melancholic Delirium." Photograph of
Geneviève Basile Legrand by Paul Regnard from Désiré-Magloire
Bourneville and Paul Regnard, *Iconographie photographique de la Salpêtrière*,
Volume 1, Paris: Aux Bureaux du Progrès Médical, Delahaye & Lecrosnier,
1877, Plate 19. Yale University, Harvey Cushing/John Hay Whitney
Medical Library.

idle chatter. She had hoarded pills while in the hospital in Poitiers,
and a few years later, at the beginning of 1865, she again attempted
suicide by trying to jump off the Puits de Grenelle, an artesian well
that used to stand in Paris, topped by a 141-foot-high cast-iron tower.
Her odd demeanor drew the attention of passersby and someone prevented her from jumping. She was taken to Necker Hospital before
being readmitted to the Salpêtrière. Both of these suicide attempts,
however, took place before Désirée was born. In the medical literature
devoted to Geneviève, no others are mentioned.

In 1871, Geneviève set out to visit her daughter, who was living with
a foster family near Avallon, in Burgundy, about 120 miles southeast
of Paris. Geneviève was "detained" by Prussian officers in Montbard,

stationed there following the Armistice of the Franco-Prussian War. Bourneville wrote that for one week "she had relations with one (?) Prussian officer, relations that resulted in a *second pregnancy*." (*Iconographie photographique de la Salpêtrière*, vol. 1, p. 56.) Bourneville used the word "detained" and added the question mark following the word "one." It's impossible to know if the "relations" were coerced or consensual. In yet another episode that reads like a chapter from a tawdry nineteenth-century novel or a *grand guignol*, she never arrived in Avallon, but instead headed back to Paris, where she gave birth to another baby girl, this time at the Hôtel-Dieu Hospital.

After a bitter dispute with a nun, Geneviève stormed out of the maternity ward before she was due to be released. She stayed with a friend in Nogent, a town on the outskirts of Paris, but since neither she nor her daughter was doing well, she returned to the city and asked to be readmitted to the Hôtel-Dieu. An unyielding clerk at the Central Hospital Bureau, the processing center for the large network of the Parisian public health-care system, refused to let her enter the Hôtel-Dieu, and she was told to go to La Charité. Geneviève refused, and shortly after she left the bureau, she suffered an attack on the street. Mother and baby took shelter at the Cité military barracks, still intact following the Franco-Prussian War. The next day, she did get permission to return to the Hôtel-Dieu, where her newborn baby died of convulsions. She was six weeks old. To add to the roster of agonies Geneviève had already suffered, she was transferred to the dreaded Sainte-Anne insane asylum before being allowed to return to the Salpêtrière at the very end of 1871.

Ecstasy

Back at the Salpêtrière, Geneviève reassumed her role as the hospital possessed woman, but her range of religious experience now included

divine apparitions and ecstatic trances. On April 5, 1874, Bourneville recorded: "Last night, G. had visions, claimed to have seen the
Virgin, Christ, etc." (*Iconographie photographique de la Salpêtrière*, vol.
1, p. 66.) The matter-of-fact tone of his sentence, in particular the
disparaging "etc." at the end, indicates just how insignificant he found
these divine apparitions. They were nothing more than an entry in
a long list of symptoms suffered by a hysteric, ones that fueled his
anticlerical campaign. In 1875, a decade after she first entered the
Salpêtrière, Geneviève began to experience ecstatic trances: "Over
the course of the year, we were witness to another variety of delirium," wrote Bourneville, "in which the religious cachet was more
pronounced. Instead of a purely melancholic delirium, accompanied
by ranting and lamentations, we were in the presence of a genuine
ecstasy." (*Iconographie photographique de la Salpêtrière*, vol. 1, p. 70.)
During her ecstasies, Geneviève took a crucifixion pose, arms out-
stretched at her side, legs together with one foot on top of the other,
or she would kneel in a classic prayer position. (See Figure 35.) She
could maintain these poses for hours at a time. Bourneville was quick
to compare his patient to "Saint Teresa and the other visionaries"
while he diagnosed Saint Teresa, Saint Catherine of Siena, and even
Joan of Arc, the latter revered as a national hero in France, as hysterics. (*Iconographie photographique de la Salpêtrière*, vol. 1, p. 70.) Henri
Legrand du Saulle, a fellow doctor at the Salpêtrière, added names to
Bourneville's list: "So many Saints and Blessed Women were nothing more than simple hysterics! If one rereads the details of the lives
of Elizabeth of Hungary in 1207; of Saint Gertrude, of Saint Bridget
(. . .) of Madame de Chantal, in 1752; of the famous Marguerite-
Marie Alacoque, and of so many others one will be easily convinced
of this truth."[25] Paul Richer was more careful when he wrote about
ecstasy, distancing himself somewhat from his colleague's anticlericalism. In discussing Geneviève's ecstasy, which he too believed was
a "morbid condition" he qualified his comments with a gentle jab at

Figure 35. "Terminal Period: Ecstasy." Photograph of Geneviève Basile Legrand by Paul Regnard from Désiré-Magloire Bourneville and Paul Regnard, *Iconographie photographique de la Salpêtrière*, Volume 1, Paris: Aux Bureaux du Progrès Médical, Delahaye & Lecrosnier, 1877, Plate 22. Yale University, Harvey Cushing/John Hay Whitney Medical Library.

Bourneville: "My intention is not to write the history of all of the famous ecstatics, nor do I have the pretention of reducing them all to the same proportions in order to make them enter into the same framework." A little later, he added another divergence of opinion from the standard at the Salpêtrière by recognizing that not all transcendent states are hysterical: "I do not contest the fact that ecstasy can be found outside of hysteria. . . ."[26]

After pious trances, Geneviève often collapsed into "erotic delirium." The Salpêtrière doctors repeatedly conflated spiritual ecstasy with erotic ecstasy, a move that placed mysticism firmly within the natural realm. "Geneviève would fall back on her bed, lift her chemise and spread her thighs; or she would address one of her attendants, abruptly leaning toward him, saying, 'Kiss me! . . . Give me! . . . Here, here's my . . .' And her gestures further accentuate the meaning of her words." (*Iconographie photographique de la Salpêtrière*, vol. 1, pp. 70–71.) According to the doctors, religious and sexual excess were often connected in women. Richer emphasized Geneviève's rapid vacillation between sexual and religious passion. "Most often," he wrote, "her hallucinations are lecherous. She sees Camille, calls out to him: 'Camille, I have never loved anyone but you.' She affects theatrical poses accompanied by these words: 'Give me your love. Don't insult me.' Or else she assumes silent poses, approaching ecstasy. She is on her knees, or seated on her bed, her eyes toward heaven, one finger raised or her hands joined together. She remains thus completely absorbed for several minutes.

"Or else she cries out: 'Dear God, save me!' Her prayer continues in an edifying manner only to be suddenly replaced by improper language and gestures."[27] The physicians believed that female sexuality and religious fervor created a breeding ground for hysteria. Marriage and family, not the convent, they argued, was the environment to contain female sexuality. Bourneville wrote of a hysteric who was released from the Salpêtrière, "married, had children and never suffered another attack." (*Iconographie photographique de la Salpêtrière,* vol. 1, p. 107, n. 1.)

Jacques Lacan was hardly the first to point out the eroticism of Bernini's famous seventeenth-century sculpture, *Saint Teresa in Ecstasy.* By the nineteenth century, it had become so common for doctors to hold up the statue as proof of the carnal nature of religious rapture that the decadent writer Huysmans lamented that his beloved saint had repeatedly been reduced to a mere hysteric and nymphomaniac: "When we consider that, in spite of incredible difficulties, she founded thirty-two nunneries, that she put them all under obedience to a rule which is a model of wisdom, a rule which foresees and rectifies the most ignored mistakes of the heart, it is astonishing to hear her treated by freethinkers as a hysterical madwoman!" Later, as a newly born-again Catholic, he denounced medical opinion that likened "the happy lucidity and unequalled genius of Saint Teresa to the extravagances of nymphomaniacs."[28]

Visitation

Bourneville assailed another saint: Marguerite-Marie Alacoque, the founder of the seventeenth-century French cult of the Sacred Heart, in a section devoted to Geneviève and her experiences with an unworldly visitor. He discussed Alacoque and quoted long passages of her hagiography, periodically interjecting clinical notes. Marguerite entered a convent, took the name Marie, and became a bride of Christ. Her husband was a jealous lover and reproached her for paying attention to anyone but him. He encouraged her to engage in many egregious forms of mortification of the flesh, including lacerating her skin by wearing iron chains and belts and drinking the bathwater of lepers. Besides these self-induced agonies, Jesus blessed Marguerite-Marie with his own wounds and she suffered from invisible stigmata:

one on her side and another around her head from where Christ had placed his crown of thorns.

Her divine husband also consoled her with his caresses. Not only did she see her lover, she heard, felt, and tasted him: "Our Savior appeared to her on the cross, radiant with love. As she was gazing upon him in rapture, he detached one of his arms and pulled the saint, who was overcome with celestial bliss, to his beloved breast and placed her lips on the wound of his heart."[29] In a later visit, one that became the foundation for the cult of the Sacred Heart, Jesus asked her to give him her heart, which he took from her body and placed in his own breast, "that ardent oven." Then, as "a token of his burning love," he removed a flame in the shape of a heart from his chest and filled the hole that Marguerite-Marie's heart had occupied. Jesus continued to visit Marguerite-Marie, who was overcome by her beloved's "special caresses" and their "amorous unions." Her mother superior initially dismissed her stories as self-aggrandizing lies told by a troublesome girl. In the end, however, a young Jesuit priest believed her and managed to convince the religious authorities of the divinity of her visions. Marguerite-Marie Alacoque was canonized in 1920.

On these same pages, Bourneville discussed another seventeenth-century nun, Madeleine Bavent. She too experienced a physical relationship with Jesus; however, in this instance, her lover turned out to be a demon disguised as Christ, and instead of becoming a saint, Madeleine Bavent was thrown into a dungeon, where she died before the authorities had the opportunity to burn her at the stake. Between her first encounter with the impostor and her death in prison, the nun's inadvertent coupling with the Devil set off a mass possession in her former convent, not unlike the famous possession in Loudun. "If we believe the theologians," wrote Bourneville, "the memory of Madeleine Bavent, wife of the Devil, must be held in contempt and booed, while that of Marie Alacoque, wife of Jesus, must be honored and venerated. This opinion is not ours. For us, both sick women were under the sad influence of the superstitions of their time." (*Iconographie photographique de la Salpêtrière*, vol. 2, p. 224.)

Bourneville's campaign to demystify religious experience and expose the barbaric superstitions of the Church was both astute and relentless. He quoted liberally from the very texts he was debunking, presenting them as evidence for his case against religion. What he failed to acknowledge, however, was that by claiming religious experience as medical symptom, he simply exchanged one patriarchal institution with another. The convent became the clinic, the priest was now a doctor. The women in his tale, whether possessed by Heaven, Hell, or hysteria, remain intractably mysterious.

The Succubus

Bourneville included the stories of Marguerite-Marie Alacoque and Madeleine Bavent in a second section devoted to Geneviève found in Volume 2 of the *Iconographie photographique de la Salpêtrière*. The chapter is entitled "Succubus," or a demon that takes the form of a beautiful woman in order to have sexual intercourse with men while they sleep. According to Bourneville, "Geneviève is a *succubus*." Oddly, the story he went on to tell cast Geneviève as the victim of an incubus, or a male demon who disguises himself in order to have sex with women, rather than a succubus herself. In any case, Bourneville's point was that, like Marguerite-Marie Alacoque and Madeleine Bavent, Geneviève experienced visits from a nocturnal lover, and like them, she not only saw her lover, but she talked with him, kissed him, felt his body on hers, and experienced "the most voluptuous sensations." Paul Richer further notes that Geneviève's "sick imagination has created an entire novel."[30]

At first Geneviève suffered from unrequited love. She had become hopelessly obsessed with one of the physicians on the ward, referred to

as "Mr. X." He appears for the first time in Volume I of the *Iconographie*.
Geneviève had run off and this time was tracked to the staff lounge of
the epileptic ward. When found, she insisted that she needed to be there,
that Dr. X. had asked her to meet him; indeed, that he had ordered her
to do so. Finally, after much arguing, her doctors escorted her back to
her room. Six weeks later, Dr. X. reappears. She confessed to her doctors "the passion" she felt for him and that he resembled her beloved
Camille: "I love him but he doesn't know it," she confided. "When I see
him, I become completely pale . . . Only he and Camille have that effect
on me . . . When Camille was courting me, it was the same thing. . . ."
(*Iconographie photographique de la Salpêtrière*, vol. 1, p. 80.) Seven weeks
later, after another escape, she insisted that she was merely obeying Dr.
X., who had "ordered her to meet him in the country." (*Iconographie
photographique de la Salpêtrière*, vol. 1, p. 88.) Bourneville conducted her
back to her room on the pretext that he was taking her to Dr. X.

In the chapter called "Succubus" of the *Iconographie*, Geneviève's
relationship with Dr. X. turns sexual. As she told it, Dr. X., who was
married, arrived at her bedside in the middle of the night on the
pretext that he was conducting medical experiments, ones involving
"genital sensations." (*Iconographie photographique de la Salpêtrière*, vol.
2, p. 203.) At first she resisted his advances, deeming it "criminal to
have sexual relations with a married man." Finally, worn down by his
persistence and her own desire, she gave in, only to be so wracked by
guilt that she refused any new contact.

More than two years later, Geneviève, who still persisted in her
belief that she was having an affair, would figure out just why she
was so drawn to the married doctor. As she told it, Mr. X., in order to
coax her back into bed with him, revealed his long-kept secret: "I am
the Camille that you miss so much, the one you have cried over for so
long!" This extraordinary revelation filled her with such joy that she
willingly threw herself into his arms. And even though she still had
qualms about the fact that he was married to someone else, her love

for Camille was so overpowering that she now found it impossible to resist him. In fact, even before he confessed, she had suspected the truth because his resemblance to her long-lost fiancé was so striking. Once he had told the truth, Camille, aka Dr. X., came to her almost every night and stayed in her bed, where they cavorted for hours, she "as amorous as a cat and he a tom cat." (*Iconographie photographique de la Salpêtrière*, vol. 2, p. 205.)

Geneviève's acknowledgment of her sexual appetite was remarkably frank for the period. She repeatedly spoke of her lust and her efforts to control it. Like Blanche, Geneviève had been pursued sexually by an employer when she was a teenager, but unlike Blanche, who had experienced the advances as unwanted and threatening, Geneviève had been conflicted and confessed that she had been obsessed. In the medical literature devoted to Geneviève, she articulated this battle repeatedly, in words that reflect a nineteenth-century morality punctured by erotic desire. Long before she gave in to Camille/Dr. X., or hallucinated that she did, she spoke of the erotic turmoil he sent her into:

> "Me, I'm not like those street walkers . . . I don't love one man one day and another the next . . . To kiss a man that one doesn't love . . . it's dirty!" Her features express disgust; she spits. "Mr. X., I know that I must never kiss him . . . I will die in a convent . . . I get pale when I see Mr. X. But I am not so stupid to tell him everything . . . I am no longer myself when I see him . . . He must not stay here much longer or I will go mad . . . I told him this morning that I want to go back to Poitiers . . . I will never be cured here as long as he's here . . . Each time that I see him, I am completely shattered . . . I will have to be kept in a cell in order not to blurt out something." (*Iconographie photographique de la Salpêtrière*, vol. 1, p. 79.)

Once she had given in to her desire, she claimed that she felt "more voluptuous sensations than she ha[d] ever felt with any other man and Camille claim[ed], on his part, that he has never felt so much pleasure as he does with her. . . ." (*Iconographie photographique de la Salpêtrière*, vol. 2, p. 207.)

Bourneville wrote about Geneviève and her imagined lover as though he were reporting the truth. Whatever the erotic passion they may have felt for one other, he noted, the relationship became increasingly tormented. "Just like the love between Marguerite-Marie Alacoque and Jesus," wrote Bourneville with an ironic wink to the reader, "the love between Geneviève and Mr. X. was not without its storms." (*Iconographie photographique de la Salpêtrière*, vol. 2, p. 220.) For example, when Geneviève tried to talk Camille/Dr. X. into running away with her, he became so angry that he dragged her into the courtyard. When she tried to resist his advances he beat her brutally. After these violent fights, she would wake in the morning stripped naked, her body covered with bite marks. Bourneville related much of this with deadpan detachment, as though he were simply recording the facts of her case. In an entry that summed up the first half of 1878, he noted: "The nocturnal relations continue, as many as six times a night: this is why she is always so tired, so pale, so dejected in the morning." (*Iconographie photographique de la Salpêtrière*, vol. 2, pp. 203–204.) This is the same narrative strategy he used when writing about saints and the demonically possessed. Thus, Marguerite-Marie Alacoque *had* lovers' quarrels with Jesus and Madeleine Bavent "also received a visit from Christ who took her as his fiancée. But it was not the real Christ, it was the fallen angel named Balban . . . , whom she served as wife for many years." (*Iconographie photographique de la Salpêtrière*, vol. 2, p. 225.) Bourneville's conviction that science trumped fantasy was so tenacious that at times he did not even bother to qualify the experiences he recorded as imaginary, or hallucinatory.

When Richer wrote about Geneviève's relationship with Camille/ Dr. X., he did so with a touch more compassion than Bourneville, noting that her cries had a startling ring of truth about them:

> Oh! Poor Gen.! Who can understand my pain? God alone . . . I ought to stop seeing him. . . . He insults me . . . I should be his wife! But he has made me his mistress. . . . I love him too much . . . everything is lost for me . . . (. . .) Yes, yes . . . I love you and I am angry . . . I want all of this to stop! . . . Just kill me . . . No one will know . . . Give me something to make me die . . . (. . .) And just think, he had the cruelty to reveal himself to me . . . Ah! . . . the night that he confessed everything, it would have been better if he had broken his leg . . . Marry me! . . . Never in my life, never will a man be anything to me . . . Oh! Camille, Camille! . . . I want to die in my pain![31]

On another occasion Richer again quoted Geneviève's torment regarding her lover: "Camille . . . Camille . . . tie me up, guillotine me, I will always love you. I have never loved anyone else! . . . Ah! the horror!"[32]

Geneviève's doctors did not believe she was having an affair with Dr. X., even though sexual relationships between interns and hysterics were not uncommon, and Geneviève had escaped from the hospital in Poitiers with the help of a doctor before running off to Paris with him. However, in this instance, there seemed to be no doubt in the physicians' minds that she was experiencing "nocturnal hallucinations," ones that were sustained for years. Many hysterics experienced them, but most were aware of the imaginary quality of their visions when they woke up in the morning. Geneviève, like Marguerite-Marie Alacoque and Madeleine Bavent, insisted on the reality of these nighttime trysts, no matter how much her doctors attempted to persuade her otherwise. "Her belief in the reality of these hallucinations," wrote Richer, "lasts beyond the time span of the attack. Gen. believes she sees Camille. We can find an explanation here, for those poor souls who insisted in the days of witchcraft, in the face of torture and being burned at the stake, in the reality of their dealings with the devil."[33] Bourneville and the accused Dr. X. energetically denied that the affair was real. Her story was preposterous. But to each objection they made, she had a logical counterargument. Camille, she insisted, would hide the moment he heard someone approaching; she deliberately chose a bed next to the heaviest sleepers; the concierge let Dr. X. in with a secret password; the night watchman would leave the door unlocked; Charcot himself was "in cahoots with Mr. X.," making it possible for him to carry on the affair with his patient. (*Iconographie photographique de la Salpêtrière*, vol. 2, p. 205.) When asked why she had not become pregnant, she responded that Camille "took precautions," and then added that she believed she had recently been pregnant and miscarried. Bourneville noted that she had had a particularly heavy menstrual period and passed clots of blood.

When the doctors reminded her that Camille died many years ago, Geneviève had a logical response. He had faked his death and fled the countryside because he did not want to be tied down to a sick woman. She knew this was true because Camille had confessed everything. "The doubt we cast on these visits," wrote Bourneville, "the irony with which her confessions are received, does not shake her own conviction in their reality. She would swear in a court of law, before God and before anyone else, that she saw Camille, that she received his embraces." (*Iconographie photographique de la Salpêtrière*, vol. 1, p. 104.) When Dr. X. laughed at her and cruelly pointed out that he had never set foot in her "dirty countryside," much less been raised there, she reproached him as a scorned lover: "How can you go back

Figure 36. "Hystero-Epilepsy: Succubus." Photograph of Geneviève Basile Legrand by Paul Regnard from Désiré-Magloire Bourneville and Paul Regnard, *Iconographie photographique de la Salpêtrière*, Volume 2, Paris: Aux Bureaux du Progrès Médical, Delahaye & Lecrosnier, 1877, Plate 39. Yale University, Harvey Cushing/John Hay Whitney Medical Library.

on your word like that?! How can you forget in the light of day the promises you made during the night?" (*Iconographie photographique de la Salpêtrière*, vol. 2, p. 204.)

Nothing her doctors said could persuade Geneviève that she was not carrying on a torrid affair with Camille/Dr. X. and the guilt she felt about sleeping with a married man was very real. She became increasingly despondent. She complained that her illicit relationship had aged her, given her wrinkles, and made her lose weight. She took to wearing a black hood and veil and referred to herself as the "fiancée of death." (See Figure 36.)

When her priest forbade her to continue the affair after her confession, Geneviève protested: "But, I want to be his wife. I don't want to stay here . . . I love him and I hate him at the same time . . . I need him so much . . . It's stronger than I am . . . I end up by giving in to him." When Bourneville asked her why she had let out a shrill scream, she answered: "A miserable creature like me deserves no pity . . . He doesn't deserve any either." And then she added the astute and undeniably true observation: "But, he is more useful to society than I am . . . Me, I only serve as a bad example." (*Iconographie photographique de la Salpêtrière*, vol. 2, p. 204.) On December 28, 1878, Geneviève, desperate and guilty, took it upon herself to write a letter to Mr. X.'s wife.

Madame,
Ah! madame, can you ever forgive me? I am guilty when it comes to you. Since I see that you know everything, I am going to be frank with you. I am going to confess everything to you. Remember that veiled woman that you saw coming out of your room on the night of August 15th? The one that you let pass by you? Well, that was me! And I know that you recognized me and that you let me go, when you could have had me arrested for the vile creature that I am. But you have kept quiet, all the while being my rival. I cannot help but

find in you a noble and generous heart to have had the courage to
speak to me when you came to the ward. But don't you ever let him
believe that this union is blessed. I will remain miserable for the rest
of my life since that is my destiny. And if after having poisoned my
existence, he lets me live in peace, I would still be miserable because
what you saw in your bedroom, that is not all there is. Almost every
night he comes to find me, begging me until I give in. And if I don't
want to, he bites me like the rabid dog that he is and he drags me
into the courtyard. You must have already realized as much because
you have seen the freshly made and cruel bite marks, and those are
not the first ones either. I have them all over my body. He has gone
so far as to burn me with matches and if you don't believe me I can
show you all of the scars. . . . (Iconographie photographique de la
Salpêtrière, vol. 2, pp. 214–215.)

Bourneville ostensibly included this letter in the *Iconographie* in
order to illustrate that while Geneviève's "demon" usually came to her
bedroom, he would sometimes whisk her away to another location,
just like the demon Balban had done when he transported Madeleine
Bavent to the witch's sabbath. It is a bizarre connection—Geneviève
meeting her lover at his apartment and Madeleine Bavent cavort-
ing with the Devil away from her convent—that reads like a pretext. Having made his point, he ended the letter with a maddening
ellipsis, leaving the reader to wonder if Geneviève left it unfinished
and unsent. Bourneville repeatedly deviated from the Salpêtrière
practice of including patients' words only to make a medical point.
By including the letter, the reader gets a rare glimpse of Geneviève's
written words, words that reveal her guilt, but also her rage against
her lot. The saga of Camille may have been an elaborate invention,
an extended hallucination, but it remained poignantly and undeniably true that Geneviève felt poisoned, beaten, and burned by a
Salpêtrière doctor.

Axel Munthe

Geneviève's claim that Dr. X. lured her off to his apartment finds an interesting counterpart in *The Story of San Michele*, the 1929 autobiography of Axel Munthe, the Swedish doctor who studied medicine under Charcot in Paris and who gave the scathing account of Charcot's hypnosis performance that I cited earlier. In Chapter 18, entitled "La Salpêtrière," he included a bizarre episode involving a patient named Geneviève. There were other patients named Geneviève at the Salpêtrière; however, Munthe claimed that this was a star of the clinic, and our Geneviève was the only one who can qualify. That said, the vignette is at least part, if not all, fiction, but it is nonetheless fascinating. As Munthe told it, as he was leaving the Salpêtrière one evening, he came across two old peasants who were looking for "their daughter Geneviève," whom they believed worked in the hospital kitchen. Moved by their wholesomeness—"they smelt of the country, of the orchard, the fields and the cow-house, it did my heart good to look at them"—the young doctor decided to help, to rescue the young woman from what he had come to believe was an unhealthy and exploitative environment. Much to Munthe's surprise, Geneviève was actually enjoying her life as a "prima donna" at the hospital and refused his offer. The doctor then devised an elaborate scheme to help the girl in spite of herself, to remove her from the corrupting influence of the Salpêtrière and send her back to the fresh air of the country. In order to carry out his plot, he asked Charcot for permission to work with Geneviève, "conducting experiments in telepathy." Permission granted, he met with her, and over the course of several sessions, he hypnotized her and planted the suggestion that she hated her life at the Salpêtrière and longed to return to the simple ways of her rural village. He then gave her the posthypnotic suggestion that she sneak out of the hospital during the midday meal when the staff would be distracted and meet him at his apartment. Everything proceeded as planned, and, emboldened by the success of this preliminary experiment, Munthe moved on to phase two of his scheme and suggested that Geneviève meet him two days later, same time, same place. However, this time, instead of returning her to the hospital afterward, he would see to it that she boarded a train back to her village. The appointed hour came and went. Geneviève did not show up.

The following day when the worried Munthe arrived at the Salpêtrière, he learned that Geneviève had suffered a violent attack that prevented her from leaving the hospital, and that Charcot wished to see him. "I entered the well-known sanctuary of the Master for the last time in my life," he wrote. "Charcot sat in his usual chair by the table, bent over the microscope. He raised his head and flashed his terrible eyes on me. Speaking very slowly, his deep voice trembling with rage, he said I had tried to lure to my house an inmate of his hospital, a deséquilibrée, half unconscious of her acts. According to her own confession, she had already been once to my house; my diabolical plan to take advantage of her a second time had only miscarried by a mere accident. It was a criminal offence, he ought to hand me over to the police but for the honour of the profession . . . he would let me off by turning me out of the hospital, he wished never to set his eyes on me again."[34]

There are facts in Munthe's account that simply do not add up, the most significant being that Geneviève was an orphan and would not have had parents come looking for her. That said, there are aspects of his story that were easily verified. Munthe was a young doctor practicing in Paris, he did study medicine at the Salpêtrière, and he was indeed expelled from the hospital by Charcot. Munthe prefaced this anecdote by mentioning a newspaper article about Charcot in *Le Figaro*—a vicious attack penned by a journalist who went by the pseudonym "Ignotus." According to Munthe, jealous students had falsely accused him of revealing hospital secrets to this journalist and implied that this explained Charcot's treatment of him. Whether Munthe was the source of any leaks is impossible to know. The press frequently targeted Charcot, and Ignotus, whose real name was Félix Platel, was a well-known conservative Catholic who did not need encouragement or ammunition from Munthe to attack Charcot. The article in question was a mean-spirited diatribe timed to appear on the front page of the most widely read newspaper in France on the very day that Charcot was nominated as a candidate for the Academy of Sciences. While Charcot was eventually elected to the Academy, the article might have done the damage it intended to do since he was defeated following its publication. Some years later, in a bizarre twist that Munthe did not mention in his book, Charcot received an anonymous letter from a paralyzed invalid asking for the great doctor's help. When Charcot arrived for the consultation, the patient confessed that he was none other than Ignotus. Charcot proceeded to treat him, but when it came time to collect payment, he condescendingly refused to accept his usual fee.[35]

Was Geneviève ever in Axel Munthe's apartment? If so, was she compelled to go there by posthypnotic suggestion, or was it yet another one of her escapes from the hospital? Why did Munthe include this episode at all? Oddly, the chapters concerning his time at the Salpêtrière were omitted from the French translation of the book. By 1929, when *The Story of San Michele* was published, Charcot's reputation was already severely tarnished, so censorship to protect his image seems unlikely. In any case, even if we believe Munthe's motives were honorable, that he wanted to rescue a woman who might have been our Geneviève, he nonetheless behaved in a shockingly imprudent manner. Was Charcot's accusation well founded? Did the young Swedish doctor lure Geneviève to his apartment in order to seduce her? I do not believe that "Dr. X." was Axel Munthe, but I confess the thought did cross my mind.

Mixing the Secular and the Divine

Bourneville's self-declared purpose for writing about religious experience was to demonstrate that otherworldly phenomenon could be explained scientifically, and to show how primitive and abusive practices rooted in ignorance and superstition had now been superseded by humane and rational medicine, selflessly exercised by caring practitioners. Had Geneviève lived two hundred years earlier, she too, he noted, would have expired at the stake. Yet, while the Salpêtrière doctors interpreted religious phenomena according to their own secular views, their conclusions were not merely a simple imposition of the natural onto the supernatural. They became a strange mixture of the two.

Despite the fact that they categorized the demonic possessions and religious ecstasies of the past as neuropathological, a practice they called "retrospective medicine," they also borrowed liberally from the vocabulary of the supernatural to categorize aspects of hysteria. The terms "stigmata," "passionate attitude," "demoniac attack," and "crucifixion pose," used to describe hysterical symptoms, are all borrowed from ecclesiastical discourse. However, rather than a simple imposition of one language onto the other, a subtle exchange took place: the possessed of the past were demystified as nineteenth-century hysterics, while nineteenth-century hysterics were remystified as the possessed of the past. Doctors replaced priests and the clinic becomes a cloister: a place for women to escape the oppressive limitations of society. In fact, Charcot, in his austere black coat, was frequently referred to as a kind of "high priest" of medicine. In a letter to his fiancée while he was a student at the Salpêtrière, the young Sigmund Freud wrote that Charcot had the air of "a worldly priest."[36]

By providing her doctors with a working model of contemporary ecstasy and demonic possession, Geneviève contributed to this pathologizing of the divine and dymystification of the demonic. What the doctors never admit is Geneviève's participation in the production of the desired symptoms. While her birth in Loudun was repeatedly mentioned, the Salpêtrière doctors never considered the possibility that their patient, who grew up immersed in the gruesome and glorious stories of a famous possession and was an indefatigable reader of the *Lives of the Saints*, had internalized these narratives and may have modeled her own behavior accordingly. For a young woman, especially one who was excluded from the accepted realm for women in the nineteenth century—home and family—possession meant power and attention, whether understood as religious or pathological. Her behavior, insisted the doctors, was identical to that of Jeanne des Anges, Marie-Marguerite Alacoque, Madeleine Bavent, the convulsionists of Saint-Médard and many others, because they were hysterics just like Geneviève, not because Geneviève was demonically or divinely possessed or even unconsciously imitating demonic or divine possession.

Louise Lateau

Geneviève developed a passionate interest in a young Belgian woman: Louise Lateau. Lateau, who was roughly Geneviève's age, was famous in Europe at the time as a stigmatic. Her story was even reported across the Atlantic, where the *New York Times* called her a "queer being."[37]

Interpretations of Lateau's behavior varied depending on who was doing the describing: she was a blessed visionary who had received the wounds of Christ, a gullible girl manipulated by a corrupt church, a charlatan hoodwinking a gullible public, a feeble-minded neurotic suffering from "Christomania," or, according to Bourneville, a grand hysteric, like Geneviève.

There was no disagreement about the facts. Louise Lateau was born in 1850 in Bois d'Haine, a small rural village in Belgium, not far from the French border. From the start, her life was marked by illness, pain, and poverty. After giving birth to Louise, her mother became so sick that she spent most of the next three years in bed. Then, when she was only two months old, Louise caught smallpox along with her father, a metalworker, who died of the disease. Two years later, she fell into a pond, almost drowned, and for the rest of her childhood suffered from headaches, fatigue, paleness, spitting up blood, and chlorosis. At fourteen, she was trampled by a cow, a bizarre accident that left her with an abscess on her torso and a crooked back. Because of her family's extreme poverty and her poor health, Louise attended school for only six months before her first communion at a convent, run, not insignificantly, by the Order of Saint Francis of Assisi, the first stigmatic. Speaking of her miserable childhood, Bourneville noted, "Isn't this an ensemble of conditions favorable to the development of the great neurosis known under the name of hysteria?"[38]

By all accounts, Louise fervently embraced each new symptom, and not only did she relish her own afflictions; she devoted herself to the suffering of others. When she was only eight, she went to work for an incapacitated old woman, and during the cholera epidemic a few years later, the young girl cared for the sick and even volunteered for the grisly job of carrying corpses to their coffins. None of her biographers question how a weak and deformed child could manage to carry a human body and place it in a coffin.

Shortly before her first stigmatization, Louise was overcome by a "diabolical obsession" that lasted for several months. She told her doctor that Satan appeared to her several times each night in myriad hideous forms and would toss her to the floor and strangle her. One night she was thrown so violently that she awoke with contusions. Her priest claimed to have witnessed the acts of the Devil reflected in Louise's face. To illustrate Lateau's demonic possession, Bourneville

Figure 37. *Hystero-Epileptic Attack: Period of Contorsions*. Paul Richer drawing based on a sketch by Charcot and engraved by Jean François Badoureau. This drawing was used by Bourneville as an illustration of Louise Lateau in *Science et miracle, Louise Lateau ou la stigmatisée belge*, Paris: Delahaye et Cie, Aux Bureaux du Progrès Médical, 1878.

included a drawing by Richer, based on a sketch by Charcot of one of his hysterical patients at the Salpêtrière.[39] (See Figure 37.)

One Friday, when she was eighteen years old, she began bleeding from her chest. The bleeding occurred again the next Friday and then, over the following Fridays, she began to feel pain in her hands and feet and circling her head. An "inner light" accompanied her symptoms and increased her desire to suffer. She lost her appetite and ate little or nothing, and constantly thought of the Passion. Every Friday the pains grew stronger, and soon she was bleeding from her hands, feet, head, and side. She developed an abrasion on her right shoulder, consistent with carrying the cross. As the stigmata appeared, she experienced ecstatic visions of the baby Jesus, the Virgin Mary, Saint

Teresa of Ávila, and Saint Francis of Assisi. During these ecstasies, Louise maintained a crucifixion pose, her arms stretched out at her sides and her feet placed one on top of the other, or she would kneel with her hands clasped in front of her. She allegedly ate nothing for years except a daily communion wafer, and she urinated two teaspoons a week. She did not defecate or sleep at all. Her stigmata and ecstasies continued every Friday with clocklike regularity until her death at the highly significant age of thirty-three.

News of the Belgian stigmatic spread, and Louise Lateau was subjected to all kinds of investigations: by priests, by doctors, by Church-appointed physicians, as well as by journalists and the merely curious. Lateau was so famous that even the renowned German cellular pathologist Rudolf Virchow weighed in on her case. He requested that she be brought to his laboratory in order to observe her according to strict scientific parameters. The Church denied his request, but this did not prevent him from presenting a paper in which he claimed that if she had not yet been exposed as a fraud, it was because her surroundings were not scientifically controlled. While the Church did not allow Louise to be sent off to a laboratory to be observed, it did allow doctors to make the trip to observe her in her home. Like Virchow, some of them suspected fraud and rigid conditions were put in place to safeguard against any attempt on the girl's part to deceive. She was closely monitored and her hands and feet were placed in special leather gloves and shoes. One physician, Dr. Warlomont, went even further in his attempt to prevent the possibility of Louise inflicting her own wounds: he created a special glass cylinder to cover her entire right arm and attached it to her skin with rubber and wax in such a way that it would be impossible to remove without rupturing the seal. He inserted her arm inside it on Thursday, and on Friday the doctors were able to watch the hemorrhages appear spontaneously, the seal unbroken.

The Church and many doctors also confirmed that Louise was

subsisting on nothing more than a daily communion wafer and a few sips of water. The Catholic delegation assigned to investigate Lateau recommended canonization. While she has not achieved sainthood, the Friends of Louise Lateau continue to campaign for her canonization. She is included in the most recent version of a catalogue published by the Vatican, *The Eucharistic Miracles of the World*. The Friends of Louise Lateau have restored her small house, which is still visited by pilgrims.

Geneviève, not surprisingly, felt an enormous affinity for Louise Lateau. Her case history notes that she incessantly talked about the Belgian mystic and talked about visiting her. On May 12, 1876, Geneviève was released from the Salpêtrière. As we know, Geneviève was in and out of the clinic. She sometimes returned to the Salpêtrière for a brief stay to avoid succumbing to an attack in the streets and being picked up by the police. However, following this particular leave, Bourneville noted that, uncharacteristically, he had neither seen nor heard from his patient for many weeks. Then in August of that year, Charcot received the following letter from a Dr. Decaesseckey in Quesnoy-sur-Deule, a town in northeastern France near the Belgian border. Dated August 12, 1876, the doctor writes:

Dear Sir,

I am taking the liberty to write to you on the subject of a patient who interests you very much: I am talking about the hystero-epileptic, Geneviève L. As she was traveling through Quesnoy, she was overcome by an attack of hystero-epilepsy that lasted from six in the evening until one in the morning and was only stopped with ovarian compression.

Before her attack, she had stopped in a cabaret, where she had, I am told, made some untoward remarks, and, because she had been drinking about a half liter of beer with people of even looser reputation than she, this was enough, in the eyes of the village inhabitants, for her to be taken for a drunk, for a woman who deserved not the least pity. This impression was in no way helped by a doctor who had little knowledge of nervous ailments.

When I saw her, she was in the throes of one of her attacks, with swelling of the abdomen, intermittent contractures, delirious reasoning, hallucinations, etc. I quickly ruled out pregnancy and epilepsy. It was by recalling your wise lessons that I was led to practice an ovarian compression.

Rapidly brought back to herself, Geneviève narrated her history to me, and I was happy to have spared this girl the humiliation and the more-than-malicious criticism that had buzzed in my ears. Given the cruelty of some people's ineptitude, it is satisfying for me to recount to you this incident, to prove to you the devotion and interest that you inspire, and to take this opportunity to acknowledge my debt to you.

Geneviève remained with me for one day, and despite my insistence that she return to Paris, she said that she wanted to visit one of her friends in Brussels and to go and say hello "to her sister Louise Lateau" as she called her, not without reason.

After her encounter with Dr. Decaesseckey, Geneviève did go to Brussels, where she had what her case history simply noted were "other adventures." Then she headed to the home of her "sister" in Bois d'Haine on foot, a distance of about forty miles. By the time she arrived, it was too late to see Louise Lateau, so she spent the night outdoors under a tree. The following morning, she approached the house but was forbidden entry. She spoke to the villagers about her desire to visit the stigmatic, but they only mocked her. No explanation is given for why she was not allowed in to see Louise Lateau. However, in an account of his own visit to the Belgian stigmatic, a British reverend named Gerald Molloy wrote of a crowd of people who had flocked to the cottage all with the intention of visiting the living stigmatic and that it was up to the village priest to select among them: "It was a troublesome and unpleasant task for the poor Curé to meet them all: to listen to their several stories, to hear their urgent petitions, and yet to refuse what they sought for so earnestly."[40] Unlike poor Geneviève, Gerald Molloy made the cut. Heartbroken, she walked back to Paris, a distance of 170 miles, sleeping in the woods and fields along the way.

Bourneville noted that he cannot guarantee that Geneviève was telling the truth, but added that, "knowing our patient as we do, there is nothing improbable about it." (*Iconographie photographique de la Salpêtrière*, vol. 1, p. 108.) Two years later, a visitor to the Salpêtrière from Brussels named Dr. Casse confirmed the veracity of the story. He quizzed Geneviève about the specifics of Louise Lateau's home, which he knew well, and according to the Belgian doctor, the details she provided about the house and the surrounding area could only come from someone who had been there. (*Iconographie photographique de la Salpêtrière*, vol. 2, p. 205.)

Unlike Geneviève, Bourneville did not travel to Bois d'Haine in order to meet Louise Lateau. He based his 1875 book, *Science et miracle: Louise Lateau ou la stigmatisée belge* (Science and Miracle: Louise Lateau or the Belgian Stigmatic), on the detailed medical and religious accounts of her case that had already been published. Not surprisingly, Bourneville argued that Lateau's miraculous manifestations were symptoms of hysteria. The insomnia, retention of urine, demonic thrashing, crucifixion poses, fasting, ecstasies, loss of feeling: all classic clinical symptoms of hysteria. In fact, Louise Lateau resembled no one so much as Geneviève. He pointed to a veritable litany of similarities between the two, from the banal—they both enjoyed reading prayer books—to the bizarre—urine retention, fasting without weight loss, and crucifixion poses. Even Lateau's stigmata were not rare at the Salpêtrière. "Are the weekly hemorrhages that Louise Lateau presents all that exceptional?" asked Bourneville. "No, hemorrhages occur frequently in hysterics."[41]

Geneviève is used repeatedly in Bourneville's book on Louise

Lateau as a clinical subject for his anticlericalism. By the third chapter of his book, Bourneville stops calling Lateau the Belgian stigmatic and begins calling her "the Belgian hysteric," as though she were his patient. The demonic visits that had left Lateau with bruises on her face had also been experienced by Geneviève: "Sometimes it happens that she [Geneviève] is projected from one side to the other and just recently she almost cracked her skull on the foot of her bed."[42] In fact, Bourneville argued that each one of Lateau's "symptoms" had been noted "countless times in Geneviève." Even the order in which they unfolded "occurs in an identical way with Geneviève." Lateau's ecstasy, "the prostration and above all the crucifixion which the pious biographers of Louise have taken to have a miraculous meaning (. . .) are absolutely like Geneviève." Both resembled the saints depicted in paintings during their ecstasies: "Such is the case with Geneviève: her hair tumbling down over her shoulders, her head tilted back, her eyes immobile and directed toward the heavens, her neck tightened, her hands joined together, as though in a position of prayer, that is her image, and certainly, in those moments, she is exactly comparable to the patient in Bois-d'Haine." Bourneville's pleasure in demystifying what the Church held most holy is palpable: "Louise Lateau and Geneviève's movements are as dignified and as religious as one could wish."[43]

Bourneville, whose express purpose was to champion the enlightening power of medicine over the dark superstitions of Catholicism, concluded: "If, in the end, in spite of all the warnings, the Belgian believers in magic drive Louise Lateau to her tomb and end up by getting her listed as one of their Saints, they should place her in the category of Martyr. It will not be the pagans who have to reproach themselves for the death of the unfortunate hysteric of Bois d'Haine, but rather those who did not want to break the chain of stigmatics that began with Francis of Assisi and who chose Louise Lateau as the victim of their fantasies and sought to exploit her sufferings as the manifestation of 'Divine Power.'"[44]

Bourneville and Geneviève's interest in Louise Lateau makes perfect sense. Geneviève identified with the Belgian girl who manifested behavior similar to her own but was worshiped for it. The ferociously anticlerical doctor was deeply invested in fighting the Church. His goal was clearly articulated: the triumph of science over superstition. Yet, beneath Bourneville's unabashed promotion of his cause is a remarkably nuanced understanding of illness. By not dismissing Louise Lateau as a fraud, as Virchow and other doctors had, Bourneville was shifting the conceptual framework for understanding disease. Charcot and his disciples argued that hysteria was a neurological disease, a "real" illness, but they also hinted at a psychogenic source for physical symptoms decades before Freud articulated his theory of the unconscious. According to Bourneville, Louise Lateau and Geneviève were afflicted not only with a disease called hysteria, but with a disease called *faith*.

Ten years after Bourneville published his book on Lateau, Joseph Delboeuf published an experiment in which a pharmacist produced blisters on a woman's arm merely by suggesting them. Then, not satisfied with mere blisters, he successfully created "sizable wounds such as those that would be brought about by pounding a nail into the flesh, in short, actual stigmata, comparable to those that have made the famous Louise Lateau so celebrated" by doing nothing more than suggesting them.[45]

Delboeuf went on to recount a similar experiment he witnessed at the Salpêtrière, one in which Charcot induced a burn on an unnamed hysteric's arm through hypnotic suggestion. He told the patient that a spot on her arm was covered with hot wax and that it was burning her: "Do you feel the fire eating at your flesh?" asked Charcot. "Yes. Oh how I suffer!" the patient responded. Charcot then told the hysteric that her skin was getting red and swollen and that by tomorrow, she would have blisters. "It's an awful burn," he declared. Delboeuf, who was color-blind, was unable to see the redness, but he did notice the swelling. A little later, when she was awakened, she felt the pain. "Oh," she cried, "I've been burned again! I must have been burned on the stove. Why aren't they more careful to keep me away from the stove during experiments?" Delboeuf had the opportunity to view the burn the following day. A wound, 2 to 3 centimeters wide, had formed. "This phenomenon," he remarked, "has profound consequences: we have not arrived at all of them. I give them over to the reader to reflect upon."[46]

Delboeuf did not spell out just what those profound consequences were. Open wounds that erupt spontaneously on women, whether induced by God or by Charcot, remain baffling. While the doctors removed Jesus and Satan as the source for these inexplicable behaviors, they did not successfully make the twitching, bleeding, ecstatic women any less mysterious. If stigmata were not a gift from Jesus, but from Charcot, was Christ being brought down to earth, or was Charcot elevating his own stature? The Salpêtrière doctors didn't debunk religion as much as they appropriated its stature. Their explicit purpose was to make the supernatural natural. Yet in the end, the source of hysterical symptoms remained as unknowable as God.

Charcot and the other Salpêtrière physicians borrowed a religious vocabulary and iconography for their own use. Louise Lateau was diagnosed as a hysteric, but Geneviève and the other hysterics were described as ecstatics and demoniacs, and, in Geneviève's particular case, as a "succubus." The word "stigmata," used by nineteenth-century doctors to describe the signs or localized spots of insensitivity on the body that would immediately identify the patient as hysterical, was taken from Christian terminology. The process used to identify true hysterics by locating stigmata repeats, in a shockingly similar way, a ritual used to identify witches in the sixteenth and seventeenth centuries. In both cases, the suspect was pricked with pins. When the needle-wielding practitioner came to a spot that was insensitive to pain, he had discovered the stigmata—proof positive that his subject was a witch or hysteric. As can be seen in the image of Blanche and other photographs that documented the nineteenth-century version of these rituals, once a stigma was located, the physician was able to pass a large needle right through the spot—on the arm or the thigh, for example—without the patient feeling a thing: "We can pierce her as deeply as possible, traverse her thigh or arm from one side to the next, without provoking any manifestation of feeling on her part."[47] In the case of Louise Lateau, doctors *and* priests pricked and poked the poor girl. As was done to Blanche and to Augustine, they pierced her flesh through and through, and like the hysteric, she showed not the slightest reaction.

Charcot's detailed classification of the hysterical attack also took from the language of religious experience. The third stage, that of the "attitudes passionnelles" which translates into something between "passionate poses" and "passionate attitudes," involved a series of shifting positions and gestures, including "the call," "supplication," "menace," "crucifixion," "beatitude," and "ecstasy." Some of the words seem deliberately vague: is the "call" a call to God, a call to prayer, or a call from a lover, as it was for Augustine? If the language was ambiguous at times, many of the photographs that illustrate these poses leave no doubt about the religious significance. Three photographs of a hysteric in the crucifixion pose, taken while she is lying down on her bed, have been placed vertically on the page, emphasizing her resemblance to Christ on the cross more strongly than if they had been mounted horizontally.[48] (See Figure 38.) The photographs of Geneviève in "ecstasy" show her kneeling on her bed, her hands clasped together as though in prayer, her eyes turned to the heavens. Her face is filled with so much light that her features are effaced, as though by a spiritual glow rather than the photographer's lamps. (See Figure 39.)

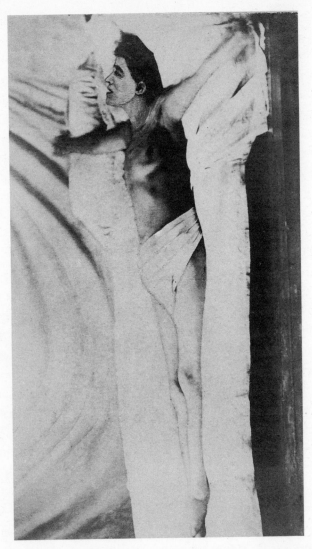

Figure 38. "Attack: Crucifixion." Photograph by Paul Regnard from Désiré-Magloire Bourneville and Paul Regnard, *Iconographie photographique de la Salpêtrière*, Volume 1, Paris: Aux Bureaux du Progrès Médical, Delahaye & Lecrosnier, 1877, Plate 6. Yale University, Harvey Cushing/John Hay Whitney Medical Library.

Figure 39. "Terminal Period: Ecstasy." Photograph of Geneviève Basile Legrand by Paul Regnard from Désiré-Magloire Bourneville and Paul Regnard, *Iconographie photographique de la Salpêtrière*, Volume 1, Paris: Aux Bureaux du Progrès Médical, Delahaye & Lecrosnier, 1877, Plate 24. Yale University, Harvey Cushing/John Hay Whitney Medical Library.

Along with his book on Louise Lateau, Bourneville published the
Bibliothèque Diabolique, (The Diabolical Library), a collection of historical texts on demonic possession and religious miracles. These books
were heavily annotated by the Salpêtrière physicians and included
the autobiography of Jeanne des Anges discussed above, which has
lengthy clinical notes by Gilles de la Tourette and Gabriel Legué,
another doctor at the Salpêtrière, and a preface written by Charcot.
The physical manifestations of the Ursuline mother superior's possession were analyzed one by one, and, like Bourneville's study of
Lateau, were shown to be perfect examples of the hysterical attack.
Jeanne des Anges had hysterical attacks, a hysterical pregnancy, hys-
terical anesthesias, hysterical vomiting, hysterical nosebleeds, hysteri-
cal expectoration, hysterical obsessions, hysterical fury, and hysterical
delusions. In fact, "Sister Jeanne's hysteria is quite complete from the
symptomatic perspective."[49]

Art

Charcot also explored the connection between science and the
religious experience in art. In several works, retrospective medicine
was applied to artistic representations of religious excess, namely *Les
démoniaques dans l'art*, (The Demonically Possessed in Art), *Les difformes et les malades dans l'art* (The Deformed and the Diseased in
Art), and *L'hystérie dans l'art* (Hysteria in Art).[50] Like the Diabolical
Library, these studies interpreted various paintings of demonic possession and religious ecstasy from the fifth through the eighteenth
centuries according to Charcot's symptomology of hysteria. In *Les
démoniaques dans l'art*, Charcot and Richer analyzed a wide variety
of paintings and emptied them of any occult content. They diagnosed postures, expressions, and contortions as various stages of the
hysterical attack, while scenes that depicted exorcisms were studied

to reveal that the priests had strategically placed their fingers on the possessed one's hysterogenic zones, and had thereby arrested the hysterical attack: "the relief brought about by the assistants, can be attributed to the compression of certain regions of the body endowed with special properties, which we have defined in hysterics under the name of hysterogenic zones."[51] A simple "ovarian compression," not divine intervention, insisted the authors, was responsible for the cessation of the attack.

Their "retrospective medicine" was flagrantly reductive. It treated centuries of various art styles, from the Byzantine to the Baroque, as though they were "naturalist" medical documents, clinical evidence for Charcot's symptomology. Charcot and Richer judged the art according to how well it depicted medical symptoms. Sometimes a work did not live up to their medical criteria. A painting by the fifteenth-century artist Bartholomew Zeitblom is criticized for depicting the hands of the demonically possessed subject incorrectly: "The limp appearance of her open hands has no reason to be there."[52] On the other hand, a sketch by Rubens was considered to be such a perfect example of hysteria that it was placed side by side with the photographs in the *Iconographie photographique de la Salpêtrière*. In fact, Charcot even used the word "photograph" to refer to this work of art, one that he believed objectively represented—even more objectively than the real women in his clinic—the contortions of a hysterical attack: "This is the most faithful photograph of the contortions of an attack of hysteria."[53] (See Figure 40.)

Unlike Geneviève and the other hysterics who frustrated the specialists with their lack of cooperation, the painting by Rubens provided a perfect static image of hysteria, a more accurate representation than the flesh-and-blood women were willing to furnish. A painting of a woman from the seventeenth century provided nineteenth-century science with an ideal version of hysteria, and, in effect, usurped the flesh-and-blood model. Representation of illness, inherent to the ill-

Figure 40. *Demoniac*. Sketch by Rubens in Désiré-Magloire Bourneville
and Paul Regnard, *Iconographie photographique de la Salpêtrière*, Volume 1,
Paris: Aux Bureaux du Progrès Médical, Delahaye & Lecrosnier, 1877,
Plate 40. Yale University, Harvey Cushing/John Hay Whitney Medical
Library.

ness itself, created a path for further representation. As in the famous
painting by Brouillet, in which a drawing of a hysteric hangs on the
wall for the painted Blanche to see—an image within an image—
signs represent other signs, and the original "fictive" character of the
affliction is further fictionalized. In fact, as the art historian Didi-
Huberman has noted, the features in Richer's drawings of his patients
resemble the face in Rubens' painting, not the hysterics he was representing.[54] On the other hand, other artists were criticized by Charcot
and Richer for not representing hysteria accurately enough.

While the doctors considered these artistic representations to be accurate medical depictions of hysteria, the hysterics in turn represented these familiar representations. Geneviève imitated not just the behavior she read about in the *Lives of the Saints*, but the postures in religious paintings. She was well known for her crucifixion poses, and Bourneville compared her ecstasy to that found in works of religious art: "Her head is thrown back, her face toward the heavens; her features, marked by extreme softness, express an ideal satisfaction; her neck is swollen, taut; her breathing appears to be suspended; the immobility of her entire body is absolute. Her hands clasped together on the upper part of her chest complete her resemblance to those perfect representations of saints that art has given us." (*Iconographie photographique de la Salpêtrière*, vol. 1, p. 70.) Madeleine Lebouc, a hysteric who spent time at the Salpêtrière at the beginning of the twentieth century under the care of Charcot's student Pierre Janet, was a stigmatic who bled from her hands, feet, and side. When a doctor remarked that the wound on her torso was on her left side, not the right as is traditionally depicted in Christian iconography, she pointed out that the Christ on the large cross in the Salpêtrière church bled from his left side.[55]

These medical texts on art and religion are important less for their avowed aim of providing evidence that the hysterical attack had always existed (and thereby fending off criticism that it only occurred within the walls of the Salpêtrière) than for the way they appropriated the religious phenomena they were fighting and thereby reintroduced Christ and Satan into hysteria. Not only did the doctors interpret historical paintings and texts about occult phenomena according to new scientific laws, they interpreted contemporary phenomena according to outdated religious criteria. For while depictions of demonic possessions and rapturous ecstasies were exposed as nothing more than varying stages of the hysterical attack, hysterical contortions and attitudes at the Salpêtrière were viewed as "demonic" and "ecstatic." The term "demonic variation" was coined to describe a hysterical attack that did not evolve in a regular fashion, that is, one that deviated from Charcot's four stages and was characterized by "the development of illogical positions." Geneviève and the hysterics who manifested such symptoms were referred to as "modern possessed women."

By appropriating the language and the imagery of religion, Charcot's particular brand of positivism ended up straying into the supernatural and the occult. Charcot's entire office—its walls and all of its furnishings—were painted black, creating, as his biographer Georges Guillain noted, "a rather lugubrious effect."[56] On these sinister walls hung engravings of scenes of demonic possession. Not surprisingly, one aspect of Charcot's public image was that of a sorcerer, a "Prince of Darkness" a "satanic savant."[57] The line that separated benevolent and humanitarian science from evil satanic forces was not clearly defined in the nineteenth-century cultural imagination. Science was understood as a wonderful and purifying power but also as a dark and threatening force that was transforming the world into a mechanized and godless place.

Faith Healing

The battle between the Church and Charcot for control of aberrant female behavior ended in a gesture toward syncretism by the doctor, but it was a gesture that did not appease the clerics. While he never fully renounced his search for an organic source of hysteria, Charcot repeatedly hinted at nonphysical explanations for the disease. Unlike many scientists of his day, or of our day, for that matter, Charcot did not accuse mystics and the demonically possessed of chicanery but accepted the reality of their spontaneous bleeding, ecstatic trances, convulsions, and other bizarre religious behaviors. At the end of his life, he added miracle cures to the list. If genuine physical symptoms could be engendered by ideas, then why not their cures? Charcot's disagreement with the Church was not about the reality of these wonders, but rather their source, which he believed was hysteria, not God or Satan. The actual source of hysteria, however, remained as elusive as any otherworldly being.

Toward the end of his career, Charcot began to inch away from his previous insistence that hysteria was a disease caused by an organic lesion, albeit one that had yet to be found, and move toward a more psychological explanation. Suggestibility had always been a symptom of hysteria, but Charcot had always claimed that biology was the underlying cause. By the late 1880s, he began to consider the possibility that ideas, not anatomical pathology, might be a source of hysterical symptoms. In 1892 he published "La Foi qui guerit" (The Faith Cure), an article that tackled the thorny topic of miracle healing and opened up a crack in his previously ironclad biomedical paradigm. This would be his last paper, and while it was met with applause by the anticlerics and derision by the Church, it was a more nuanced argument than the Salpêtrière School's reductive naturalism, and it ended the great positivist's career on a decidedly ambivalent note. Faith healing, Charcot maintained, exists. However, in an assertion designed to damage Christian dogma, he pointed out that Jesus and Catholic saints were not alone in their ability to miraculously cure the sick, since documented cases of faith healing had been known to occur throughout time and throughout religions.

While Charcot never explicitly referred to the famous sanctuary Lourdes in his text, there are several veiled references that would have been immediately apparent to contemporary readers. He began the article by referring to a "famous author" whose recent visit to a religious sanctuary had received much attention in the press. French readers in 1892 would have known that Charcot meant Émile Zola's trip to Lourdes, a visit he made in order to conduct research for the novel he published in 1894 called *Lourdes*. While these references would have been obvious to late-nineteenth-century readers,

Charcot's omission of the name Lourdes is still odd. As he grappled to delineate the boundaries that separate biology from culture, he seemed aware that he was venturing into territory that was not just medical, but epistemological. Hysterics repeatedly challenged scientific objectivity with their flawlessly executed symptoms of diseases they did not possess, their extraordinary ability to do the medically impossible. Lourdes was something of a bugaboo for Charcot, a site for mass hysteria. While Lourdes no doubt had its share of religious charlatans and sham healings, it also produced, according to Charcot, genuine healing, and he was deeply interested in the mechanism behind these cures. However, he needed to proceed in such a way that his interest would not be confused with an endorsement of the supernatural. His refusal to even mention the name Lourdes reflected his deep ambivalence and caution.

The rise of Lourdes as a healing sanctuary coincided with the rise of hysteria at the Salpêtrière School. The glory days of scientific positivism were also the glory days of Lourdes. The first national pilgrimages to the shrine began in 1870, the same year that Charcot established a hysteria service at the hospital and the same year he began lecturing on the disease. By the time Charcot wrote "The Faith Cure," tens of thousands of pilgrims were visiting each year. Lourdes as a site of miracles, however, began several decades earlier. Ten years before Louise Lateau experienced her first apparition, another desperately poor and sick peasant girl had her own visitation.[58] In 1858 the fourteen-year-old Bernadette Soubirous had a series of visions of the Virgin Mary, or the "lady in white," as Bernadette referred to her, close to a grotto not far from home. Her mother and the local authorities accused Bernadette of making up stories, but when people began to flock to the grotto and reported that they had been healed by a small freshwater spring found inside, the Church investigated. Bernadette's claim that the apparition told her "I am the Immaculate Conception" proved extremely useful to the pope because he had recently decreed the Immaculate Conception— Mary was born free from original sin—Roman Catholic dogma. The fact that Bernadette was French was also advantageous, given that the church had enormously weakened in France after the Revolution. In 1876, the same year Geneviève visited the home of Louise Lateau, the pope declared the grotto in Lourdes a holy site, launching mass pilgrimages that continue to this day. As was the case with Louise Lateau, there were doctors who insisted that Bernadette was a hysteric. Auguste Voisin, a physician at the Salpêtrière, argued that she was a "hallucinating child" who had been locked away in a convent in Nevers to hide her condition.[59] Medical attempts to discredit her seemed to have little effect on Bernadette's believers or on the enormous appeal of the sanctuary. Bernadette died in the convent in Nevers in 1878, and her body, exhumed on three separate occasions, was said to have resisted decay. In 1925 she was beatified and her corpse, coated in wax, was placed on display in the convent in Nevers, where it can still be visited. In 1933, Bernadette was canonized as a saint. Louise Lateau, who had heard nothing particularly useful during her visits with the Virgin, has yet to receive the honor.[60]

The Vatican proceeded cautiously with Lourdes. In a concession to the power medicine had gained over the course of the nineteenth century, it established a Medical Bureau at the shrine in 1883 to investigate any purported healing that took place. Lourdes is the only Christian sanctuary in the world that has such an office. The bureau was especially wary of ailments whose origin might be hysterical or "nervous" and might be cured by mere suggestion rather than by divine intervention. In order to register their cures as miraculous, patients were required to bring a signed document from a doctor certifying the organic nature of their suffering and stating that secular treatment had been tried and had failed. Only then would it be recorded in the registers as a gift from Heaven. The bureau recognized thousands of cures as miraculous. Cancer, clubfoot, blindness, pleurisy, diphtheria, elephantiasis, eczema, influenza, gangrene, scoliosis, necrosis, tuber-culosis, rickets, rheumatism, lupus, "general debility," and more than a hundred other diseases were entered into the registers as cured by the holy waters at Lourdes. And in spite of the bureau's reluctance to recognize ailments whose origin was not certified as organic, Section 16 in the "Statistics of Cures" is devoted to "Nervous Diseases." Neuralgia, sciatica, epilepsy, hysteria, Saint Vitus' dance, neurasthenia, hallucination, obsession, catalepsy, and exophthalmic goiter, now called Grave's disease, all met the criteria and were listed among the miraculous cures.[61] The inclusion of nervous disorders in the records, when the bureau was known to discriminate against them, is perhaps not so strange: out of the thousands of cures recorded, only 255 were categorized as "nervous," including several that have since been moved to other diagnostic categories.

The Vatican has been far more selective than the Medical Bureau of Lourdes. Out of the thousands of cures it deemed miraculous, only sixty-seven of them have been recognized by the Vatican, the most recent in 2005 for a case of mitral valve stenosis. Out of the sixty-seven, fifty-four of the healed people are women.[62]

Charcot acknowledged that Lourdes had alleviated the symptoms of patients of his that he had been unable to help, and at times he had even sent them there himself. "I have seen patients return from fashionable sanctuaries," he wrote, "sent there with my consent after I had failed to inspire faith healing myself. I have examined their limbs which were afflicted only a few days before with paralysis or contractures, and I have witnessed the gradual disappearance of localized sensory stigmata that almost always persist for a short while after the healing of the paralysis or contracture."[63] According to Dr. Gustave Boissarie, head of the Medical Bureau between 1892 and 1914, Charcot sent between fifty to sixty patients there every year.[64] It seems Charcot's hysterics were not only traveling between the clinic and the carnival, but they were traveling between the clinic and Lourdes as well.

The *Annales de Notre-Dame de Lourdes* even devoted a special section to "Salpêtrière Patients."[65] Boissarie eagerly accepted the Salpêtrière patients in part because of Charcot's fame. In his medical history of Lourdes, he devoted a section to Charcot's "incurable" hysterics and wrote about a certain Céleste Mériel, who had arrived at the sanctuary paralyzed, deaf, and mute. Three days later, she was completely cured and returned to the Salpêtrière not as a patient but to work as a "ward girl."[66] Boissarie kept in touch with Mériel and visited her twice at the Salpêtrière. While her recovery met the Lourdes Medical Bureau's criteria for miraculous cure, her name is not among the sixty-seven listed by the Vatican.

Charcot believed that miracle cures, whether they were brought about at Lourdes or in the clinic, were the result of "autosuggestion." Every step of the process of going on a pilgrimage to a religious sanctuary such as Lourdes conspired to encourage healing through suggestion, from the money spent to undertake the journey, to the trappings of the site itself with its relics, religious souvenirs, crowds of believers, and cast-off crutches, and most importantly, the patient's expectations of being healed. Charcot had witnessed spontaneous healing, or "miracle cures," at the Salpêtrière on many occasions. Hysterical symptoms were known to move suddenly from one part of the body to another and at times to disappear altogether. His clinic was filled with women who were sporadically mute, blind, and paralyzed. His clinic was also filled with women who, like Céleste Mériel, moved between the wards and the staff rooms, between patient and employee. According to Charcot, intense emotions could trigger these cures, especially when the emotion was what he referred to as "religious excitation." Justine Etchevery, a famous patient who had entered the Salpêtrière with an incurable hysterical contracture that left one side of her body completely paralyzed, was suddenly cured after eight years in the hospital, after being, in Charcot's words "mixed up in a religious ceremony that deeply moved her."[67] In another instance, a paraplegic patient was cured when Charcot commanded her to get up and walk. The woman, who had been paralyzed for many years, left her bed and walked across the room.[68] To Charcot's dismay, these events were interpreted by Catholics as miracles rather than as demystifications of the supernatural, as he had intended. In fact, a popular Catholic weekly covered these and other events at the Salpêtrière and referred to them as Charcot's miracle healings.[69]

Besides the contractures and paralyses that were so common among hysterics, other hysterical symptoms were also subject to faith healing. In his article, Charcot mentioned an American doctor named Fowler who had been very successful at curing "neurotic breast tumors," some of them as large as an egg, through faith healing. Discussing one of his patients, whose breast tumors had disappeared during a lecture at the New York Neurological Society, Dr. Fowler noted, "Like all women of similar temperament, she had a fetich-like-faith [sic] in her regular medical attendant."[70] In the clinic and in a religious sanctuary, faith could heal symptoms of all kinds, from tumors to paralyses, as long as the ailment's origin was hysterical. As Charcot wisely remarked, in all the records of miraculous cures he had consulted, he had never come across one instance of "faith healing that had been able to make an amputated limb grow back."[71]

Although in "The Faith Cure" Charcot accepted the reality of miraculous healing, he did not give any ground to the Church. The cure was produced by the patient's faith, not by God. However, if he didn't yield to religion, he did, though not explicitly, concede some territory to his old nemesis from Nancy, Hippolyte Bernheim. Bernheim had argued all along that suggestion, via hypnosis, could play a therapeutic role, something Charcot and the Salpêtrière School had vociferously denied. However, that is precisely what Charcot articulated as the mechanism behind faith cures in his article. What he did not fully acknowledge, however, was his own power to heal through suggestion. Unlike Lourdes, which was and continues to be devoted to healing, the Salpêtrière under Charcot was a center for observation and documentation and he had never been especially interested in whether a patient got well or not.[72] Yet in "The Faith Cure," Charcot wrote that a doctor must take into account the medical imperative to heal and therefore must not discriminate against cures that work. In other words, if faith healing could work, the doctor must prescribe it.

Like Lourdes, where cast-off crutches lay in plain view of the sick pilgrims who flocked there, the Salpêtrière had its own set of expectations for its ill patients, reinforced with its own visual aids. Those who went to Lourdes expected to be cured. The hysterics at the Salpêtrière were expected to become better hysterics by presenting better symptoms; they were not expected to get better. In fact, when Geneviève wanted to punish Charcot, she withheld her symptoms, just as Augustine had refused to be hypnotized. On October 31, 1878, Geneviève became extremely jealous of another patient, who was providing wonderful symptoms and was therefore receiving more attention than she was. Geneviève caused some kind of unspecified trouble. As Bourneville recounted: "Mr. Charcot strongly reprimanded her. She was deeply mortified. Under the influence of this intense emotion, her rachialgia [a spinal affliction] disappeared completely and *we were unable to provoke an attack*." (*Iconographie photographique de la Salpêtrière*, vol. 2, p. 205, emphasis added.) Bourneville added in a footnote that this was not the first time her anger toward her doctors had resulted in the disappearance of her symptoms. Two months later, Geneviève appears again to have withheld her symptoms out of spite. And once again, the target of her anger was Charcot: "She was in the laboratory," wrote Bourneville, "and as she was being insufferable, Mr. Charcot sent her away. For her this was a terrible insult; she was deeply offended." An hour later, when Bourneville checked on her, he noted that she was still furious and that "full sensitivity had completely returned, her rachialgia no longer exists, and it is impossible to provoke an attack." (*Iconographie photographique de la Salpêtrière*, vol. 2, p. 207.)

Expectations are powerful. Placebos are often just as effective as "real" medicine. Hysterics blurred the boundaries between the real and the unreal, taunting biomedical objectivity. Charcot's star patients were not those who were cured, but those who presented with the best symptoms. Lourdes's star patients were the ones who walked away completely healed. Perhaps if Charcot had lived longer (he died unexpectedly less than a year after "The Faith Cure" was published), he would have continued to pursue the possibility that the same mechanisms that caused hysteria could cure it. He had set out determined to subject hysteria to an "anatomo-pathological" model, and he ended his career acknowledging that something more elusive was at play. "The Faith Cure" ends with a decidedly unscientific quote from Shakespeare's *Hamlet*: "There are more things in heaven and earth / Than are dreamt of in your philosophy."

I do not know what happened to Geneviève. After 1878, the Salpêtrière registers show no further admittances or releases, nor do the hospital records document her death. The very last entry for Geneviève in the *Iconographie* was on Christmas Day, 1878: "The visits [between Geneviève and Camille/Mr. X.] continue: sometimes they have violent quarrels, sometimes they get along well. The frequency of their sexual relations has increased. She experiences more pleasure than she ever has with any other man. As for Camille, he claims that he has never had such intense climaxes as he does with her." (*Iconographie photographique de la Salpêtrière*, vol. 2, p. 208.) And with that, all information about Geneviève stops. Maybe she left the Salpêtrière and went on a pilgrimage to Lourdes. Or maybe, because of her rage toward Charcot, she no longer needed Lourdes.

In fact, after that fateful day, when Charcot expelled her from the laboratory, Bourneville did not record another hysterical symptom for Geneviève. Her affair with Camille/Dr. X. continued, but she did not suffer another seizure, contortion, contracture, paralysis, anesthesia, rachalgia, ischuria: not so much as a twitch is noted. Perhaps Charcot had inadvertently cured one of his star patients.

EPILOGUE: HYSTERIA REVISITED

While writing this book, I kept an ever-growing file of clippings from newspapers and magazines that resonated with the medical lives of Blanche, Augustine, and Geneviève. While hysteria has supposedly disappeared, these stories seem to belie its current status as a defunct disease. After the September 11 attacks on the World Trade Center, for example, Margaret Talbot wrote an article for the *New York Times Magazine* on outbreaks of rashes in otherwise healthy children and adolescents in elementary and middle schools across the United States.[1] During that period of heightened fear, these rashes were not taken lightly. After all, these were the days when U.S. postal workers wore gloves to sort and deliver the mail. Local and federal health officials were called in to investigate; schools were evacuated and cleaned; environmental experts monitored the air, the ducts, and even the books inside the affected schools. The press swarmed and speculated about bioterrorism and chemical warfare. But in the end, after all of the medical and environmental tests available had been exhausted, no germ or chemical was found to explain the mysterious itchy red bumps. The rashes were an instance of mass psychogenic illness, another name for mass hysteria.

Then there was the vexing fact that not *all* children were coming down with the rashes. Girls accounted for the vast majority of cases; at one point, 100 percent of the afflicted students were girls.

It is no longer medically acceptable to explain this demographic by arguing that females are somehow biologically inferior to males, more predisposed to psychosomatic symptoms. Gary Small, a psychiatrist who studies mass psychogenic illness, has been booed at medical conventions when he points out the undeniable truth that there is a preponderance of girls and women in these kinds of outbreaks.[2]

Women are also more likely to suffer from chronic fatigue syndrome, a condition for which 60 to 65 percent of cases are women. Chronic fatigue syndrome is an illness that has fought hard to shed its image as the "yuppy flu," a disorder of entitled whiners. While more accepted than it once was, the condition continues to provoke suspicion in the medical community. Patients, confronted by skeptical doctors, have organized to champion their cause, with support groups that publish lists of doctors sympathetic to the illness, and a campaign to change the name from chronic fatigue, with its benign and malingering implications, to the more dire sounding "myalgic encephalomyelitis." Researchers searched for a biomarker, and when the Epstein-Barr virus was found in many patients with chronic fatigue, the movement felt vindicated. The problem with Epstein-Barr, however, is that almost everybody, the energetically spry as well as the fatigued, has the antibodies in their blood. Research has yet to uncover a definitive cause. Chronic fatigue currently occupies the medical status of syndrome, with syndrome defined as a cluster of idiopathic symptoms, and is one of three conditions listed in the *Merck Manual* under a separate category: "Special Subjects: Syndromes of Uncertain Origin."[3]

The advocates of chronic fatigue syndrome adamantly resist any implication that their symptoms might be hysterical. Unlike the golden age of the Salpêtrière, when hysteria was a disease worthy of the attention of one of the most renowned physicians of the day, few today want to hear that their suffering cannot be traced to an organic or chemical source. The term "hysterical" has become pejorative, and patients experience it as an egregious dismissal of their suffering. Doctors no longer use the word, even though a large number—by some accounts 40 percent—of the complaints patients consult physicians about, remain medically unexplained. The term "functional" is often applied to these instances, a euphemism for "hysterical." The word "hysterical" is so disparaged that when Elaine Showalter included chronic fatigue and Gulf War syndromes as examples of new incarnations of hysteria in her book *Hystories*, she received not only hate mail, but also death threats. Charcot's hysteria received the attention it did precisely because he believed it to be a disease worthy of medical research. Blanche, Augustine, and Geneviève were thought of, and thought of themselves, as patients who were afflicted with a real disease. When banished from the hysteria ward to the ward for insane women, the hysterics suffered not only from the lack of privileges and freedom this punishment entailed, but also from the scathing humiliation of being classified, if only temporarily, as mad, not hysterical.

Our medical model is essentially the same one that Charcot established, but the status of hysterical, or "functional," disorders has been demoted. Symptoms that can be traced to a biological source via blood tests, imaging, biopsies, etc., or to environmental contaminants, are thought of as real; those that elude medical testing are deemed "not real." They might end up classified as psychiatric disorders, or as syndromes. While Charcot never found the lesion for hysteria, and he did articulate the theory of a psychogenic origin, he always insisted that hysteria was a neurological disease. In other words, while Charcot believed that emotional trauma or suggestion could produce a paralysis, for example, he understood that hysterical paralysis to be neurological. It was not spurned as fake, but taken seriously. After decades of Freudianism, in which medically inexplicable symptoms were understood as physical conversions of unconscious conflicts, we have entered an era that in many ways resembles Charcot's. We are now in the process of assigning concrete, rather than unconscious, sources to just about every aspect of human behavior. But, unlike Charcot, we no longer treat symptoms that have no biological origin with dignity. The sufferers of chronic fatigue syndrome are not misguided in their insistence that a virus, or a chemical, or something concrete either in their bodies or in their environment is causing their suffering. Without that, they are cast aside as complainers who take time away from doctors who have patients with "real" conditions to see.

More and more, mental illness is thought of as a biological glitch: a "chemical imbalance" in the brain, for example, or a troublesome gene. Psychiatrists, armed with a checklist of symptoms, classify patients according to one of the ever-shifting diagnoses in the DSM. Once the patient is diagnosed, the doctor prescribes the appropriate medication, designed to counteract the sufferer's lopsided chemistry. Since the 1980s, psychiatrists, whose training once included extensive coursework in psychotherapy, have been educated to classify symptoms and prescribe medication. As Dr. Daniel Carlat wrote in the *New York Times Magazine*, today's psychiatrists are taught to focus on symptoms as though they were objective medical findings, "much the way internists view blood-pressure readings or potassium levels."[4] Charcot's pupils at the Salpêtrière School would be surprisingly at home in contemporary psychiatric residency programs. Instructed in Charcot's anatomoclinical method, they too focused on classifying symptoms and searching for organic causes. Increasingly, people who visit doctors because they are sad, tired, moody, worried, excited, distracted, disorganized (or excessively organized), angry, or shy, are told that they are victims of their biology. Their treatment is less likely to be psychological therapy and more likely to involve taking a pill. And, like Charcot's hysterics, individuals who are told their suffering is biological rather than psychological, a medical problem that can be corrected pharmacologically, experience their suffering as more legitimate.

Never mind that that the theory of a chemical imbalance as the cause of these emotional troubles is on just as shaky ground as Charcot's elusive lesion. The studies that originally posited the thesis that a lack of serotonin caused depression, for example, have now largely been discredited. Nonetheless, kept alive by pharmaceutical companies and the press, the theory continues to be widely accepted. Antidepressants, taken not only for depression but also for anxiety, chronic fatigue syndrome, and a whole range of other disorders, are among the top-selling drugs of all time.[5] Millions of people pop a pill every day, including children, to help improve their moods or their focus. While hysteria was the epidemic of Charcot's time, depression is the epidemic of our era: one out of every ten Americans takes an antidepressant. And, like hysteria, the overwhelming majority of people who are diagnosed with and treated for depression are women: the numbers range from two to three times as high.[6] Women are also far more likely than men to be prescribed some form of psychotropic medication.[7]

Why do women suffer from illnesses such as chronic fatigue, mass psychogenic illness, and depression in far larger numbers than men? This fact is something of an embarrassment to the medical community, because, unlike the nineteenth century, it is no longer acceptable to argue that women are inherently unstable and predisposed to illness. Explanations tend to hinge on the social. While our culture is far more egalitarian than Charcot's was, women continue to be denied full equality, which, not surprisingly, leads to unhappiness. Women are also more likely to seek help than men, having been taught from an early age to be more comfortable with expressing their emotions. Talbot suggests that the psychogenic rashes spread from girl to girl not because they have more delicate constitutions than boys, but because girls are more social and talk about their feelings with each other.[8] Most incidents of mass hysteria have occurred in women who are in cloistered communities: schools, barracks, factories, and convents. At the Salpêtrière, it was not uncommon for the entire ward to break out in hysterical fits when one patient succumbed to an attack.

Biological explanations for female instability are nonetheless alive and well. When the United States Congress recently passed the health-care reform bill, Speaker of the House Nancy Pelosi remarked, "From now on, being a woman will no longer be considered a preexisting condition." While she was referring to one of the many unscrupulous ways that insurance companies deny coverage to their clients, her comment speaks to larger issues. The condition of being a woman is still understood to be one that can at any moment veer out of control and is therefore in need of medical regulation. The female reproductive cycle, from menstruation to pregnancy to menopause, is viewed as vulnerable to pathology, and virtually every aspect has been medicalized. Hormones, chemicals that are necessary for all human beings, male as well as female, are construed as inherently problematic for women. Premenstrual syndrome and the more recent, and more extreme, "premenstrual dysphoric disorder" and postpartum depression are all conditions thought to be triggered by a woman's "raging hormones." Men who are feeling depressed or anxious are not told that their hormones are to blame. Much has been written about how pharmaceutical companies manufacture diseases in order to create new markets for drugs. More attention, however, needs to be drawn to the fact that women are targeted more often for this manipulation than men are.

Men, of course, also suffer from chronic, debilitating, and contagious symptoms that cannot be traced to a specific organic or chemical source. Significantly, the most notable recent example of this contains the alleged source in its name: Gulf War syndrome. The men who experienced the syndrome may very well have been exposed to some toxic chemical, either through the vaccines they received from the U.S. military or from exposure to chemicals on the battlefield in Iraq. However, every test conducted has failed to produce evidence to support this contention. Unlike chronic fatigue syndrome, whose very name implies a kind of feminine languishing, a self-inflicted weariness, Gulf War syndrome connotes masculine battle wounds and points directly to the cause. Soldiers have always suffered both physical and emotional scars that linger long after they leave the battlefields. Civil War soldiers came down with "soldier's heart," World War I veterans returned to civilian life with shell shock, Vietnam War veterans came home with posttraumatic stress disorder, and more recently, we have Gulf War syndrome. These shifts in nomenclature of what are in many ways versions of the same disorder reflect the movement in our psychiatric culture away from the unconscious toward the biological. Soldier's heart, shell shock, and posttraumatic stress disorder leave no doubt about the psychic nature of the suffering. Gulf War syndrome has no such acknowledgment.

Among the many illnesses that remain medically unexplained, there are still cases of what looks like Charcot's hysteria, in which patients suffer from paralysis, numbness, muscle contractions, impaired hearing and vision, seizures, and aphonia that cannot be explained by a known neurological disease, or by feigning. These symptoms are no longer called hysteria, but "psychogenic pain disorder," "undifferentiated somatoform disorder," or "conversion disorder," and like hysteria, they afflict women far more often than men, with some studies showing the rate to be ten times as high.[9] However, unlike the epidemic that occurred in the nineteenth century, these new disorders are quite rare. More commonly, contemporary incarnations of hysteria take the form of complaints that can be verified only through what the patient claims to experience: fatigue, mood changes, sadness, and pain. The medical historian Edward Shorter argues that as neurology became more sophisticated in its understanding of organic motor phenomena, hysteria lost its ability to simulate neurological symptoms convincingly. Pain and fatigue, which are ultimately subjective, represent one more stage in hysteria's flight from the pursuit of an organic medical diagnosis.[10]

Charcot, of course, never located the sought-after organic source for hysteria. The medical model on which he based his theory—one of an inside lesion that produced outside symptoms—functioned brilliantly with a range of neurological diseases that he defined. Multiple sclerosis, ALS, and Parkinson's disease, for example, all yielded to this approach. Yet, no matter how beautifully Blanche, Augustine, and Geneviève manifested their symptoms, a biological origin for hysteria was not found. Charcot did not have the opportunity to perform autopsies on these women, but he did analyze the corpses of countless other hysterics: in each case, their brains and spinal cords revealed no flaws to account for their seizures and other motor disorders. Charcot did not, however, abandon his research as failed. Hysteria remained for him a disease that warranted serious study, and he considered hysterical symptoms to be no less real than those produced by Parkinson's disease, for example.

Charcot's critics chose to discredit his entire hysteria enterprise. Hysteria as defined by the great neurologist, they concluded, was not only a medical mistake but also a national embarrassment. Soon after his death, Charcot lost his standing as the preeminent doctor of the day and was cast aside as either a practitioner of shoddy science, or worse, a charlatan. Along with Charcot's dethroning, the hysterics of the Salpêtrière lost their status as medical celebrities and were once again disparaged as malingerers, frauds, madwomen, or, to the contrary, they were reclassified as "genuine" patients with "real" neurological disorders that had been misdiagnosed as hysterical.

We are still stuck in a mind-body medical paradigm that classifies illness as "real" or "not real." We live in a culture that privileges illness with so-called "real" origins. Yet, when confronted with hysterical disorders, this paradigm is woefully inadequate. Charcot recognized this, and years before Janet and Freud developed the idea of unconscious motivations, he acknowledged the power of traumatic memory in the production of physical symptoms. In one of his Tuesday lectures, he spoke of "psychic paralysis" and, rather than dismissing it as madness, accorded it medical legitimacy: "I want to speak about these strange paralyses that have been designated as psychic paralyses, paralyses arising from an idea, and paralyses resulting from imagination. I did not say, and make note of this, 'imaginary paralyses,' because, in short, these motor weaknesses that develop as a result of a psychic disturbance are just as real as those arising from an organic lesion."[11] For Charcot, "hysterical" did not mean "unreal." We stand to learn an important lesson from him.

The recent development of more sophisticated brain-imaging techniques has challenged our understanding of illness, and, I believe, these are developments that would not have surprised Charcot. We now know, for example, that not only do placebos work to diminish symptoms such as pain and depression, but that their impact can be viewed in the brain with PET scans. Imaging reveals that the "endogenous endorphin" system in the brains of subjects who receive a placebo is activated in an identical manner as it is in those who took an antidepressant.[12] In another study cited by Carlat, patients with obsessive-compulsive disorder were divided into two groups. Half were treated with Prozac, the other half received psychotherapy. All of the patients improved equally. The test subjects' brains were scanned both before and after their treatments, and the imaging revealed that the patients treated with psychotherapy had identical shifts in their brain circuits as those treated with Prozac.[13]

Clearly, it is time to rethink the mind-body paradigm. Soldiers who return from the battlefield with debilitating but idiopathic symptoms are afflicted with something "real," just as Blanche, Augustine, and Geneviève suffered from an actual disease. The schoolgirls' rashes were not imaginary because the cause was psychogenic. Charcot understood this when he insisted that psychic paralysis was just as real as paralysis caused by an organic lesion. The source might not be the same, but the symptom itself is no less genuine because of it.

Blanche, Augustine, and Geneviève suffered countless indignities as patients in Charcot's hysteria ward. Charcot was an imperious authority figure who treated the hysterics at the Salpêtrière as medical specimens. Yet, unlike "hysterical" patients today, their suffering was never dismissed as not real. Furthermore, these women actively participated in the hysteria project. They provided the material—authentic neurological symptoms that arose from "psychic disturbances"—for Charcot's research, research that was abruptly suspended and unfortunately discredited when he died in 1893. While flawed, Charcot's work on hysteria should not be dismissed as a medical mistake. By acknowledging hysterical authenticity, he did nothing less than articulate a new paradigm for illness, one that superseded the tenacious mind-body model that we are still muddling about in. Perhaps it is time to pick up where Charcot left off. It is time to exonerate hysteria.

ACKNOWLEDGMENTS

When I began my research for this book, I had no formal training as a medical historian, and therefore relied heavily on the archivists, librarians, and staff of the various institutions I consulted. I am especially indebted to the wonderful staff at the Archives de l'Assistance Publique in Paris, in particular to the archivists Sophie Riché and Maïlys Mouginot. Their expertise, generosity, and enthusiasm for the material made my research there not only fruitful but also extremely enjoyable. Their help often went beyond professional duty. I am grateful for their advice on how to compose the written request required in order to access material protected by French privacy laws, for the overseas assistance offered when I was obligated to return to New York before an elusive document had been secured, for assistance deciphering the elaborate curlicues of nineteenth-century French handwriting, for the fascinating tour I was given of the vast cellar where many of the hospital records are held, and for many other instances of kindness and generosity.

Véronique Leroux-Hugon, the head librarian of the Bibliothèque Charcot at the Salpêtrière Hospital in Paris, helped me navigate Charcot's magnificent collection, donated to the Faculty of Medicine by his son Jean-Baptiste Charcot. The gift included not only Charcot's manuscripts and private library of more than 20,000 volumes but also his ornately carved bookshelves, desk chair, and other pieces of furniture and artifacts from his home on the Boulevard Saint-Germain—objects that have transformed the reading room into something of a shrine to the neurologist. As Jean-Baptiste Charcot stated in his speech at the inauguration of the library, the soul of his father seems to haunt the place.

I am also indebted to the librarians and staff at the Archives Départementales de Vienne in Poitiers, the Archives de Paris, the Bibliothèque Nationale, the Bibliothèque de l'Arsenale, the New York Academy of Medicine Library, and the Henry Cushing/John Hay Whitney Medical Library at Yale University.

Thank you to Nan Graham, who encouraged me to turn what I believed would be an obscure academic project into a trade book proposal. Jill Goldman and Vicki Kennedy gave me the opportunity to discuss an early incarnation of this book during an informal lecture they arranged in Los Angeles. The questions and comments from that evening helped me sharpen my arguments and articulate my ideas. Toby Gelfand; Andrew Scull; Dianne Hunter; Meighan Gale; Jean-Claude Monad; and Jean-Louis Dardé, director of the Centre Hospitalier Gerard Marchant in Toulouse, all kindly provided advice and information. Françoise Schein, Paul Windey, Olivia Custer, Michel Feher, and Amanda Bay were helpful in a variety of ways, including, but certainly not limited to, providing me with shelter on my many research trips to Paris. I owe immense gratitude to Ellen Flamm and Richard Peterson, who have repeatedly and generously offered a haven for writing in Nantucket. Andrew Ohanesian gave me calm technical support during several alarming computer crises, and for that I am extremely grateful.

I would like to thank the following individuals for their generous assistance with the images in this book: Arlene Shaner at the Historical Collections in the Malloch Rare Book Room at the New York Academy of Medicine; Toby Appel and Florence Gillich at the Henry Cushing/John Hay Whitney Medical Library at Yale University; Cécile Swiatek at the Bibliothèque Interuniversitaire Scientifique Jussieu, Université Pierre et Marie Curie; and Sonja Poncet at the Musée d'Histoire de la Médecine in Paris.

This book is better because of my editor at Norton, Jill Bialosky. She suggested that I write the epilogue and understood, even when I did not, that this addition would be an improvement. I am also extremely grateful to my editor at Bloomsbury, Alexandra Pringle, for her enthusiastic and patient support. I must also thank my agents, Sarah Chalfant and Jin Auh. Sarah was convinced that my idea should become a book and offered encouragement during the long process of it becoming so. Jin's enthusiasm for my work, and gentle prodding, helped me finish. Thank you as well to Alison Liss at Norton, Alexa von Hirschberg at Bloomsbury, and Jordyn Ostroff at the Wylie Agency for many instances of assistance on practical matters, and to Fred Wiemer, who improved the manuscript with his skillful copyediting and must be credited with helping me avoid embarrassing mistakes.

Finally, I must acknowledge my family. I am enormously indebted to my sister, Siri Hustvedt, who read this entire book in manuscript form—some sections more than once—and offered her insight and advice on matters both big and small. I have been the lucky beneficiary of her kindness and wisdom since the day I was born. I would like to thank my parents for providing a home filled with books where ideas and intellectual curiosity mattered. I owe my desire to immerse myself in the stories of people too often denied a voice to my late father, who died while I was writing this book, and I owe my desire to pursue French studies to my mother. I also want to thank my husband, Jon Kessler, who has supported me in far too many ways to list, and my daughter, Juliette Hustvedt Kessler, who cheerfully traipsed through French cemeteries on my behalf and, somewhat less cheerfully, endured many hushed afternoons in French libraries. This book is dedicated to her.

NOTES

Part One: Charcot

1. While many authors are credited throughout this book, I am especially indebted to the extensive research and philosophical perspectives of Christopher G. Goetz, Michel Bonduelle, Toby Gelfand, Mark S. Micale, Ian Hacking, Elaine Showalter, Georges Didi-Huberman and Edward Shorter.

2. Charcot did not write his memoirs and there is not much known about his childhood. Georges Guillain, a successor to Charcot's chair at the Salpêtrière, published a biography of Charcot in 1955. While he had never met Charcot, he knew some of his students and his son, Jean-Baptiste Charcot. Georges Guillain, *J.-M. Charcot: His Life, His Work*, trans. Pearce Bailey (New York: Harper & Brothers, 1959). A more recent biography, *Charcot: Constructing Neurology*, by the neurologists Christopher Goetz and Michel Bonduelle and the historian Toby Gelfand, provides a more comprehensive and engaging study of the man and his career. Christopher G. Goetz, Michel Bonduelle, Toby Gelfand, *Charcot, Constructing Neurology*, New York: Oxford University Press, 1995. Henri F. Ellenberger, in his classic book *The Discovery of the Unconscious*, mentions that Charcot had a speech impediment as a child, which, if true, might help to explain his shyness. The remark is unattributed, and I have not seen it mentioned anywhere else. Henri F. Ellenberger, *The Discovery of the Unconscious* (New York: Basic Books, 1970), p. 89.

3. Henri Meige, cited in Guillain, *J.-M. Charcot*, p. 23.

4. Charcot's student, Henri Meige, wrote an essay on how Charcot's artistic skills—his ability to discern physical anomalies—served him well as a clinician. See Henri Meige, *Charcot artiste* (Paris: Masson & Cie., 1925).

5. Many of Charcot's drawings have been preserved by the Charcot Library at the Salpêtrière Hospital in Paris.

6.   Sigmund Freud, "Charcot," in *The Freud Reader*, ed. Peter Gay (New York: Norton, 1989), p. 49.

7.   Michel Foucault and the anti-psychiatry historians have pointed out that new forms of restraint—the straitjacket for example, or the psychological oppression of Pinel's moral treatment—replaced iron chains in this restructuring of the asylum. See, for example, Michel Foucault, *Madness and Civilization: A History of Insanity in the Age of Reason* (New York: Vintage, 1973.) For much of my information on the history of the Salpêtrière, I am indebted to Mark S. Micale's "The Salpêtrière in the Age of Charcot: An Institutional Perspective on Medical History in the Late Nineteenth Century," *Journal of Contemporary History* 20, no. 4 (1985): 703–731.

8.   The generation of doctors at the Salpêtrière between Pinel and Charcot include Esquirol, Moreau de la Tour, Trélat, Legrand du Saulle, Baillarger, Lasègue, Falret, and Delasiauve.

9.   Freud quotes Charcot in French: *"Faudrait y retourner et y rester"* (I must return there and stay there). Sigmund Freud, "Charcot," in *The Freud Reader*, p. 49.

10.   Freud, "Charcot," in *The Freud Reader*, p. 49.

11.   Jean-Martin Charcot, "Hospice de la Salpêtrière: Réouverture des conférences cliniques de M. Charcot," in *Progrès Médical* 8 (November 27, 1880): 970. Cited by Edward Shorter in *From Paralysis to Fatique: A History of Psychosomatic Illness in the Modern Era* (New York: Free Press, 1992), p. 169.

12.   Jean-Martin Charcot, *Oeuvres complètes*, vol. 4 (Paris: Aux Bureaux du Progrès Médical, Lecrosnier & Babé, 1880), p. 14, cited in Goetz, Bonduelle, and Gelfand, *Charcot*, p. 67.

13.   Freud includes the quote in French: *"La théorie c'est bon, mais ça n'empêche pas d'exister."* Sigmund Freud, "Charcot," in *The Freud Reader*, p. 50.

14.   For a detailed account of Charcot's major contributions to neurology, see Goetz, Bonduelle, and Gelfand, *Charcot*, chap. 4, pp. 97–134.

15.   Jean-Martin Charcot, *Oeuvres complètes*, vol. 4, pp. 4–5, cited in Goetz, Bonduelle, and Gelfand, *Charcot*, p. 122.

16.   Charcot's success within the medical academic world of Paris was by no means instantaneous. He worked for twenty years after his internship ended before he became a member of the Paris medical faculty. For a thorough description of his struggle to gain a professorship, see Goetz, Bonduelle, and Gelfand, *Charcot*, chap. 2, pp. 31–61.

17.   Mark S. Micale "The Salpêtrière in the Age of Charcot: An Institutional Perspective on Medical History in the Late Nineteenth Century," *Journal of Contemporary History* 20, no. 4 (1985): 713–714.

18. Sigmund Freud, letter to Martha Bernays, cited in Goetz, Bonduelle, and Gelfand, *Charcot*, p. 280.

19. Sigmund Freud, *Letters of Sigmund Freud*, trans. Tania Stern and James Stern (New York: Basic Books, 1960), pp. 196–197.

20. Léon Daudet, cited in Guillain, *J.-M. Charcot*, p. 33.

21. The anecdote involving the grand duke, Gambetta, and Charcot's monkey is based on personal communication from Charcot's granddaughter to the authors of *Charcot: Constructing Neurology*. They also include a photograph from the family archives of Charcot holding his pet monkey protectively inside his coat. See Goetz, Bonduelle, and Gelfand, *Charcot*, pp. 271–272.

22. Jean-Martin Charcot, "De l'influénce des lesions traumatiques sur le développement des phénomènes d'hystérie locale," *Progrès Médical*, May 4, 1878, cited in Goetz, Bonduelle, and Gelfand, *Charcot*, p. 173.

23. Briquet, quoted in *La leçon de Charcot: Voyage dans une toile* (Paris: Catalogue de l'exposition organisée au Musée de l'Assistance Publique, 1986), p. 69. All translations are my own, unless otherwise noted.

24. "Hystérie" in *Dictionnaire encyclopédique des sciences médicales*, 1885, ed. A. Dechambre (Paris: Masson, 1889), p. 240.

25. Guillain, *J.-M. Charcot*, p. 136.

26. Désiré-Magloire Bourneville and Paul Regnard, *Iconographie photographique de la Salpêtrière*, vol. 3 (Paris: Delahaye & Cie., 1879), pp. 3–4.

27. Freud, "Charcot," in *The Freud Reader*, pp. 49–50.

28. Jean-Martin Charcot, "Leçon d'ouverture," *Progrès Médical* 10 (May 6, 1882): 336.

29. Charcot, *Oeuvres complètes*, vol. 3, p. 15.

30. See Micale, "The Salpêtrière in the Age of Charcot," p. 721.

31. Charles Féré, "J.-M. Charcot et son oeuvre," *Revue des Deux Mondes*, vol. 122 (March 1, 1894): 415.

32. Pierre Janet cited in Guillain, *J.-M. Charcot*, p. 55.

33. Freud, "Charcot," in *The Freud Reader*, p. 52.

34. Jean-Martin Charcot, *Leçons du mardi à la Salpêtrière* (Paris: Delahaye & Lecrosnier, 1887–1888), p. 204.

35. See, for example, Henri Legrand du Saulle, *Les hystériques: État physique et état mental: Actes insolites, délictueux, et criminels* (Paris: Baillière, 1891), p. 46.

36. Jules Claretie and Guy de Maupassant are cited by Mark S. Micale, "Discourses of Hysteria in Fin-de-Siècle France," in *The Mind of Modernism*, ed. Mark S. Micale (Stanford, Calif.: Stanford University Press, 2004), p. 4.

37. See Jan Goldstein, "The Hysteria Diagnosis and the Politics of Anticlerical-

ism in Late Nineteenth-Century France," *Journal of Modern History* 54, no. 2 (June, 1982): 209–239. Some historians have explained this dramatic rise on late-nineteenth-century social demands on women. In this view, hysteria is the natural result of women internalizing the cult of female invalidism by producing a disease without organic cause that also served as a covert movement of resistance and rebellion. See, for example, Barbara Ehrenreich and Deirdre English, *For Her Own Good: 150 Years of the Experts' Advice to Women* (Garden City, N.Y.: Doubleday, 1978), pp. 133–140. See also Carroll Smith-Rosenberg, "The Hysterical Woman: Sex Roles and Role Conflict in 19th-Century America," *Social Research* 39 (Winter 1972): 652–678. While she does not deny the validity of this understanding, Goldstein interprets the proliferation of hysteria diagnoses as an attempt to further the interests of the fledgling discipline of psychiatry, and exposes its political connections to anticlericalism. Goldstein, pp. 212–213.

38. Debove, cited in Guillain, *J.-M. Charcot*, p. 74.

39. Henri F. Ellenberger, *The Discovery of the Unconscious* (New York: Basic Books, 1970), p. 94.

40. The Babinski sign is a pathological plantar reflex that is indicative of corticospinal tract damage. If the big toe moves up when the sole of the foot is stimulated, it indicates a problem in the central nervous system. Babinski published his attack on Charcot's description of hysteria in 1909. See Joseph Babinski, "Démembrement de l'hystérie traditionelle: Pithiatisme," *Semaine Médicale* 29 (1909): 3–8.

41. Pierre Marie, Edouard Brissaud, A. J. Souques, Albert Pitres, Alexis Joffroy, and Henri Meige were among the prominent members of the Salpêtrière School who rejected Charcot's theory of hysteria, a theory that they had eagerly promoted while he was alive. See Mark S. Micale, "On the 'Disappearance of Hysteria'" *Isis* 84 (1993): 496–526.

42. Georges Guinon, cited in Christopher C. Goetz, "The Salpêtrière in the Wake of Charcot's Death," *Archives of Neurology* 45 (1988): 444.

43. Sigmund Freud and Josef Breuer published *Studies on Hysteria* in 1895.

44. Jacques Lacan, cited in Micale, "On the 'Disappearance of Hysteria,'" p. 498.

Part Two: Blanche

1. Jean-Martin Charcot, "Isolation in the Treatment of Hysteria" in *Clinical Lectures on Diseases of the Nervous System*, vol. 3, trans. Thomas Savill (London:

New Sydenham Society, 1889), p. 368. Also see Ilza Veith, *Hysteria: The History of a Disease* (Chicago: The University of Chicago Press, 1965), p. 235.

2. Charles Richet, "Les Démoniaques d'aujourd'hui," *Revue des Deux Mondes* 37 (January 15, 1880): 344.

3. Tardieu quoted by Georges Gilles de la Tourette in *Traité clinique et thérapeutique de l'hystérie d'après l'enseignement de la Salpêtrière* (Paris: E. Plon, Nourrit & Cie., 1891), p. 490.

4. Gilles de la Tourette, *Traité clinique et thérapeutique*, pp. 489–490.

5. Georges Didi-Huberman refers to the Salpêtrière as a kind of "factory that manufactured hysteria." See Georges Didi-Huberman, *Invention de l'hystérie* (Paris: Macula, 1982). This book has been translated into English by Alisa Hartz: *Invention of Hysteria* (Cambridge, Mass.: MIT Press, 2003).

6. Désiré-Magloire Bourneville and Paul Regnard, *Iconographie photographique de la Salpêtrière*, vol. 3 (Paris: Bureau du Progrès Médical, Delahaye & Lecrosnier, 1879–1880), p. 6. Case histories of the hysterics were published in three volumes in the *Iconographie photographique de la Salpêtrière* (Photographic Iconography of the Salpêtrière). Because I quote from this source so extensively, I will from this point forward use in-text citations.

7. See Pierre Buiral and Guy Thuillier, *La Vie quotidienne des domestiques en France au XIXe siècle* (Paris: Hachette, 1978), pp. 176–177.

8. Love stories between interns and hysterics can be found in nineteenth-century newspapers, novels, and plays. See, for example, Jules Claretie, *Les amours d'un interne* (Paris: Dentu, 1881); Leon Daudet, *Les morticoles* (Paris: Charpentier, 1894); and André de Lordes, "Une leçon à la Salpêtrière," in *Théâtre d'épouvante* (Paris: Charpentier & Fasquelle, 1909).

9. See Micale, "The Salpêtrière in the Age of Charcot," p. 709.

10. Jules Claretie, *Les amours d'un interne* (Paris: E. Dentu, 1883), p. 140.

11. Joseph Delboeuf, "Une visite à la Salpêtrière," *Revue de Belgique* 54 (1886): 122–123.

12. Jean-Martin Charcot, *L'hystérie*, selection and introduction by Étienne Trillat (Paris: L'Harmattan, 1998), pp. 50–51. Martha Noel Evans points out that ovarian compression was used recently in France. Étienne Trillat, she notes, "recounts that he utilized it with one of his hysterical patients at the Maison Blanche Hospital. She was having convulsions and, not knowing what else to do in the circumstance, he tried Charcot's technique. It worked; the convulsions ceased." See Martha Noel Evans, *Fits and Starts: A Genealogy of Hysteria in Modern France*, Ithaca, N.Y., and London: Cornell University Press, 1991), p. 29.

13. Paul Richer, *Études cliniques sur la grande hystérie ou hystéro-épilepsie* (Paris: Delahaye & Lecrosnier, 1885), p. 230.

14. Richer, *Études cliniques*, p. 147.

15. Delboeuf, "Une visite à la Salpêtrière," p. 258.

16. Dermagraphism, or dermographism, as it is sometimes spelled, is still a medical term, although not one deliberately induced by physicians. In the AMA Family Medical Guide, it is listed as an allergic reaction, and is defined as follows: "Dermographism is a type of hives usually caused by scratching the skin. It consists of long, raised, narrow wheals that exactly follow the lines where scratching or rubbing has occurred. It is relatively easy to confirm the cause of this type of allergic reaction, even though sometimes the wheals do not appear on the skin until several hours after the irritation that caused the marks to form." See *The American Medical Association Family Medical Guide*, 3rd ed. (New York: Random House, 1994), p. 244.

17. Ernst Mesnet, "Autographisme et stigmates," *Revue de l'hypnotisme et de la psychologie physiologique* (1889–1890): 322–323.

18. G. Dujardin-Beaumetz, "Note sur des troubles vaso-moteurs de la peau observés sur un hystérique" *L'union médicale* 144, no. 9 (December 1879): 920. This article is reprinted in *Parachute* 35 (June–August 1984): 13–14.

19. See "Démence précoce catatonique dermographisme" in *Nouvelle iconographie photographique de la Salpêtrière*, vol. 17, plate 27.

20. There are no photographs of dermagraphism included in the *Iconographie photographique de la Salpêtrière*, but images of the phenomenon were published in the later *Nouvelle iconographie de la Salpêtrière*, as well as in other medical journals. This image is from an article by the doctor Ernst Mesnet published in a journal devoted to hypnotism. See Ernst Mesnet, "Autographisme et stigmates," *Revue de l'hypnotisme experimentale et thérapeutique* (1889–1890): 321–335, figure 2.

21. T. Barthélémy, *Étude sur le dermagraphisme ou dermoneurose toxivasomotrice* (Paris: Société d'Éditions Scientifiques, 1893), pp. 83–84. See also, Georges Didi-Huberman, "L'incarnation figurale de la sentence (note sur la peau 'autographique')," *Scalène*, no. 2 (October 1984): 143–169.

22. Contemporary—and criminal—versions of dermagraphism have occurred recently. In 2000, for example, a New York obstetrician used his scalpel to carve his initials on a woman's abdomen. For his defense, he argued that the caesarian section he performed was a work of art worthy of signing. A surgeon in Kentucky was sued in 2003 for branding the initials of his alma mater, the University of Kentucky, onto a woman's uterus during a hysterectomy. Apparently, he too was proud of his work, because he videotaped the engrav-

ing and sent it to the patient. See Edward Wong, "Doctor Carved His Initials into Patient, Lawsuit Says," *New York Times*, January 22, 2000; and Anabelle Garay, Associated Press, "Surgeon: UK Brand Was a Guide," *Kentucky Post*, January 29, 2003.

23. According to Ilza Veith, "this 'group practice' was attended by elaborate ceremony, which strongly appealed to the jaded tastes of his well-born patients in the French capital. The healing rituals took place in a heavily curtained room. . . . Mesmer made his appearance with the accompaniment of soft mournful music. He slowly passed among his patients, draped in a lavender-colored silken robe or suit, fixing his eyes upon each in turn and touching them with his hands or with a long magnetized iron wand, which he always carried with him." See Ilza Veith, *Hysteria: The History of a Disease* (Chicago: University of Chicago, 1965), pp. 222–223.

24. Gilles de la Tourette, *Traité clinique et thérapeutique*, p. 459.

25. F. W. H. Myers, "Dr. Jules Janet on Hysteria and Double Personality," in *Proceedings of the Society for Psychical Research* 6 (1889): 216, emphasis added.

26. Jean-Martin Charcot, *Oeuvres complètes*, vol. 9 (Paris: Aux Bureaux du Progrès Médical, Lecrosnier & Babé, 1890), p. 310.

27. Charcot, *Oeuvres complètes*, vol. 9, p. 310.

28. W. J. Morton, *New York Medical Record*, 1881, cited by Esther M. Thorton in *Hypnotism, Hysteria, and Epilepsy: An Historical Synthesis* (London: William Heinemann, 1976), p. 147.

29. Paul Regnard, "L'anesthésie hystérique," in *Les maladies épidémiques de l'esprit. Sorcellerie, magnétisme, morphinisme, délire des grandeurs* (Paris: E. Plon, Nourrit et Cie, 1887), p. 77.

30. Claretie, *Les amours d'un interne*, p. 178.

31. W. J. Morton, *New York Medical Record*, 1881, cited by Esther M. Thorton in *Hypnotism, Hysteria and Epilepsy*, p. 147.

32. Georges Gilles de la Tourette and Paul Richer, "Hypnotisme" in *Dictionnaire encyclopédique des sciences médicales* (Paris: G. Masson, 1889), p. 94.

33. Gilles de la Tourette and Richer, "Hypnotisme" in *Dictionnaire encyclopédique des sciences médicales*, p. 95.

34. Gilles de la Tourette and Richer, "Hypnotisme" in *Dictionnaire encyclopédique des sciences médicales*, p. 95.

35. See Guillaume-Benjamin Amand Duchenne de Boulogne, *Mécanisme de la physionomie humaine; ou, Analyse éléctro-physiologique de l'expression des passions, applicable à la pratique des arts plastiques* (Paris: Renouard, 1862). English translation by R. Andrew Cuthbertson. *The Mechanism of Human Facial Expression* (New York: Cambridge University Press, 1990). Charcot describes

this procedure in his "Leçons sur la métallothérapie et l'hypnotisme," in *Oeuvres complètes*, vol. 9. See also, Gilles de la Tourette and Richer, who reprint this lesson verbatim in their article "Hypnotisme" in *Dictionnaire encyclopédique des sciences médicales*, pp. 96–97.

36. Charcot, "Leçons sur la métallothérapie et l'hypnotisme," p. 442. Gilles de la Tourette and Richer reprint this passage as well, underscoring their complete devotion to the theories of their master. Gilles de la Tourette and Richer, "Hypnotisme" in *Dictionnaire encyclopédique des sciences médicales*, pp. 96–97.

37. Charcot, *Oeuvres complètes*, vol. 3, p. 337.

38. Gilles de la Tourette and Richer, "Hypnotisme," in *Dictionnaire encyclopédique des sciences médicales*, pp. 88–89, emphasis added.

39. Dr. Foveau de Courmelles, *L'hypnotisme* (Paris: Hachette, 1890), p. 91.

40. Gilles de la Tourette and Richer, "Hypnotisme," p. 79.

41. W. J. Morton, *New York Medical Record*, 18, (1880). Quoted by E. M. Thornton, *Hypnotism, Hysteria, and Epilepsy: An Historical Synthesis* (London: William Heinemann Medical Books Limited, 1976), pp. 145–46.

42. Delboeuf, "Une visite à la Salpêtrière," p. 258.

43. Alfred Binet, *Alterations of Personality*, trans. Helen Green Baldwin (New York: D. Appleton & Co., 1896), p. 249.

44. Binet, *Alterations of Personality*, p. 251.

45. Binet, *Alterations of Personality*, p. 252.

46. Georges Gilles de la Tourette, *L'hypnotisme et les états analogues au point de vue médico-légal* (Paris: Plon, 1889), pp. 131–132, emphasis added.

47. Delboeuf, "Une visite à la Salpêtrière," p. 139.

48. Delboeuf, "Une visite à la Salpêtrière," p. 263.

49. Gilles de la Tourette, *L'hypnotisme et les états analogues*, pp. 127–128.

50. See Alfred Binet and Charles Féré, *Animal Magnetism* (London: Kegan Paul, Trench & Company, 1887), pp. 239–240. This anecdote is also recounted in *The Psychology of Reasoning Based on Experimental Researches in Hypnotism* by Alfred Binet, trans. Adam Gowans Whyte (Chicago: Open Court Publishing Co., 1899), p. 59.

51. Gilles de la Tourette, *L'hypnotisme et les états analogues*, pp. 139–140; also recounted in Pierre Janet, *Psychological Healing: A Historical and Clinical Study*, trans. Eden Paul and Cedar Paul (London: G. Allen & Unwin, 1925), p. 184.

52. Delboeuf, "Une visite à la Salpêtrière," p. 269.

53. Delboeuf, "Une visite à la Salpêtrière," p. 269.

54. Gilles de la Tourette, *L'hypnotisme et les états analogues*, p. 155.

55. Gilles de la Tourette, *L'hypnotisme et les états analogues*, p. 155.

56. Jules Claretie, "Chroniques Parisiennes," *Le Temps*, July 11, 1884.

57. Hugues le Roux, "La vie à Paris," *Le Temps*, April 30, 1887.

58. Gilles de la Tourette, *L'hypnotisme et les états analogues*, pp. 131–135.

59. Gilles de la Tourette, *L'hypnotisme et les états analogues*, pp. 376–380.

60. For an in-depth analysis of the Gabrielle Bompard trial, see Ruth Harris, "Murder Under Hypnosis in the Case of Gabrielle Bompard: Psychiatry in the Courtroom in Belle Époque Paris," in *The Anatomy of Madness*, vol. 2, *Institutions and Society*, ed. William F. Bynum, Roy Porter, and Michael Shepherd (London: Routledge, 1985).

61. Léon Daudet and André de Lorde, for example, provide detailed accounts of these demonstrations in their work. See Leon Daudet, *Les Morticoles* (Paris: Charpentier, 1894); André de Lordes, "Une leçon à la Salpêtrière," in *Théâtre d'épouvante* (Paris: Charpentier & Fasquelle), 1909.

62. Among the regulars to attend Charcot's lectures were Rudolphe Virchow, the founder of cellular pathology; Dom Pedro d'Alcántra, the emperor of Brazil; the grand dukes of Russia; the Cardinal Lavigerie; the Prefect of Police Lépine; as well as the politicians Alfred Naquet, Antonin Proust, and Waldeck-Rousseau; the artists Jérome, Rochegrosse, Dalou, and Falguière; and Garnier, the architect of the eponymous opera house in Paris. See Guillain, *J.-M. Charcot*, pp. 32–33.

63. Axel Munthe, *The Story of San Michele* (London: John Murray, 1962) (first published 1929), pp. 200, 204.

64. Alphonse Daudet, "A la Salpêtrière," in *Trois souvenirs: Au Fort-Montrouge, À la Salpêtrière, Une leçon* (Paris: Librairie Borel, 1896), pp. 51–55.

65. Charles Richet, "Les démoniaques d'aujourd'hui" in *Revue des Deux Mondes* 37 (January 15, 1880): p. 343.

66. Jules Claretie, *Le Temps*, July 11, 1884 and Delboeuf, "Une visite à la Salpêtrière," p. 124.

67. *A History of Private Life: From the Fires of Revolution to the Great War*, ed. Michelle Perrot, trans. Arthur Goldhammer (Cambridge, Mass.: Belknap Press of Harvard University Press, 1990), p. 630.

68. In the interview, she is asked, "Have you not already been to the Salpêtrière, and was it not in order to do research?" "Yes," she responded, "I went to the Salpêtrière when I was preparing for Adrienne Lecouvreur." The journalist adds that "she uttered these last words nervously, with real emotion. Our interviewee is obviously troubled by this topic and has not succeeded very well in disguising her trouble." See, "Une heure chez Sarah Bernhardt," *La Chronique Médicale* 4, no. 19 (October 1, 1897): p. 614.

69. I am grateful to Toby Gelfand, who directed me to Jane Avril's memoirs. They

were published in *Paris-Midi* in serial form in August 1933 and have been preserved at the Bibliothèque de l'Arsenale in Paris. All citations are from these unnumbered pages. Michel Bonduelle and Toby Gelfand wrote about Jane Avril's experience at the Salpêtrière in "Hysteria Behind the Scenes: Jane Avril at the Salpêtrière," *Journal of the History of the Neurosciences* 8, no. 1 (1999), pp. 35–42.

70. Saint Guy's dance, also called Sydenham's chorea, is a nervous system disorder that causes involuntary movements and muscle contractions.

71. Jane Avril writes that she stayed at the Salpêtrière for two years. Bonduelle and Gelfand's research determined that she was hospitalized for eighteen months: December 28, 1882, until July 11, 1882. Bonduelle and Gelfand, "Hysteria Behind the Scenes," p. 37, fn. 3.

72. Marguerite Bottard worked as a nurse at the Salpêtrière for sixty years. She received many honors for her years of service, including the title of Chevalier of the Legion of Honor, rarely awarded to women at that time. Bottard began working at the Salpêtrière in 1841, and for the rest of her life she rarely left the hospital grounds. She worked as Charcot's head nurse for his entire tenure at the hospital. "For thirty years, maybe more," he said during one of the ceremonies held to honor her dedication to the hospital, "you and I have walked everyday side by side in this great asylum of human misery that is called the Salpêtrière Hospital. . . ." She retired in 1901 when she was eighty, but she continued to live at the Salpêtrière. In 1898, when she received the Chevalier award, she said, "I am very happy, and have only one regret, that Mr. Charcot is no longer here." Charcot and Bottard are cited in the catalogue for an exhibition at the Museum of the Assistance Publique in Paris, *La leçon de Charcot: Voyage dans une toile*, 1986, pp. 67–68.

73. Avril incorrectly wrote "Baumville" instead of Bourneville.

74. Jean-Martin Charcot, *Leçons sur les maladies du système nerveux faites à la Salpêtrière*, vol. 3 (Paris: A. Delahaye et Lecrosnier, 1883), p. 17.

75. Gelfand and Bonduelle note that Avril wrote her memoirs forty years after Charcot's death, and the debates about hysteria in his ward were long past. "It is difficult to imagine that these memoirs sought to fuel a polemic or argue a point." They also point out that "one must keep in mind that Jane Avril wrote fifty years after the fact. It seems likely that her retrospective narrative was colored to some extent by the debates and, eventually, the skepticism about the authenticity of Charcot's hysterical patients that had arisen during that long interval." Bonduelle and Gelfand, "Hysteria Behind the Scenes," p. 39.

76. In this last novel, the teenage daughter of a wealthy bourgeois couple falsely accuses her father's friend of raping her.

77. Among Charcot's prescriptions for Alphonse Daudet was a painful "suspension" treatment in which the patient was literally suspended from the ceiling in a contraption of straps and pulleys. Daudet describes it as follows: "Hung up in the air by Seyre's apparatus. In the evening, at Keller's, the suspension of the poor ataxia patients is sinister. There is the Russian, hung up seated in a chair. Two brothers; and the little man of dark complexion, kicking his legs about. I remain as long as four minutes in the air, and for two am held up only by my jaws. Pain in my teeth. Then, when I am let down and unfastened, there is a horrible uncomfortable sensation in the region of my back and neck, as if my whole spine were melting. I am obliged to crouch down and straighten up gradually, as—it seems to me—the spine, which has been stretched, goes back into place. No perceptible curative effect." Alphonse Daudet, *Suffering*, trans. Milton Garver (New Haven, Conn.: Yale University Press, 1934), pp. 22–23.

78. For a fascinating account of the lives of Jean-Baptiste Charcot, Léon Daudet, and Jeanne Hugo, see Kate Cambor, *Gilded Youth: Three Lives in France's Belle Epoque* (New York: Farrar, Straus & Giroux, 2009).

79. Daudet, *Les morticoles*, p. 144.

80. Daudet, *Les morticoles*, p. 144.

81. Daudet, *Les morticoles*, p. 40.

82. Daudet, *Les morticoles*, p. 145.

83. Daudet, *Les morticoles*, pp. 145–146.

84. Daudet, *Les morticoles*, p. 146.

85. Cited in Christopher G. Goetz, Michel Bonduelle, and Toby Gelfand, *Charcot: Constructing Neurology* (New York and Oxford: Oxford University Press, 1995), p. 291.

86. Dr. Georges Barral wrote the preface to *Le faiseur d'hommes* by Yveling RamBaud and Dubut de Laforest. See Yveling RamBaud and Dubut de Laforest, *Le faiseur d'hommes* (Paris: C. Marpan & E. Flammarion, 1884). Dr. J. Gérard, however, moved in the opposite direction when he asked Dumas fils to write the preface to his medical thesis on "fécondation artificielle," artificial insemination, a practice that was the subject of heated debates during this period.

87. See Jacques Léonard, *La vie quotidienne du médicin de province au XIXe siècle* (Paris: Hachette, 1977), p. 336, n. 2.

88. For a provocative study of Richet's article, see Janet Beizer's "Femme-texte et roman hystérique," in *Revue Internationale de Psychopathologie*, no. 4 (1991): 351–359.

89. Richet, "Les démoniaques d'aujourd'hui," p. 346.

90. Richet, "Les démoniaques d'aujourd'hui," p. 348.

91. Alfred Binet, *Alterations of Personality*, trans. Helen Green Baldwin (New York: D. Appleton & Co., 1896), p. 249.

92. I managed to find a copy of *La fille maudite* (written in 1876 by an Émile Richebourg). However, in the book I found, there are no characters named Fabrice or Madame de la Rivière. It is, however, a tawdry novel full of mistaken identities, stolen babies, and murders, and the doctor's error is understandable, perhaps not unlike a doctor today mistaking a patient's fascination with Jacqueline Suzanne as being with Jackie Collins. The point being made is that Blanche was a reader of sensational romance novels, and reading fiction of any kind was considered a health threat for women.

93. Joseph Delboeuf, *Magnétiseurs et médecins* (Paris: Félix Alcan, 1890), pp. 56–57.

94. There are many paintings dating from the late nineteenth century that depict beautiful nude or seminude female patients, unconscious and displayed before the penetrating gazes of fully clothed male physicians. See, for example, *Avant l'opération* (1887) by Henri Gerveux, in the Musée de l'Assistance Publique, Paris; *Le laboratoire d'électrothérapie à la Salpêtrière* (1887) by Vierge in *Le Monde Illustré*, August 14, 1887; *J. C. G. Lucae and His Assistants Dissecting a Female Cadaver*, 1864, by J. H. Hasselhorst; and *Premiers traitements du cancer par rayons X* by G. Chicotot, in the Musée des Hôpitaux in Paris.

95. J. L. Signoret has provided the names for each person in the painting, many of whom were readily recognizable by the late-nineteenth-century audience but are unfamiliar to the contemporary viewer. See "Variété historique: Une leçon clinique à la Salpêtrière" (1887), *Revue Neurologique* 12 (1983): 687–701.

96. Hugues Le Roux, "La vie à Paris," *Le Temps*, April 30, 1887.

97. The Salon of 1887 included 5,318 paintings by 2,521 artists.

98. In comparison, a recent Whitney Biennial in New York City had an attendance of 185,710. Even the very successful 2003 Matisse and Picasso show at the Museum of Modern Art, open for a month longer than the 1887 Salon, had fewer visitors.

99. Gilles de la Tourette, *L'hypnotisme et les états analogues*, p. 441.

100. *Les Soirées Litteraires*, no 114, 1 (January 1, 1882): 72.

101. Gilles de la Tourette, *L'hypnotisme et les états analogues*, p. 443.

102. Charcot, *Oeuvres complètes*, vol. 9, p. 479.

103. For example, Carl Hansen of Copenhagen, who had been thoroughly denounced as a charlatan, was now an honored guest of medical and scientific societies. For further discussion on the interconnection of carnival spectacles

and medical spectacles, see Jacqueline Carroy, *Hypnose, suggestion et psychologie: L'invention de sujets* (Paris: Presses Universitaires de France, 1991).

104. Gilles de la Tourette, *L'hypnotisme et les états analogues*, p. 384.

105. In Gilles de la Tourette's book *L'hypnotisme et les états analogues au point de vue médico-légal*, only one male subject is mentioned—the exception that proves the rule.

106. Gilles de la Tourette, *L'hypnotisme et les états analogues*, p. 442.

107. Paul-Louis Ladame, "La nécessité d'interdire les séances publiques d'hypnotisme," in Edgar Bérillon, *Premier congrès international de l'hypnotisme* (Paris, 1889), p. 30. Cited by Bertrand Méheust, *Somnambulisme et médiumnité*, vol. 1, *Le défi du magnétisme animal*, (Le Plessis-Robinson: Institut Synthélabo, 1998), p. 526.

108. Gilles de la Tourette, *L'hypnotisme et les états analogues*, p. 449.

109. Alfred d'Hont (Donato), "*Revue générale des sciences physio-psychologiques, présentant le tableau permanent des découvertes et des progrès accomplis pendant l'année 1886*," (A General Overview of the Physiopsychological Sciences Including a Table of the Discoveries and Progress Accomplished in 1886) (Paris, 1886).

110. Joseph Delboeuf, "Réponse de M. Delboeuf au rapport de M. Ladame," in *Premier congrès international de l'hypnotisme*, p. 49, cited by Bertrand Méheust, Somnambulisme et médiumnité, vol. 1, *Le défi du magnétisme animal*, pp. 527–528.

111. Pierre Janet, *Psychological Healing*, p. 192.

112. See Donato's preface to Edouard Cavailhon's *La fascination magnetique*, p. xxxii, cited by Ruth Harris, "Murder and Hypnosis in the Case of Gabrielle Bompard: Psychiatry in the Courtroom in Belle Époque Paris" in *The Anatomy of Madness: Institutions and Society*, vol. 2, p. 227.

113. "Hypnotism in Paris," *The Lancet*, July 29, 1884, pp. 163–165.

114. Gilles de la Tourette, *L'hypnotisme et les états analogues*, p. 414.

115. Gilles de la Tourette, *L'hypnotisme et les états analogues*, p. 416.

116. Gilles de la Tourette, *L'hypnotisme et les états analogues*, p. 164.

117. Gilles de la Tourette, *L'hypnotisme et les états analogues*, p. 441. A 200-franc downpayment was not an insignificant sum for a hysteric from the Salpêtrière. It was more than the 180-franc annual income of a ward girl.

118. Joseph Delboeuf, *Magnétiseurs et médecins* (Paris: Félix Alcan, 1890), p. 123.

119. Gilles de la Tourette, *L'hypnotisme et les états analogues*, p. 389.

120. Gilles de la Tourette, *L'hypnotisme et les états analogues*, p. 95.

121. Delboeuf, "Une visite à la Salpêtrière," p. 258.

122. Gilles de la Tourette, *L'hypnotisme et les états analogues*, pp. 124–125.

123. César Lombroso, *Hypnotisme et spiritisme* (Paris: Flammarion, 1920), p. 13.

124. Alfred Binet and Charles Féré, "L'hypnotisme chez les hystériques: Le transfert psychique," *Revue Philosophique* 19 (1885): 3.

125. Joseph Delboeuf, "Une visite à la Salpêtrière," p. 143.

126. Binet and Féré, "L'hypnotisme chez les hystériques," p. 7.

127. Delboeuf, "Une visite à la Salpêtrière," p. 140.

128. Binet and Féré, "L'hypnotisme chez les hystériques," p. 10.

129. Binet and Féré, "L'hypnotisme chez les hystériques," p. 10.

130. Binet and Féré, "L'hypnotisme chez les hystériques," p. 9.

131. Richer and Gilles de la Tourette, "Hypnotisme," in *Dictionnaire encyclopédique des sciences médicales*, p. 96.

132. Delboeuf, "Une visite à la Salpêtrière," p. 126.

133. Alfred Binet and Charles Féré, "La polarisation psychique," *Revue Philosophique*, vol. 19 (1885): 383.

134. Binet and Féré, "La polarisation psychique," pp. 384–385.

135. Joseph Babinski, "Recherches servant à établir que certaines manifestations de l'hystérie peuvent être transmises d'un sujet à l'autre sous l'influence de l'aimant," *Le Progrès Médical*, vol. 4 (1886): 1010–1011.

136. Jules Janet, "L'hystérie et l'hypnotisme d'après la théorie de la double personnalité," *Revue Scientifique*, May 19, 1888, pp. 616–623. At the time, "double personality" was used to describe a condition that would later be called "multiple personality," although, as the name implies, the afflicted suffered from two, not multiple, personalities.

137. Félida X in Etienne Eugène Azam, *Hypnotisme, double conscience et alteration de la personnalité*, preface de Jean-Martin Charcot (Paris: J. B. Baillière, 1887).

138. Janet, "L'hystérie et l'hypnotisme," pp. 616–617.

139. Janet, "L'hystérie et l'hypnotisme," p. 618.

140. Janet, "L'hystérie et l'hypnotisme," p. 619.

141. Janet, "L'hystérie et l'hypnotisme," p. 619.

142. Janet, "L'hystérie et l'hypnotisme," pp. 619–620.

143. Janet, "L'hystérie et l'hypnotisme," p. 621.

144. Janet, "L'hystérie et l'hypnotisme," pp. 621–622.

145. Janet, "L'hystérie et l'hypnotisme," p. 623.

146. Jules Janet, "Un cas de l'hystérie grave," *Revue de l'hypnotisme et de la psychologie physiologique* (1889): 342.

147. F. W. H. Myers. "Dr. Jules Janet on Hysteria and Double Personality," *Proceedings of the Society for Psychical Research*, vol. 6 (1889): 216–221.

148. Georges Guinon and Sophie Woltke, "De l'influence des excitations sensitives et sensorielles dans les phases cataleptique et somnambulique du grand hypnotisme," *Nouvelle iconographie de la Salpêtrière,* vol. 4 (1891): 77–88.

149. Gilbert Ballet, "La Suggestion hypnotique au point de vue médico-legal," in *Gazette Hebdomadaire de Médecine et de Chirurgie* 28, 2nd series (1891).

150. Léon Daudet, "Devant la douleur," in *Souvenirs et polémiques* (Paris: Robert Laffont, 1992), p. 161.

151. For an account of Rose Kamper's attack on Gilles de la Tourette, see Georges Guinon, "Attentat contre le docteur Gilles de la Tourette," *Le Progrès Médical,* vol. 18 (1893): 446. For biographical information about Gilles de la Tourette, see Paul Legendre, "Gilles de la Tourette, 1857–1904," *Bulletins et Mémoires de la Société Médicale des Hôpitaux de Paris* 21, no. 3 (1905): 1298–1311.

152. The Swedish writer Per Olav Enquist has written a novel based very loosely on Blanche Wittmann's life. In Enquist's book, the fictional Blanche is educated, has an English father who is an apothecary, goes to work as the laboratory assistant of Marie Curie, and murders Charcot. See Per Olav Enquist, *The Book about Blanche and Marie,* trans. Tiina Nunnally (New York: The Overlook Press, 2006).

153. A. Baudouin, "Quelques souvenirs de la Salpêtrière," *Paris Médical* 21 (1925): 517–520.

154. Edward Shorter, in his fascinating book on the history of psychosomatic illness, maps the rise of a pandemic of paralyses during the nineteenth century, He also introduces the term "symptom pools," or a "culture's collective memory of how to behave when ill." See Edward Shorter, *From Paralysis to Fatigue: A History of Psychosomatic Illness in the Modern Era* (New York: Free Press, 1992).

155. Ian Hacking appropriates the term "ecological niche" to analyze how fugue and other transient mental illnesses arise at a given moment under specific environmental conditions. See Ian Hacking, *Mad Travelers* (Charlottesville: University of Virginia Press, 1998).

156. Baudoin, "Quelques souvenirs," p. 520.

Part Three: Augustine

1. Roland Barthes, *Camera Lucida: Reflections on Photography,* trans. Richard Howard (New York: Hill and Wang, 1981), pp. 5–6.

2. Philippe L. Gross, and S. I. Shapiro, *Tao of Photography: Seeing Beyond Seeing* (Berkeley: Ten Speed Press, 2001), p. 62.

3. On wet-nursing, see George D. Sussman, *Selling Mothers' Milk: The Wet-Nursing Business in France, 1715–1914* (Urbana: University of Illinois Press, 1982).

4. The City of Paris had a municipal Bureau of Wet Nurses that paid a minimum wage directly to the wet nurse and collected the salary from the infant's father. This establishment significantly cut down on the infant mortality rate, since unpaid wet nurses had in the past neglected their charges. The Bureau of Wet Nurses of the City of Paris existed until 1876, when the supervision of wet nurses became a national, rather than a municipal, responsibility.

5. Alexandre Mayer, *De la création d'une société protectrice de l'enfance pour l'amélioration de l'espèce humaine par l'éducation du premier âge* (Paris: Librairie de Sciences Sociales, 1865), pp. 4–5, cited by George D. Sussman, *Selling Mothers' Milk*, p. 122.

6. Bourneville does not tell us when this happened, but Richer notes that she was ten years old. Paul Richer, *Études cliniques sur l'hystéro-épilepsie ou grande hystérie* (Paris: Delahaye et Lecrosnier, 1881), p. 95.

7. Niépce was born with the more common name Joseph. He later changed it to Nicéphore. Historians of photography agree that the French inventor Joseph Nicéphore Niépce, from Chalon-sur-Saône, France, produced the first permanent photograph, but they disagree somewhat about the year of that discovery. Depending on the source, it is dated from as early as 1822 to as late as 1827. Nicéphore Niépce and his brother Claude also invented an internal combustion engine that they successfully used to power a boat against the current of the Saône River. See Beaumont Newhall, *The History of Photography* (New York: Museum of Modern Art, 1982), p. 13. For more on the date of the first recorded photograph, see Denis Bernard and André Gunthert: *L'instant rêvé, Albert Londe* (Nîmes: Chambon, 1993). The Maison Nicéphore Niépce, a museum devoted to the inventor, places the development of the first permanent photograph between 1824 and 1826.

8. The early days of photography were marked by feuds and jealousy. Archer did not patent his technique, but published the recipe in a chemistry journal in 1851, and it quickly made both the daguerrotype and the calotype obsolete. Talbot stubbornly insisted that his patent covered Archer's technique and any photographer using it owed him a licensing fee. While Talbot lost his many legal battles, Archer earned nothing from his invention that revolutionized photography, and he died penniless in 1857. Daguerre did not patent his invention either, but the French government provided him with a pension and offered a detailed description of the method to the world as a gift.

9. Like Archer, Disdéri died penniless. While he had patented his invention, it was nevertheless imitated all over the world, and he ended up impoverished, blind, and deaf in a public hospital in Nice.

10. For more on the early application of photography to psychiatry, see Sander Gilman, *Seeing the Insane* (New York: John Wiley, 1982), chap. 14.

11. Cited by André Parent, "Duchenne de Boulogne: A Pioneer in Neurology and Medical Photography," *Canadian Journal of Neurological Sciences* 32, no. 3 (August 2005): 371. I am indebted to André Parent for much of my information on Duchenne.

12. Guillaume-Benjamin-Amand Duchenne de Boulogne, *Album de photographies pathologiques complémentaire du livre intitulé de l'électrisation localisée* (Paris: Baillière, 1862), p. 5. Cited by Parent, "Duchenne de Boulogne," p. 373.

13. Guillaume-Benjamin-Amand Duchenne de Boulogne, *Mécanisme de la physionomie humaine, ou, Analyse éléctro-physiologique de l'expression des passions, applicable à la pratique des arts plastiques* (Paris: J. Renouard, 1862). English translation by R. Andrew Cuthbertson. *The Mechanism of Human Facial Expression* (New York: Cambridge University Press, 1990), p. 7.

14. Some of Duchenne's photographs were used by Charles Darwin in *The Expression of the Emotions in Man and Animals*.

15. Jean-Martin Charcot, cited in Christopher G. Goetz, Michel Bonduelle, and Toby Gelfand, *Charcot: Constructing Neurology* (New York: Oxford University Press, 1995), p. 67.

16. On the relationship between Charcot and Duchenne, see Irwin M. Siegel, "Charcot and Duchenne: Of Mentors, Pupils, and Colleagues," *Perspectives in Biology and Medicine* 43, no. 4 (Summer 2000): 541–547.

17. In a literary exploration of neurological pathology, Émile Zola's Rougon-Macquart series trace the degeneration of an original nervous taint through six generations of two families.

18. This article, written in collaboration with Valentin Magnan, addressed homosexuality, or "sexual inversion," thought to be a degenerative condition, and as the authors of *Charcot: Constructing Neurology* point out, Magnan seems to have been the main writer. These authors also point to the fact that Charcot was not a member of any of the societies devoted to mental medicine. See Goetz, Bonduelle, and Gelfand, *Charcot: Constructing Neurology*, pp. 208–209.

19. See Bernard Brais, "Désiré-Magloire Bourneville and French Anticlericalism During the Third Republic," in *Doctors, Politics, and Society*, ed. Dorothy Porter and Roy Porter (Amsterdam: Rodopi, 1993), p. 112. Brais's article provides a fascinating account of Bourneville's work as a medical reformer.

20. Brais, "Désiré-Magloire Bourneville and French Anticlericalism During the Third Republic," pp. 115–116.

21. Désiré-Magloire Bourneville, "Avant-Propos," *Revue photographique des hôpitaux de Paris* (Paris: A. Delahaye, 1869), p. 2.

22. Charcot, *Oeuvres complètes*, vol. 9, p. 269.

23. Charcot, *Oeuvres complètes*, vol. 1, p. 387. This lecture, "De la chorée rythmique hystérique," was delivered in November of 1877 and first published in *Progrès Médical*, February 9, 1878.

24. Paul Richer, *Études cliniques sur l'hystéro-épilepsie ou grande hystérie* (Paris: Delahaye et Lecrosnier, 1881), pp. 11–12.

25. Richer, *Études cliniques sur l'hystéro-épilepsie*, pp. 11–12.

26. Richer, *Études cliniques sur l'hystéro-épilepsie*, p. 12.

27. Richer, *Études cliniques sur l'hystéro-épilepsie*, p. 28.

28. Richer, *Études cliniques sur l'hystéro-épilepsie*, p. 41.

29. Richer, *Études cliniques sur l'hystéro-épilepsie*, p. 73.

30. Jean-Martin Charcot, *L'hystérie*, ed. Étienne Trillat (Paris: L'Harmattan, 1998), p. 121.

31. See Denis Bernard and André Gunthert, *L'instant rêvé: Albert Londe* (Nîmes: J. Chambon, 1993).

32. Charcot, *Oeuvres complètes*, vol. 9, p. 296.

33. Jean-Martin Charcot, *L'hystérie*, ed. Étienne Trillat (Paris: L'Harmattan, 1998), p. 119.

34. Richer, *Études cliniques sur l'hystéro-épilepsie*, p. 97.

35. Josef Breuer and Sigmund Freud, *Studies on Hysteria*, ed. James Strachey (New York: Basic Books, 1957), p. 7.

36. "Review of *Iconographie photographique de la Salpêtrière*," *British Medical Journal* 1, no. 962 (June 7, 1879): 856.

37. Richer, *Études Cliniques sur l'hystéro-épilepsie*, p. 379.

38. Richer, *Études cliniques sur l'hystéro-épilepsie*, p. 378.

39. Stage hypnotists still perform this stunt. YouTube carries several clips featuring subjects that are hypnotized to be as "stiff as a board." In one video, a man is placed between two chairs and a young woman from the audience is called up to the stage to stand on his torso.

40. The term "placebo" had been used in medicine since the late eighteenth century to refer to a remedy that was given to please rather than to heal.

41. Anne Harrington is the editor of a fascinating book that addresses the placebo effect. See *The Placebo Effect: An Interdisciplinary Exploration* (Cambridge, Mass.: Harvard University Press, 1997).

42. Augustine's decision to disguise herself as a boy in order to escape from the Salpêtrière may have been inspired by Madame de la Motte, the infamous protagonist in an intrigue that became known as the Affair of the

Diamond Necklace. Madame de la Motte caused a scandal in the court of Louis XVI—one of many sordid affairs that helped to bring about the French Revolution—when she concocted an elaborate ruse to steal an extremely valuable diamond necklace. She feigned a close friendship between herself and Marie Antoinette (a deceit that added to the many malicious rumors that circulated at the end of the eighteenth century regarding the queen's licentiousness) and claimed that the queen wanted to purchase the jewels. Once Madame de la Motte had her hands on the necklace, she and her accomplices dismantled the jewelry and sold the diamonds. When the crime was discovered, Madame de la Motte was publically whipped and tortured (she was branded with the letter "V" for *voleuse*—French for thief), and imprisoned for life in the Salpêtrière, from which she, like Augustine, escaped, dressed as a man.

43. For much of my information on Bourneville, I am indebted to Bernard Brais's article "Désiré-Magloire Bourneville and French Anticlericalism During the Third Republic."

44. Breton began his medical studies in 1913 and worked as an orderly during World War I. He was fascinated by psychiatric disorders and later studied with Joseph Babinski at the neurological center at La Pitié Hospital in Paris. In the 1962 redaction of *Nadja*, Breton wrote that he had "great memories" of his time with Babinski: "I am proud of the liking he showed me—even if this in no way induced him to predict for myself a grand future in medicine!—and in my own way, I think I have taken advantage of his teaching, to which the end of the first *Manifeste du surréalisme* paid tribute." Breton, quoted in Jacques Philippon and Jacques Poirer, *Joseph Babinski* (New York: Oxford University Press, 2009), p. 45.

45. Louis Aragon and André Breton, "La cinquantière de l'hystérie," *La Revolution Surréaliste*, no. 11 (March 1928).

46. See Elaine Showalter, *The Female Malady: Women, Madness, and English Culture, 1830–1980* (New York: Pantheon, 1985); Georges Didi-Huberman, *Invention of Hysteria*, trans. Alisa Hartz (Cambridge, Mass.: MIT Press, 2003); and Lisa Appignanesi, *Mad, Bad, and Sad: Women and the Mind Doctors* (New York: Norton, 2008).

47. An Internet search reveals many more examples of creative work inspired by Augustine. She figures in a poem by Helen Kitson, and in 2001 the artist Dick Jewell, playing with the Surrealist celebration of the fiftieth anniversary of hysteria, celebrated the 123rd anniversary of hysteria by recreating some of Regnard's photographs of Augustine entitled *Hysteric Glamour*. "Augustine: Anti-Hommage" (2004) by Veronika Bökelmann; "Hysteria! A Subversive

Practice" (2004) by Miki Malör; and "X: The Rise and Fall of an Asylum Star" (2002) by Jill Dowse are just some of the performance pieces inspired by Augustine that I found.

Part Four: Geneviève

1. *Soeur Jeanne des Anges, supérieure du couvent des Ursulines de Loudun: Auto-biographie,* 1644, Préface, J.-M. Charcot, texte annoté et publié par Gabriel Legué et Georges Gilles de la Tourette, (Grenoble: Editions Jérome Millon, 1990), p. 26.
2. *Soeur Jeanne des Anges, supérieure du couvent des Ursulines de Loudun,* p. 30.
3. According to the historian Rachel Fuchs, there were several reasons for the fact that adoptions in nineteenth-century France were rare. Foremost were ideas of blood rights and inheritance. Couples with children did not want to dilute their biological children's inheritance, and childless couples did not want a nonblood relative to inherit their estate. Moreover, since most abandoned children were illegitimate, they were considered to be socially unacceptable. Nineteenth-century scientific notions of biologically inherited traits included moral behavior, therefore a child of an unwed mother was thought to be predisposed to be morally deviant. See Rachel Fuchs, *Abandoned Children: Foundlings and Child Welfare in Nineteenth-Century France* (Albany: State University of New York Press, 1984), p. 30.
4. The cobbler was named Pierre Peimeur; the tailor was Charles Vincent.
5. The councilor general decided that beginning on January 1, 1834, all foundlings abandoned in the Department of Vienne would no longer be accepted in any hospice other than the one in Poitiers.
6. One minister, who was sent from Paris to inspect the institution, recommended reducing the dimensions of the "*tour*" because children as old as eight or even ten were being left inside. He proposed making the space a size that would accommodate newborns only. This recommendation was indeed implemented and the size reduced so that only the tiniest bodies would fit inside. In order to further reduce the numbers, he recommended that the "*tour*" only be opened for limited hours each night and that a policeman be posted nearby to record the name of the mother and "encourage" her to take her child back.
7. The current Parisian telephone directory lists 13 people with the last name Basile, and 699 with the name Legrand.
8. In 1843 the schedule of payment to foster parents in the Department of Vienne was as follows: From birth to one year, 84 francs per year or 7.8 francs

per month; from one to three years, 78 francs per year or 6.50 per month; from three to six years, 66 francs per year or 5.50 per month; from six to nine years, 54 francs per year or 4.50 per month; and from nine to twelve years, 30 francs per year or 2.50 per month.

9. In Beaumont, I did find a male Camille who had died on May 27, 1857, but he was only two years old at the time of death.

10. See Yannick Ripa, *Women and Madness: The Incarceration of Women in Nineteenth-Century France,* trans. Catherine du Peloux Menagé (Minneapolis: University of Minnesota Press, 1990), p. 123.

11. See Ripa, *Women and Madness,* p. 84.

12. See Hillel Shwartz, "The Three-Body Problem and the End of the World," in *Fragments of a History of the Human Body,* pt. 2, pp. 407–465.

13. For more on the anticlerical movement and medicine, see Jan Goldstein, *Console and Classify: The French Psychiatric Profession in the Nineteenth Century* (Cambridge: Cambridge University Press, 1987), pp. 361–377.

14. For an English translation of Huysmans' hagiography, see J.-K. Huysmans, "Selections from Saint Lydwine of Shiedam," trans. Agnes Hastings, in *The Decadent Reader: Fiction, Fantasy, and Perversion from Fin-de-Siècle France,* ed. Asti Hustvedt (New York: Zone Books, 1998), pp. 1007–1062.

15. See, for example, Joan Jacob Brumberg, *Fasting Girls: The History of Anorexia Nervosa* (Ontario: New American Library, 1988); Walter Vandereycken and Ron van Deth, *From Fasting Saints to Anorexic Girls: The History of Self-Starvaton* (London: The Athlone Press, 1994); Rudolph Bell, *Holy Anorexia* (Chicago: University of Chicago Press, 1985); Caroline Walker Bynum, *Holy Feast and Holy Fast: The Religious Significance of Food to Medieval Women* (The New Historicism: Studies in Cultural Poetics, 1) (Berkeley: University of California Press, 1987).

16. *La Possession de Jeanne Fery* (1584), Bibliothèque Diabolique (Paris: A. Delahaye & Lecrosnier, 1886), p. 10, n. 3.

17. *La Possession de Jeanne Fery,* p. 68, n. 1.

18. In 1837, an American medical journal wrote about the convulsionists: "One was stretched on the ground, and the stoutest men that could be found were directed to trample with all their might and main upon her body; kicking the chest and stomach, and attempting to tread down the ribs with their heels. So violent were these exertions, that it is related that a hunchbacked girl was thus kicked and trampled into a goodly shape.

"The next exercise was what they called the plank, and consisted in laying a deal board on the patient while extended upon the back, and then getting as many athletic men as could stand upon it, to press the body down; and in this endeavour they seldom showed sufficient energy to satisfy the sufferer, who was constantly calling for more pressure.

"Next came the experiment of the pebble, a diminutive name they were pleased to give to a paving-stone weighing two-and-twenty pounds, which was discharged upon the girl's stomach and bosom, from as great a height as possible. This terrific blow was frequently inflicted upwards of a hundred times, while the astonished by-standers were terrified by the hollow sound re-echoed by the enthusiast at every blow. (. . .) It further appears that the convulsionist, who was of the gentle sex, at each stroke would exclaim in ecstacy, 'Oh, how nice!' 'Oh, how it does me good!' 'Oh, dear brother hit away—again—again!' (. . .) One of these young ladies, who was not easily satisfied, jumped with impunity into a fire, an exploit which obtained her the glorious epithet of Sister Salamander. The names that these amiable devotees gave to each other were somewhat curious. They all strove to imitate the whining and wheedling of spoiled children, or petted infants; one was called L'Imbécille, antoher L'Aboyeuse, a third La Nisette, and they used to beg and cry for barley-sugar and cakes; barley-sugar signified a stick big enough to fell an ox, and cakes meant paving-stones." *American Journal of the Medical Sciences,* vol. 21 (Philadelphia: Carey, Lea & Blanchard, 1837), pp. 274–275.

19. "De par le Roi, défense à Dieu, De faire miracle en ce lieu." *American Journal of the Medical Sciences,* vol. 21 (Philadelphia: Carey, Lea & Blanchard, 1837), p. 275.

20. *New York Times,* February 26, 1882.

21. See Robert Beverly Hale's introduction to Paul Richer, *Artistic Anatomy,* trans. and ed. Robert Beverly Hale (New York: Watson-Guptill Publications, 1986).

22. Richer, *Études cliniques sur l'hystéro-épilepsie,* p.79.

23. Richer, *Études cliniques sur l'hystéro-épilepsie,* p. 79, emphasis added.

24. Richer, *Études cliniques sur l'hystéro-épilepsie,* pp. 7–8.

25. Henri Legrand du Saulle, *Les hystériques: État physique et état mental; actes insolites, délictueux et criminels* (Paris: Librairie J. B. Baillière & fils, 1883), p. 224.

26. Richer, *Études cliniques sur l'hystéro-épilepsie,* p. 321.

27. Richer, *Études cliniques sur l'hystéro-épilepsie,* pp. 114–115.

28. J.-K. Huysmans, *En Route,* trans. C. Kegan Paul (London: Kegan Paul, Trench, Trübner, 1908), pp. 74, 242.

29. *Histoire de la bienheureuse Marguerite-Marie,* etc., de M. l'abbé, Em. Bougaud, 4th ed., 1876, p. 199, cited by Bourneville, *Iconographie photographique de la Salpêtrière,* vol. 2, p. 223.

30. Richer, *Études cliniques sur l'hystéro-épilepsie*, p. 12.
31. Richer, *Études cliniques sur l'hystéro-épilepsie*, pp. 125–126.
32. Richer, *Études cliniques sur l'hystéro-épilepsie*, p. 124.
33. Richer, *Études cliniques sur l'hystéro-épilepsie*, p. 130.
34. Axel Munthe, *The Story of San Michele* (London: John Murray, 1929), pp. 210–211.
35. The anecdote about Charcot refusing payment from Platel, first recorded by his student Alexandre-Achille Souques in *Charcot intime*, 1925, is retold in Christopher G. Goetz, Michel Bonduelle, and Toby Gelfand, *Charcot: Constructing Neurology* (New York, Oxford: Oxford University Press, 1995), p. 252.
36. *Letters of Sigmund Freud*, selected and edited by Ernst L. Freud, translated by Tanya and Jay Stern (New York: Basic Books, 1960), p. 175.
37. See "A Fasting Girl," *New York Times*, November 5, 1874; "Louise Lateau the Stigmatist," *New York Times*, May 18, 1879, and September 18, 1883; and her obituary, "Death of a Queer Being," *New York Times*, September 18, 1883. Lateau is also compared to Mollie Fancher, a young woman from Brooklyn who became a famous "fasting girl," in a newspaper article with the cumbersome title "Hysteria and Its Causes; Some Observations on the Fancher Case. Peculiarities of Hysterical Patients, the Prevalence of the Malady, Credulous Medical Practitioners, the Case of Louise Lateau Recalled," *New York Times*, December 15, 1878. On Mollie Fancher, see Abram H. Dailey, *Mollie Fancher, The Brooklyn Enigma: An Authentic Statement of Facts in the Life of Mary J. Fancher, the Psychological Marvel of the Nineteenth Century: Unimpeachable Testimony of Many Witnesses* (Brooklyn: Press of Eagle Book Printing Dept., 1894). Also see Michelle Stacey's lively and enjoyable account, *The Fasting Girl: A True Medical Mystery* (New York: Putnam, 2002).
38. Désiré-Magloire Bourneville, *Science et Miracle: Louise Lateau ou la Stigmatisée Belge* (Paris: Delahaye, 1875), p. 8.
39. Bourneville, *Science et Miracle*, p. 41.
40. Gerald Molloy, *A Visit to Louise Lateau* (London: Burns, Oates, & Co., 1873), p. 22.
41. Bourneville, *Science et Miracle*, p. 26.
42. Bourneville, *Science et Miracle*, p. 19.
43. Bourneville, *Science et Miracle*, pp. 42–43.
44. Bourneville, *Science et Miracle*, p. 75.
45. Delboeuf, "Une visite à la Salpêtrière," p. 134.
46. Delboeuf, "Une visite à la Salpêtrière," pp. 136–137.
47. G. Dujardin-Beaumetz, "Note sur des troubles vaso-moteurs de la peau

observés sur un hystérique," *L'union médicale* 144 (December 9, 1879): 921. This article is reprinted in *Parachute*, no. 35 (June–August 1984): 13–14.

48. Georges Didi-Huberman pointed out this shift in orientation in the postface "Charcot, l'histoire et l'art," in Jean-Martin Charcot and Paul Richer, *Les démoniaques dans l'art* (Paris: Macula, 1984), p. 164.

49. *Autobiographie, Soeur Jeanne des Anges*, text annotated and published by Gabriel Legué and Georges Gilles de la Tourette, *Progrès Médical* (Paris: Delahaye & Lecrosnier, 1886), p. 99.

50. Indeed, this kind of "retrospective medicine" spawned an entire genre of books in which historical figures and events were interpreted according to current medical theories. For example, Docteur Cabanès authored a number of extremely popular works, such as *The Revolutionary Neurosis*, *The Unknown Marat*, and *The Secret Cabinet of History*, which includes chapters with titles such as "The Pathological Case of Jean Jacques Rousseau," "The Autopsy of Charlotte Corday," and "The Madness of the Divine Marquis." See Docteur Cabanès, *Le cabinet secret de l'histoire* (Paris: Albin Michel).

51. Charcot and Richer, *Les démoniaques dans l'art*, p. 87.

52. Charcot and Richer, *Les démoniaques dans l'art*, p. 22.

53. Charcot, *Oeuvres complètes*, vol. 9, p. 296.

54. Charcot and Richer, *Les démoniaques dans l'art*, p. 159.

55. Paul Janet, *De l'angoisse à l'extase* vol. 1 (Paris: Alcan, 1926), p. 476, cited by Didi-Huberman in Charcot and Richer, *Les démoniaques*, p. 147.

56. Guillain writes that a few years after Charcot died, he was shown his office: "It was kept then exactly as it was in Charcot's time. The room, which was not very large, was illuminated by a single window, and the only furniture in the room was a wardrobe for the clothes of Charcot, a table, an office chair, and several other chairs. The entire room and all of the furnishings were painted in black. On the walls were several engravings by Raphael and by Rubens and a large portrait with a dedication from the English neurologist John Hughlings Jackson. The entire ensemble produced a rather lugubrious effect, but it is worth remembering that many great discoveries were made and developed in this office of Charcot's." Georges Guillain, *J. M. Charcot: His Life, His Work*, trans. P. Bailey (New York: Paul B. Hoeber, 1959), p. 52.

57. For more on Charcot as a dark figure, see Jacqueline Carroy, *Hypnose, suggestion, et psychologie: L'invention de sujets* (Paris: Presses Universitaires de France, 1991), p. 59. Carroy also includes a popular image that depicts a sinister-looking Charcot inside the gaping jaws of a skull; see p. 165.

58. For much of my information on Bernadette Soubirous and Lourdes, I am

indebted to Ruth Harris's informative and moving book *Lourdes: Body and Spirit in the Secular Age* (New York: Penguin, 1999).

59. Auguste Voisin, *L'union médicale*, June 27, 1872. Voisin's accusation was met with angry rebuttals from the bishop of Nevers, as well as from doctors who had cared for Bernadette. Some of these rebuttals are reprinted in the appendix of the book by George Bertrin, *Lourdes: A History of its Apparitions and Cures*, trans. Mrs. Philip Gibbs (New York: Benziger Brothers, 1908), pp. 289–292.

60. The cause for Louise Lateau's beatification, one of the steps taken in order to become a saint, was opened in 1991.

61. This list of diseases that were allegedly cured in Lourdes is taken from the much longer list found in the book by Georges Bertrin, the archivist of medical records at Lourdes. See Bertrin, *Lourdes*, pp. 293–296.

62. Gustave Boissarie, the director of the Medical Bureau at Lourdes from 1892 to 1914, writes that in 1905 alone there were between 1,000 and 1,500 miracle cures. See Gustave Boissarie, *L'oeuvre de Lourdes* (Paris: Ancienne Maison Charles Douniol, 1908), p. 2. For a list of the cures that have been recognized by the Church as miraculous, see the official Web site of Lourdes: http://www.lourdes-france.org/upload/pdf/gb_guerisons.pdf.

63. Jean-Martin Charcot, "La foi qui guérit," reprinted in *Les démoniaques dans l'art suivi de la foi que guérit* (Paris: Macula, 1984), p. 121.

64. Gustave Boissarie, *Lourdes: Historie médicale, 1858–1891* (Paris: Librairie Victor Lecoffre, 1891), pp. 18–19.

65. See Mark S. Micale, *Approaching Hysteria: Disease and Its Interpretations* (Princeton, N.J.: Princeton University Press: 1995), p. 276.

66. Boissarie, *Lourdes*, pp. 258–259.

67. Charcot, *Oeuvres complètes*, vol. 9, p. 289.

68. Charcot, *Oeuvres complètes*, vol. 1, p. 356.

69. *Une Semaine Religieuse de Paris* 44, no. 1141 (November 20, 1875): 657–658.

70. "Neurotic Tumours of the Breast, read before the New York Neurological Society," January 7, 1890, *Medical Record*, February 15, 1890, p. 179, cited by Charcot in "La foi qui guérit," reprinted in *Les démoniaques dans l'art suivi de la foi que guérit* (Paris: Macula, 1984), p. 120.

71. Charcot, "La foi qui guérit," reprinted in *Les démoniaques dans l'art suivi de la foi que guérit*, p. 112.

72. As Mark Micale notes in his book on hysteria, the wealthy could consult Charcot privately and take the waters at spas, while the populations of both Lourdes and the Salpêtrière were made up largely of the same demographic: poor dispossessed women. See Micale, *Approaching Hysteria*, pp. 262–294.

Epilogue: Hysteria Revisited

1. Margaret Talbot, "Hysteria, Hysteria," *New York Times Magazine*, June 2, 2002, p. 46.

2. Gary Small, a psychiatrist at the University of California at Los Angeles, cited by Talbot.

3. The two other conditions are "multiple chemical sensitivity syndrome," in which individuals, 85 to 90 percent of them women, have shifting complaints attributed not to a virus but to environmental toxins, and Gulf War syndrome, the controversial illness that afflicted veterans from the 1991 Gulf War.

4. Daniel Carlat, "Mind over Meds," *New York Times Magazine*, April 19, 2010, p. 40.

5. See Louis Menand, "Head Case," *The New Yorker*, March 1, 2010.

6. See Brant Wenegrat, *Illness and Power: Women's Mental Disorders and the Battle Between the Sexes* (New York: New York University Press, 1995), pp. 15–20. Wenegrat mentions the Amish exception to this ratio. Among the Amish, men and women are equally afflicted with depression, p. 17.

7. Joan Busfield, *Men, Women, and Madness: Understanding Gender and Mental Disorder* (New York: New York University Press, 1996), p. 3.

8. Margaret Talbot, "Hysteria, Hysteria," p. 46.

9. American Psychiatric Association, *Diagnostic and Statistical Manual of Mental Disorders*. 4th ed., text revised (Washington, D.C.: American Psychiatric Association, 2000). See also "Conversion Disorder," sec. 15, chap. 186, in *The Merck Manual of Diagnosis and Therapy*, ed. Mark H. Beers, M.D., and Robert Berkow, M.D. (Whitehouse Station, N.J.: Merck Research Laboratories, 1999).

10. Edward Shorter, *From Paralysis to Fatigue: A History of Psychosomatic Illness in the Modern Era* (New York: Free Press, 1992).

11. Charcot cited by Georges Guillain, *J.-M. Charcot, 1825–1893: His Life, His Work*, ed. and trans. by Pearce Bailey (New York: Paul B. Hoeber, 1959), p. 140, emphasis added.

12. Carlat, "Mind over Meds."

13. Carlat, "Mind over Meds." For a far more in-depth analysis of the recent developments in neuroscience, as well as the philosophical implications of this research, see my sister Siri Hustvedt's book *The Shaking Woman or a History of My Nerves* (New York: Henry Holt, 2010).

BIBLIOGRAPHY

Acocella, Joan Ross. *Creating Hysteria: Women and Multiple Personality Disorder.* San Francisco: Jossey-Bass, 1999.

Appignanesi, Lisa. *Mad, Bad, and Sad: Women and the Mind Doctors.* New York: W. W. Norton, 2008.

Aragon, Louis, and André Breton. "La cinquantière de l'hystérie." *La Revolution Surréaliste* 11 (March 1928).

Avril, Jane. "Mes mémoires." *Paris-Midi*, August 1933.

Azam, Étienne Eugène. *Hypnotisme, double conscience et alterations de la personnalité: le cas Félida X.* Préface de Jean-Martin Charcot. Paris J. B. Baillière, 1887.

Babinski, Joseph. "Démembrement de l'hystérie traditionelle: pithiatisme." *Semaine Médicale* 29 (1909): 3–8.

———. "Recherches servant à établir que certaines manifestations de l'hystérie peuven être transmises d'un sujet à l'autre sous l'influence de l'aimant." *Progrès Médical* 4 (1888): 1010–1011.

Baer, Ulrich. *Spectral Evidence: The Photography of Trauma.* Cambridge, Mass.: MIT Press, 2002.

Ballet, Gilbert. *Médecine légale l'expertise médico-légale et la question de responsabilité (discussion du rapport sur).* Geneva: Société Générale d'Imprimerie. 1907.

———. "La Suggestion hypnotique au point de vue medico-legal." *Gazette hebdomadaire de médecine et de chirurgie* 28 (1891): 522–525, 534–538.

Bannour, Wanda. *Jean-Martin Charcot et l'hystérie.* Paris: Editions Métailié, 1992.

Barthélémy, T. *Étude sur le dermagraphisme ou dermoneurose toxivasomotrice.* Paris: Société d'Éditions Scientifiques, 1893.

Barthes, Roland. *Camera Lucida: Reflections on Photography.* New York: Hill & Wang, 1981.

Bartholomew, Robert E. *Little Green Men, Meowing Nuns, and Head-Hunting Panics: a Study of Mass Psychogenic Illness and Social Delusion.* Jefferson, N.C.: McFarland, 2001.

Baudouin, A. "Quelques souvenirs de la Salpêtrière." *Paris Médical* 21 (1925): 517–520.

Beizer, Janet. "Femme-texte et roman hystérique." *Revue Internationale de psychopathologie* 4 (1991): 351–359.

———. *Ventriloquized Bodies: Narratives of Hysteria in Nineteenth-century France*. Ithaca N.Y.: Cornell University Press, 1994.

Bell, Rudolph M. *Holy Anorexia*. Chicago: University of Chicago Press, 1985.

Berlillon, Edgar. "Neurasthénie grave traitée avec success par la suggestion hypnotique." *Revue de l'hypnotisme et de la psychologie physiologique* (1889–1890): 336–338.

Bernard, Denis, and André Gunthert. *L'instant rêvé: Albert Londe*. Nîmes: J. Chambon, 1993.

Bernheim, Hippolyte. *De la suggestion dans l'état hypnotique et dans l'état de veille: 1884*. Paris: L'Harmattan, 2004.

Bernheimer, Charles. "Huysmans: Syphilis, Hysteria, and Sublimation." In *Figures of Ill Repute: Representing Prostitution in Nineteenth-Century France*, 234–265. Cambridge, Mass.: Harvard University Press, 1989.

Bertrin, Georges. *Lourdes: A History of Its Apparitions and Cures*. Translated by Agnes Gibbs. New York: Benziger Brothers, 1908.

Binet, Alfred. *Alterations of Personality*. Translated by Helen Green Baldwin. New York: D. Appleton, 1896.

———. *The Psychology of Reasoning Based on Experimental Researches in Hypnotism*. Translated by Adam Gowans Whyte. London: K. Paul, Trench, Trübner, 1899.

Binet, Alfred, and Charles Féré. *Animal Magnetism*. London: K. Paul, Trench, Trübner, 1887.

———. "L'Hypnotisme chez les hystériques: Le transfert psychique." *Revue Philosophique* 19 (1885): 1–25.

———. "Les paralysies par suggestion." *Revue Scientifique* (July 12, 1884): 45–49.

———. "La Polarisation psychique." *Revue Philosophique* 19 (1885): 369–402.

———. "Recherches expérimentales sur la physiologie des mouvements chez les hystériques." *Archives de Physiologie Normale et Pathologique* 10, series 3 (1887): 320–373.

Boissarie, Gustave. *Lourdes: Histoire médicale, 1858–1891*. Paris: Lecoffre, 1891.

Boissarie, Prosper. *L'oeuvre de Lourdes*. Paris: Ancienne Maison Charles Douniol, 1908.

Bonduelle, Michel. "Charcot et les Daudet." *La Presse Médicale* 22, no. 32 (October 23, 1993): 1641–1648.

Bourneville, Désiré-Magloire. *De la contracture hystérique permanente*. Paris: A. Delahaye, 1872.

———. *Laïcisation de l'Assistance Publique conférence faite a l'Association Philotechnique le 26 décembre 1880*. Paris: Aux Bureau du Progrès Médical, 1881.

———, ed. *La Possession de Jeanne Fery*. Paris: Bureaux du Progrès Médical, 1886.

———. *Recherches cliniques et thérapeutiques sur l'épilepsie et l'hystérie compte rendu des observations recueillies à la Salpêtrière de 1872 à 1875*. Paris: A. Delahaye, 1876.

———, ed. *Revue photographique des hôpitaux de Paris: Bulletin médical publié sous le patronage de l'administration de l'assistance publique*. Paris: Adrien Delahaye, 1869.

———. *Science et miracle: Louise Lateau ou la stigmatisée belge*. Paris: A. Delahaye, 1875.

Bourneville, Désiré-Magloire, and Paul Regnard. *Iconographie photographique de la Salpêtrière*. Paris: Aux Bureaux du Progrès Médical, Delahaye & Lecrosnier, 1876.

———. *Iconographie photographique de La Salpêtrière*. Paris: Progrès Médical, 1877.

———. *Iconographie photographique de la Salpêtrière*. Paris: Delahaye & Lecrosnier, 1878.

———. *Iconographie photographique de la Salpêtrière*. Paris: Delahaye & Lecrosnier, 1879.

Brais, Bernard. "Désiré-Magloire Bourneville and French Anti-Clericalism during the Third Republic." In *Doctors, Politics, and Society: Historical Essays*. Edited by Dorothy Porter and Roy Porter, 107–139. Amsterdam: Rodopi, 1993.

Breton, André. *Nadja*. Translated by Richard Howard. New York: Grove, 1960.

Breuer, Josef, and Sigmund Freud. *Studies on Hysteria*. New York: Basic Books, 1957.

———. Translated by James Strachey. *Studies on Hysteria*. London: Penguin, 1991.

Briquet, Paul. *Traité clinique et thérapeutique de l'hystérie*. Paris: J.-B. Baillière & Fils, 1859.

British Medical Journal (June 7, 1879): 856.

Brumberg, Joan Jacobs. *Fasting Girls: The Emergence of Anorexia Nervosa as a Modern Disease*. Cambridge, Mass.: Harvard University Press, 1988.

Buiral, Pierre, and Guy Thuiller. *La vie quotidienne des domestiques en France au XIXe siècle*. Paris: Hachette, 1978.

Burq, Victor. *Métallothérapie: Nouveau traitement des maladies nerveuses, paralysies, rheumatisme chronique, spasmes, névralgies, chlorose, hystérie, hypochondrie, délire, monomanie, etc.; des convulsions de l'enfance, du choléra, des crampes des cholériques, etc. par les applications métalliques*. Paris: G. Baillière, 1853.

Burton, Richard. *Holy Tears, Holy Blood: Women, Catholicism, and the Culture of Suffering in France, 1840–1970*. Ithaca, N.Y.: Cornell University Press, 2004.

Busfield, Joan. *Men, Women, and Madness: Understanding Gender and Mental Disorder*. New York: New York University Press, 1996.

Bynum, Caroline Walker. *Holy Feast and Holy Fast: The Religious Significance of Food to Medieval Women*. London: University of California, 1987.

Bynum, W. F., Roy Porter, and Michael Shepherd. *The Anatomy of Madness: Essays in the History of Psychiatry*. London: Tavistock Publications, 1985.

Cabanès, Auguste. *Le cabinet secret de l'histoire*. Paris: Albin Michel, 1905.

Cambor, Kate. *Gilded Youth: Three Lives in France's Belle Époque*. New York: Farrar, Straus & Giroux, 2009.

Carlat, Daniel. "Mind over Meds." *New York Times Magazine*, April 25, 2010.

Carroy, Jacqueline. *Les personnalités doubles et multiples: Entre science et fiction.* Presses Universitaires de France, 1993.

Carroy-Thirard, Jacqueline. "Figures de femmes hytériques dans la psychiatrie française au 19e siècle." *Psychanalyse à l'université* 4 (1978–1979): 313–324.

———. *Hypnose, suggestion, et psychologie: L'invention de sujets.* Paris: Presses Universitaires de France, 1991.

———. "Hystérie, théâtre, literature au dix-neuvième siècle." *Psychanalyse à l'université* 7 (March 1982): 299–316.

Cavailhon, Edouard. *La fascination magnetique.* Paris: Dentu, 1882.

Certeau, Michel de. *The Possession at Loudun.* Translated by Michael B. Smith. Chicago: University of Chicago Press, 2000.

Charcot, J. M. *Charcot, the Clinician: The Tuesday Lessons: Excerpts from Nine Case Presentations on General Neurology Delivered at the Salpêtrière Hospital in 1887–88 by Jean-Martin Charcot.* Translation and commentary by Christopher G. Goetz. New York: Raven Press, 1987.

———. *Clinical Lectures on Diseases of the Nervous System: Delivered at the Infirmary of La Salpêtrière.* Translated by Thomas Savill. Vol. 3. London: New Sydenham Society, 1889.

Charcot, Jean-Martin. "De la chorée rythmique hystérique." *Progrès Médical* (February 9, 1878).

———. "Hospice de la Salpêtrière: Réouverture des conférences cliniques de M. Charcot." *Progrès Médical* 8 (November 27, 1880).

———. *L'hystérie.* Edited by Étienne Trillat. Paris: L'Harmattan, 1998.

———. *Leçons sur les maladies du système nerveux faites à la Salpêtrière.* Edited by Désiré-Magloire Bourneville. Vol. 1. Paris: A. Delahaye & Lecrosnier, 1880.

———. *Leçons sur les maladies du système nerveux faites à la Salpêtrière.* Edited by Désiré-Magloire Bourneville. Vol. 2. Paris: A. Delahaye & Lecrosnier, 1880.

———. Leçons sur les maladies du système nerveux faites à la Salpêtrière. Edited by Charles Féré. Vol. 3. Paris: A. Delahaye & Lecrosnier, 1883.

———. *Oeuvres Complètes: Leçons sur les maladies du système nerveux.* Edited by Désiré-Magloire Bourneville. Vol. 1. Paris: Lecrosnier et Babé, Bureaux du Progrès Médical, 1872–1873.

———. *Oeuvres Complètes: Leçons sur les maladies du système nerveux.* Edited by Désiré-Magloire Bourneville. Vol. 2. Paris: Lecrosnier et Babé, Bureaux du Progrès Médical, 1877.

———. *Oeuvres complètes: Leçons sur les maladies du système nerveux.* Vol. 3. Edited by Joseph Babinski, Charles Féré, Georges Guinon, Pierre Marie, and Georges Gilles de la Tourette. Paris: Lecrosnier et Babé, Bureaux du Progrès Médical, 1887.

———. *Oeuvres complètes: Leçons sur les localisations dans les maladies du cerveau et de la moelle épinière*. Vol. 4. Edited by Désiré-Magloire Bourneville and Edouard Brissaud. Paris: Lecrosnier et Babé, Bureaux du Progrès Médical, 1880.

———. *Oeuvres complètes: Hémorragie et ramollissement du cerveau. Métallothérapie et hypnotisme. Électrothérapie*. Edited by Désiré-Magloire Bourneville. Vol. 9. Paris: Lecrosnier et Babé, Bureaux du Progrès Médical, 1890.

Charcot, Jean-Martin, and Paul Richer. *Les Démoniaques dans l'art: Suivi de la foi qui guérit*. Paris: Macula, 1984.

———. *Les difformes et les malades dans l'art*. Paris: Lecrosnier & Babé, 1889.

Claretie, Jules. "Chroniques Parisiennes." *Le Temps*, July 11, 1884.

———. *Les amours d'un interne*. Paris: Dentu, 1881.

———. *La Vie à Paris, 1881*. Paris: Havard, 1882.

Clayman, Charles B. *The American Medical Association Family Medical Guide*. New York: Random House, 1994.

Copjec, Joan. "Flavit et Dissipati Sunt." *October* 18 (Fall 1981): 21–40.

Crabtree, Adam. *From Mesmer to Freud: Magnetic Sleep and the Roots of Psychological Healing*. New Haven, Conn.: Yale University Press, 1993.

Cuvelier, André. *Hypnose et suggestion: De Liébeault à Coué*. Nancy: Presses Universitaires de Nancy, 1987.

Dailey, Abram H. *Mollie Fancher, the Brooklyn Enigma: An Authentic Statement of Facts in the Life of Mary J. Fancher, the Psychological Marvel of the Nineteenth Century: Unimpeachable Testimony of Many Witnesses*. Brooklyn, N.Y.: Press of Eagle Book Printing Dept., 1894.

Darwin, Charles. *The Expression of the Emotions in Man and Animals*. Chicago: University of Chicago, 1965.

Daudet, Alphonse. *La Doulou, la vie: Extraits des carnets inédits de l'auteur*. Nîmes: Lacour, 2004.

———. *Suffering, 1887–1895*. Translated by Milton Garver. New Haven, Conn.: Yale University Press, 1934.

———. *Trois souvenirs: Au fort-montrouge, à la Salpêtrière, une leçon*. Paris: Librairie Borel, 1896.

Daudet, Léon. "Devant la douleur." In *Souvenirs et polémiques*, edited by Bernard Oudin, pp. 143–265. Paris: Laffont, 1992.

———. "Fantômes et vivants." In *Souvenirs et polémiques*. edited by Bernard Oudin, pp. 7–141. Paris: Laffont, 1992.

———. *Les morticoles*. Paris: Charpentier, 1895.

———. *Quand vivait mon père*. Paris: B. Grasset, 1940.

Daudet, Leon, and Bernard Oudin. *Leon Daudet: Souvenirs et polémiques: Souvenirs, député de Paris, Paris vécu, le stupide XIXe siècle*. Paris: Robert Laffont, 1992.

"Death of a Queer Being." *New York Times*, Sept 18, 1883.

Delboeuf, Joseph. *L'hypnotisme: Devant les chambres legislatives belges*. Paris: Félix Alcan, 1892.

———. *Magnétiseurs et médecins*. Paris: F. Alcan, 1890.

———. *Le sommeil et les rêves et autres textes*. Paris: Fayard, 1993.

———. "Une visite à la Salpêtrière." *Revue de Belgique* 54 (1886): 139–147; 258–278.

De Marneffe, Daphne. "Looking and Listening: The Construction of Clinical Knowledge in Charcot and Freud." *Signs* (Autumn 1991): 71–110.

D'Hont (Donato), Alfred. *Revue générale des sciences physiopsychologiques, présentant le tableau permanent des découvertes et des progrès accomplis pendant l'année 1886*. Paris, 1886.

Diagnostic and Statistical Manual of Mental Disorders: DSM-IV-TR. Washington, D.C.: American Psychiatric Association, 2000.

Didi-Huberman, Georges. "The Figurative Incarnation of the Sentence (Notes on the 'Autographic' Skin)." *Journal: A Contemporary Art Magazine* (Spring 1987): 66–70.

———. "L'incarnation figurale de la sentence (note sur la peau 'autographique')." *Scalène* 2 (1984): 143–69.

———. *Invention de l'hystérie: Charcot et l'iconographie photographique de la Salpêtrière*. Paris: Macula, 1982.

———. "Une notion du 'corps-cliché' au XIX siècle." *Parachute* 35 (June, July, August 1984): 8–14.

Donato. "Preface." In *La fascination magnétique* by Edouard Cavailhon, vii–lxx. Paris: Dentu, 1882.

Drinka, George Frederick. *The Birth of Neurosis: Myth, Malady, and the Victorians*. New York: Simon & Schuster, 1984.

Dubarry, Armand. *Les déséquilibrés de l'amour*. 11 vols. Paris: Chamuel, 1898–1902.

Dubut de Laforest, Jean-Louis. *Les derniers scandales de Paris: Grand roman dramatique inédit*. 37 vols. Paris: Fayard Frères, 1890–1900.

Duchenne, G.-B. *Mécanisme de la physionomie humaine, ou, analyse électro-physiologique de l'expression des passions*. Paris: J. Renouard, 1862.

———. *The Mechanism of Human Facial Expression*. Translated and edited by R. Andrew Cuthbertson. Cambridge: Cambridge University Press, 1990.

Duffin, Jacalyn. *Medical Miracles: Doctors, Saints, and Healing in the Modern World*. Oxford: Oxford University Press, 2009.

Dujardin-Beaumetz, G. "Note sur des troubles vaso-moteurs de la peau observés sur un hystérique." *L'union Médicale* 144 (December 9, 1879): 917–922.

Ehrenreich, Barbara, and Deirdre English. *For Her Own Good: 150 Years of the Experts' Advice to Women*. Garden City, N.Y.: Anchor Books, 1978.

Elkins, James. *Photography Theory*. New York: Routledge, 2007.

Ellenberger, Henri F. *The Discovery of the Unconscious: The History and Evolution of Dynamic Psychiatry*. New York: Basic Books, 1970.

Enquist, Per Olav. *The Book about Blanche and Marie*. Translated by Tiina Nunnally. New York: The Overlook Press, 2006.

Evans, Martha Noel. *Fits and Starts: A Genealogy of Hysteria in Modern France.* Ithaca, N.Y.: Cornell University Press, 1991.

"A Fasting Girl." *New York Times*, November 5, 1874.

Favazza, Armando R. *Bodies Under Siege, Self-Mutilation and Body Modification in Culture and Psychiatry.* Baltimore: Johns Hopkins University Press, 1996.

Ferber, Sarah. "Charcot's Demons: Retrospective Medicine and Historical Diagnosis in the Writings of the Salpêtrière School." In *Illness and Healing Alternatives in Western Europe*, edited by Marijke Gijswijt-Hofstra, Hilary Marland, and Hans de Waardt, 120–140. London: Routledge, 1997.

Finger, Stanley. *Minds Behind the Brain: A History of the Pioneers and Their Discoveries.* Oxford: Oxford University Press, 2000.

Foucault, Michel. *The Birth of the Clinic: An Archaeology of Medical Perception.* Translated by A. M. Sheridan Smith. New York: Vintage Books, 1994.

———. *Madness and Civilization: A History of Insanity in the Age of Reason.* New York: Vintage, 1973.

Foveau de Courmelles, François Victor. *Hypnotism.* Translated by Laura Ensor. Philadelphia: David Mackay, 1891.

Féré, Charles. "J.-M. Charcot et son oeuvre." *Revue des deux mondes* 112 (March 1, 1894).

Freud, Sigmund. *The Freud Reader.* Edited by Peter Gay. New York: W. W. Norton, 1989.

———. *Letters of Sigmund Freud.* Edited by Ernst L. Freud. Translated by Tanya and Jay Stern. New York: Basic Books, 1975.

Fuchs, Rachel Ginnis. *Abandoned Children: Foundlings and Child Welfare in Nineteenth-century France.* Albany: State University of New York, 1984.

———. *Poor and Pregnant in Paris: Strategies for Survival in the Nineteenth Century.* New Brunswick, N.J.: Rutgers University Press, 1992.

Furse, Anna. *Augustine (Big Hysteria).* Amsterdam: Harwood Academic, 1997.

Gamjee, A. "Account of Demonstration of Hystero-Epilepsy Given by Professor Charcot." *British Medical Journal* 2 (1878): 454–458.

Garay, Anabelle. "Surgeon: UK Brand Was a Guide." *Kentucky Post*, January 29, 2003.

Gauchet, Marcel, and Gladys Swain. *Le vrai Charcot: Les chemins imprévus de l'inconscient.* Paris: Calmann-Lévy, 1997.

Gelfand, Toby. "Medical Nemesis, Paris, 1894: Léon Daudet's Les Morticoles." *Bulletin of the History of Medicine* 60 (1986): 155–76.

———. "The 'Secret' of Medical Miracles: Zola's *Lourdes* and Charcot's *La Foi qui guérit*." *Excavatio* 19, nos. 1–2 (2004): 251–271.

Gelfand, Toby, and Michel Bonduelle. "Hysteria Behind the Scenes: Jane Avril at the Salpêtrière." *Journal of the History of the Neurosciences* 8.1 (1999): 35–42.

Gilles de la Tourette, Georges. *L'hypnotisme et les états analogues au point de vue médico-légal: Les états hypnotiques et les états analogues, les suggestions criminelles, cabinets de somnambules et sociétés de magnétisme et de spiritisme, l'hypnotisme devant la loi.* Paris: Plon, Nourrit & Cie., 1889.

———. "Jean-Martin Charcot." *Nouvelle iconographie de la Salpêtrière* 6 (1893): 241–250.

———. *Traité clinique et thérapeutique de l'hystérie d'après l'enseignement de la Salpêtrière: Hystérie normale ou interparoxystique.* Paris: E. Plon, Nourrit & Cie., 1891.

———. "The Wonders of Animal Magnetism." *North American Review.* Edited by Allen Thorndike Rice. Vol. 146 (1888), 131–143.

Gilles de la Tourette, Georges, and Paul Richer. "Hypnotisme." In *Dictionnaire encyclopédique des sciences médicales.* Edited by A. Dechambre. Paris: Masson, 1889.

———. "Note sur les caractères clinique des paralysies psychiques expérimentales (paralysies par suggestion)." *Progrès Médical* (March 29, 1884): 241–242.

Gilman, Sander L. *Seeing the Insane.* New York: John Wiley, 1982.

Gilman, Sander L., Helen King, Roy Porter, George Rousseau, and Elaine Showalter. *Hysteria Beyond Freud.* Berkeley: University of California Press, 1993.

Glucklich, Ariel. "Self and Sacrifice: A Phenomenological Psychology of Sacred Pain." *Harvard Theological Review* 92, no. 4 (October 1999): 479–506.

Goetz, Christopher G. "Charcot and the Myth of Misogyny." *Neurology* 52 (May 12, 1999): 1678–686.

———. "The Salpêtrière in the Wake of Charcot's Death." *Archives of Neurology* 45 (1988).

———. "Visual Art in the Neurologic Career of Jean-Martin Charcot." *Archives of Neurology* 48 (1991): 421–25.

Goetz, Christopher G., Michel Bonduelle, and Toby Gelfand. *Charcot: Constructing Neurology.* New York: Oxford University Press, 1995.

Goldstein, Jan. *Console and Classify: The French Psychiatric Profession in the Nineteenth Century.* Cambridge: Cambridge University Press, 1987.

———. "The Hysteria Diagnosis and the Politics of Anticlericalism in Late Nineteenth-Century France." *Journal of Modern History* 54.2 (1982): 209–239.

Goncourt, Edmund, and Jules Goncourt. *Mémoires de la vie littéraire.* Paris: Fasquelle & Flammarion, 1956.

Gordon, Rae Beth. "From Charcot to Charlot: Unconscious Imitation and Spectatorship in French Cabaret and Early Cinema." In *The Mind of Modernism: Medicine, Psychology, and the Cultural Arts in Europe and America, 1880–1940.* Edited by Mark S. Micale, 93–124. Stanford, Calif.: Stanford University Press, 2004.

———. *Why the French Love Jerry Lewis: From Cabaret to Early Cinema.* Stanford, Calif.: Stanford University Press, 2001.

Grasset, Joseph. "Hystérie." In *Dictionnaire encyclopédique des sciences médicales.* Edited by A. Dechambre. Paris: Masson, 1889.

Gross, Philippe L., and S. I. Shapiro. *The Tao of Photography: Seeing Beyond Seeing.* Berkeley, Calif.: Ten Speed, 2001.

Guillain, Georges. *J.-M. Charcot: 1825–1893: Sa vie, son oeuvre*. Paris: Masson, 1955.

———. *J.-M. Charcot, 1825–1893: His Life, His Work*. Edited and translated by Pearce Bailey. New York: Paul B. Hoeber, 1959.

Guinon, Georges. "Attentat contre le docteur Gilles de la Tourette." *Progrès Médical* 18 (1893): 446.

Guinon, Georges, and Sophie Woltke. "De l'influence des excitations sensitives et sensorielles dans les phases cataleptique et somnambulique du grand hypnotisme." *Nouvelle iconographie de la Salpêtrière*. Vol. 4 (1891): 77–88.

Guiral, Pierre, and Guy Thuillier. *La Vie quotidienne des domestiques en france au XIXe siècle*. Paris: Hachette, 1978.

Gunning, Tom. "In Your Face: Physiognomy, Photography, and the Gnostic Mission of Early Film." In *The Mind of Modernism: Medicine, Psychology, and the Cultural Arts in Europe and America, 1880–1940*, edited by Mark S. Micale, 141–171. Stanford, Calif.: Stanford University Press, 2004.

Hacking, Ian. "*Automatisme Ambulatoire*: Fugue, Hysteria, and Gender at the Turn of the Century." In *The Mind of Modernism: Medicine, Psychology, and the Cultural Arts in Europe and America, 1880–1940*. Edited by Mark S. Micale, 125–137. Stanford: Stanford University Press, 2004.

———. *Mad Travelers: Reflections on the Reality of Transient Mental Illnesses*. Charlottesville: University of Virginia Press, 1998.

———. *Rewriting the Soul: Multiple Personality and the Sciences of Memory*. Princeton, N.J.: Princeton University Press, 1995.

Harrington, Anne. *The Cure Within: A History of Mind-Body Medicine*. New York: W. W. Norton, 2008.

———. "Hysteria, Hypnosis, and the Lure of the Invisible: The Rise of Neo-Mesmerism in Fin-de-Siècle French Psychiatry." In *The Anatomy of Madness: Essays in the History of Psychiatry*. Edited by Roy Porter, Michael Shepherd, and William F. Bynum. London: Tavistock Publications, 1985.

———. *Medicine, Mind, and the Double Brain: A Study in Nineteenth-Century Thought*. Princeton, N.J.: Princeton University Press, 1987.

———. "Metals and Magnets in Medicine: Hysteria, Hypnosis, and Medical Culture in Fin-de-Siècle Paris." *Psychological Medicine* 18.1 (February 1988): 21–38.

———. *The Placebo Effect: An Interdisciplinary Exploration*. Cambridge, Mass.: Harvard University Press, 1997.

Harris, Ruth. *Lourdes: Body and Spirit in the Secular Age*. New York: Viking, 1999.

———. "Murder and Hypnosis in the Case of Gabrielle Bompard: Psychiatry in the Courtroom in Belle Époque Paris." In *The Anatomy of Madness: Essays in the History of Psychiatry*. Edited by Roy Porter, Michael Shepherd, and William F. Bynum. London: Tavistock Publications, 1985.

———. "Melodrama, Hysteria, and Feminine Crimes of Passion in the Fin-de-Siècle." *History Workshop Journal* 25 no. 1 (1988): 31–63.

———. *Murders and Madness: Medicine, Law, and Society in the Fin de Siècle*. Oxford: Oxford University Press, 1989.

Hugues Le Roux. "La Vie à Paris." *Le Temps*, April 30, 1887.

Hunter, Dianne. *The Makings of Dr. Charcot's Hysteria Shows: Research Through Performance* (Studies in Theatre Arts, Vol. 4). New York: Edwin Mellon Press, 1998.

Hustvedt, Asti, ed. *The Decadent Reader: Fiction, Fantasy, and Perversion from Fin-de-Siècle France*. New York: Zone Books, 1998.

Hustvedt, Siri. *The Shaking Woman or a History of My Nerves*. New York: Henry Holt, 2010.

Huysmans, J.-K. *En Route*. Translated by C. Kegan Paul. London: Kegan Paul, Trench, Trübner, 1908.

"Hypnotism in Paris." *The Lancet* 29 (July 1884): 163–164.

"Hysteria and Its Causes: Some Observations on the Fancher Case: Peculiarities of Hysterical Patients; the Prevalence of the Malady; Credulous Medical Practitioners; The Case of Louise Lateau Recalled." *New York Times*, Dec. 15, 1878.

Ignotus (Baron Félix Platel). "Cabotinage." *Le Figaro*, April 18, 1883.

Janet, Jules. "L'hystérie et l'hypnotisme d'après la théorie de la double personnalité." *Revue scientifique* (May 19, 1888): 616–623.

———. "Un cas de l'hystérique grave." *Revue de l'hypnotisme et de la psychologie physiologique* (1889): 339–342.

Janet, Pierre. *De l'angoisse à l'extase: Études sur les croyances et les sentiments*. Paris: F. Alcan, 1926.

———. *L'état mental des hystériques: Les stigmates mentaux des hystériques: Les accidents mentaux des hystériques: Etudes sur divers symptomes hystériques: Le traitement psychologique de l'hystérie*. Paris: Ancienne Librairie Germer Baillière, 1911.

———. *Psychological Healing: A Historical and Clinical Study*. Translated by Eden Paul and Cedar Paul. London: G. Allen & Unwin, 1925.

Jeanne des Anges. *Soeur Jeanne des Anges: Supérieure du couvent des Ursulines de Loudun (XVIIe siècle): Autobiographie d'une hystérique possédée*. Edited and annotated by Georges Gilles de la Tourette and Gabriel Legué. Paris: Charpentier, 1886.

Knibiehler, Yvonne, and Catherine Fouquet. *La femme et les médecins: Analyse historique*. Paris: Hachette Littérature Générale, 1983.

Kushner, Howard I. *A Cursing Brain?: The Histories of Tourette Syndrome*. Cambridge, Mass.: Harvard University Press, 1999.

Lachapelle, Sofie. "Between Miracle and Sickness: Louise Lateau and the Experience of Stigmata and Ecstasy." *Configurations* 12, no. 1 (Winter 2004): 77–105.

Laqueur, Thomas Walter. *Making Sex: Body and Gender from the Greeks to Freud*. Cambridge, Mass.: Harvard University Press, 1990.

Lasègue, Charles. *De la folie à deux à l'hystérie et autres états*. Paris: L'Harmattan, 1998.

Lefebvre, Ferdinand. *Louise Lateau of Bois d'Haine: Her Life, Her Ecstasies, and Her Stigmata*. Translated by J. Spencer Northcote. London: Burns & Oates, 1873.

Legendre, P. "Gilles de la Tourette, 1857–1904." *Bulletins et Mémoires de la Société Médicale des Hôpitaux de Paris* 21, no. 3 (1905): 1298–1311.

Legrand du Saulle, Henri. *Les hystériques: État physique et état mental; actes insolites, délictueux, et criminels.* Paris: Baillière, 1891.

Lemonnier, Camille. *L'hystérique.* Paris: Séguier, 1996.

Léonard, Jacques. *La médecine entre les savoirs et les pouvoirs: Histoire intellectuelle et politique de la médecine française au XIXe siècle.* Paris: Aubier-Montaigne, 1981.

———. *La vie quotidienne du médecin de province au XIXe siècle.* Paris: Hachette, 1977.

Leroux-Hugon, Véronique. "L'évasion manquée de Geneviève, ou des aléas de la traduction." *Frénésie: Histoire, Psychiatrie, Psychanalyse* 2 (1991): 103–112.

Les Soirées Litteraries 114 (January 1, 1882).

Lombroso, Cesare. *Hypnotisme et spiritisme.* Paris: Flammarion, 1920.

Lombroso, Cesare, and Guglielmo Ferrero. *The Female Offender.* Littleton, Colo.: Fred B. Rothman, 1980.

Lorde, André de. *Théâtre d'épouvante.* Paris: Librairie Charpentier & Fasquelle, 1909.

"Louise Lateau the Stigmatist." *New York Times,* May 18, 1879.

Maître, Jacques. *Anorexies religieuses, anorexie mentale: Essai de psychanalyse sociohistorique: De Marie de l'Incarnation à Simone Weil.* Paris: Les Éditions du Cerf, 2000.

———. *Une inconnue célèbre: La Madeleine Lebouc de Janet.* Paris: Anthropos, 1993.

———. *Les stigmates de l'hystérique et la peau de son évêque: Laurentine Billoquet (1862–1936).* Paris: Anthropos, 1993.

Mayer, Alex. *De la création d'une société protectrice de l'enfance pour l'amélioration de l'espèce humaine par l'éducation du premier âge.* Paris: Librairie des Sciences Sociales, 1865.

Mazzoni, Cristina. *Saint Hysteria: Neurosis, Mysticism, and Gender in European Culture.* Ithaca, N.Y.: Cornell University Press, 1996.

Méheust, Bertrand. *Somnambulisme et médiumnité: Le défi du magnétisme.* vol. 1. Le Plessis-Robinson: Institut Synthélabo pour le Progrès de la Connaissance, 1999.

———. *Somnambulisme et médiumnité: Le choc des sciences psychiques.* vol. 2. Le Plessis-Robinson: Institut Synthélabo pour le Progrès de la Connaissance, 1999.

Meige, Henry. *Charcot artiste.* Paris: Masson & Cie., 1925.

Menand, Louis. "Head Case." *The New Yorker,* March 1, 2010.

Merskey, Harold. "Hysteria: The History of an Idea." *Canadian Journal of Psychiatry* 28 (1983): 428–433.

Mesnet, Ernst. "Autographisme et stigmates." *Revue de l'hypnotisme experimental et thérapeutique* (1889–1890): 321–335.

Meyer, Philippe. *Sommeils indiscrets: Roman.* Paris: Orban, 1990.

Micale, Mark S. *Approaching Hysteria: Disease and Its Interpretations.* Princeton, N.J.: Princeton University Press, 1995.

———. "Discourses of Hysteria in Fin-de-Siècle France." In *The Mind of Modernism:*

Medicine, Psychology, and the Cultural Arts in Europe and America, 1880–1940. edited by Mark S. Micale, 71–92. Stanford: Stanford University Press, 2004.

———. "Introduction: The Modernist Mind—A Map." In *The Mind of Modernism: Medicine, Psychology, and the Cultural Arts in Europe and America, 1880–1940,* edited by Mark S. Micale, 1–19. Stanford: Stanford University Press, 2004.

———. "On the 'Disappearance of Hysteria.'" *Isis* 84 (1993): 496–526.

———. "The Salpêtrière in the Age of Charcot: An Institutional Perspective on Medical History in the Late Nineteenth Century." *Journal of Contemporary History* 20.4 (1985): 703–731.

Molloy, Gerald. *A Visit to Louise Lateau in the Summer of 1872 with a Short Account of Her Life and a Description of Her Stigmas and Her Ecstasy.* London, 1873.

Munthe, Axel. *The Story of San Michele.* London: John Murray, 1975.

Musée de l'Assistance Publique de Paris (catalogue.) Paris: Musée de L'assistance Publique, 1987.

Myers, F. W. H. "Dr. Jules Janet on Hysteria and Double Personality." In *Proceedings of the Society for Psychical Research.* vol. 6, 216–221. London: Society for Psychical Research, 1882.

Myers, Frederic W. H. *Human Personality and Its Survival of Bodily Death.* London: Longmans, Green & Co, 1903.

Newhall, Beaumont. *The History of Photography: From 1839 to the Present.* New York: Museum of Modern Art, 1982.

Owen, A. R. G. *Hysteria, Hypnosis, and Healing: The Work of J.-M. Charcot.* New York: Garrett Publications, 1971.

Parent, André. "Duchenne De Boulogne: A Pioneer in Neurology and Medical Photography." *Canadian Journal of Neurological Sciences* 32.3 (2005): 369–377.

Perrot, Michelle, ed. *A History of Private Life: From the Fires of Revolution to the Great War.* Translated by Arthur Goldhammer. Cambridge, Mass.: Harvard University Press, 1990.

Philippon, Jacques, and Jacques Poirier. *Joseph Babinski: A Biography.* Oxford: Oxford University Press, 2009.

Regnard, Paul. *Les Maladies de épidemiques de l'esprit: Sorcellerie, magnétisme, morphinisme: Délire des grandeurs.* Paris: E. Plon, Nourrit & Cie., 1887.

"Reports, La Salpêtrière Hospital (Paris), Cases of Hysteria and Hystero-epilepsy, with Hemi-Anaesthesia and Other Neurotic Disturbance (Under the Care of Professor Charcot)." *British Medical Journal* 2 (October 12, 1878): 561–563.

"Review of Iconographie photographique de la Salpêtrière." *British Medical Journal* 1.962 (June 7, 1879): 856–857.

Richebourg, Émile. *La fille maudite.* Montréal: Moderne, 1954.

Richer, Paul. *Artistic Anatomy.* Translated and edited by Robert Beverly Hale. New York: Watson-Guptill Publications, 1986.

———. *Études cliniques sur l'hystéro-épilepsie ou grande hystérie*. Paris: A. Delahaye & É. Lecrosnier, 1881.

Richer, Paul, and Jean-Martin Charcot. *Les démoniaques dans l'art*. Edited by Georges Didi-Huberman. Paris: Macula, 1984.

Richet, Charles. "Les démoniaques d'aujourd'hui." *Revue des Deux Mondes* 37 (January 15, 1880): 340–372.

———. "Ruther Experiments in Hypnotic Lucidity or Clairvoyance." *Journal of the Society for Psychical Research* VI (1889–1890): 66–83.

Ricou, Philippe, Véronique Leroux-Hugon, and Jacques Poirier. *La bibliothèque Charcot à la Salpêtrière*. Paris: Pradel, 1993.

Ripa, Yannick. *Women and Madness: The Incarceration of Women in Nineteenth-Century France*. Translated by Catherine du Peloux Ménage. Minneapolis: University of Minnesota, 1990.

Schwartz, Hillel. "The Three-Body Problem and the End of the World." In *Fragments for a History of the Human Body*. Edited by Michel Feher, Ramona Naddaff, and Nadia Tazi. Vol. 2, New York: Zone Books, 1989. 407–465.

La Semaine Religieuse de Paris, November 20, 1875.

Shorter, Edward. *From Paralysis to Fatigue: A History of Psychosomatic Illness in the Modern Era*. New York: Free Press, 1992.

———. *A History of Psychiatry: From the Era of the Asylum to the Age of Prozac*. New York: John Wiley, 1997.

Showalter, Elaine. *The Female Malady: Women, Madness, and English Culture, 1830–1980*. New York: Pantheon, 1985.

———. *Hystories: Hysterical Epidemics and Modern Media*. New York: Columbia University Press, 1997.

Siegel, Irwin M. "Charcot and Duchenne: Of Mentors, Pupils, and Colleagues." *Perspectives in Biology and Medicine* 43.4 (Summer 2000): 541–547.

Sigerson, George. "A Lecture on Certain Phenomena of Hysteria Major Delivered at the Salpêtrière on November 17th by Professor Charcot." *British Medical Journal* 2 (November 30, 1878): 789–791.

Signoret, J. L. "Variété historique: Une leçon clinique à la Salpêtrière." *Revue Neurologique* 12 (1983): 687–701.

Silverman, Debora. *Art Nouveau in Fin-de-Siècle France: Politics, Psychology, and Style*. Berkeley: University of California Press, 1989.

Simon-Dhouailly, Nadine. *La leçon de Charcot: Voyage dans une toile: Exposition organisée au Musée de l'Assistance Publique de Paris, 17 septembre–31 décembre 1986*. Paris: Musée de l'Assistance Publique, 1986.

Sontag, Susan. *On Photography*. New York: Farrar, Straus & Giroux, 1977.

Souques, Achille. *Charcot intime*. Paris: Masson, 1925.

Spitzer, Robert L. *DSM-IV-TR Casebook: A Learning Companion to the Diagnostic and*

Statistical Manual of Mental Disorders, Fourth Edition, Text Revision. Washington, D.C.: American Psychiatric Pub., 2002.

Stacey, Michelle. *The Fasting Girl: A True Victorian Medical Mystery.* New York: Jeremy P. Tarcher/Putnam, 2002.

Sussman, George D. *Selling Mothers' Milk: The Wet-Nursing Business in France, 1715–1914.* Urbana: University of Illinois Press, 1982.

Szabo, Jason. "Seeing Is Believing? The Form and Substance of French Medical Debates over Lourdes." *Bulletin of the History of Medicine* 76 (2002): 199–230.

Talbot, Margaret. "Hysteria, Hysteria." *New York Times Magazine,* June 2, 2002.

Thornton, Esther M. *Hypnotism, Hysteria, and Epilepsy: An Historical Synthesis.* London: Heinemann Medical, 1976.

Thuillier, Jean. *Monsieur Charcot de la Salpêtrière.* Paris: R. Laffont, 1993.

Trepsat, L. "Démence précoce catatonique avec pseudo-oedème compliqué." *Nouvelle Iconographie de la Salpêtrière* XVII (1904): 193–199.

Trillat, Étienne, and Guy Maruani. *De l'hystérie à la psychose: Du corps à la parole.* Paris: L'Harmattan, 1999.

Tuke, Daniel Hack. *Illustrations of the Influence of the Mind upon the Body in Health and Disease, Designed to Elucidate the Action of the Imagination.* London: J. & A. Churchill, 1872.

———. *Sleep-Walking and Hypnotism.* London: J. & A. Churchill, 1884.

"Une Heure Chez Sarah Bernhardt." *La chronique médicale* 4.19 (October 1897): 609–616.

Vandereycken, Walter, and Deth Ron. Van. *From Fasting Saints to Anorexic Girls: The History of Self-Starvation.* London: Athlone, 1994.

Veith, Ilza. *Hysteria: The History of a Disease.* Chicago: University of Chicago Press, 1965.

Voisin, Auguste Felix. *De l'hypnotisme et de la suggestion hypnotique dans leur application au traitement des maladies nerveuses et mentales.* Paris: A. Reiff, 1886.

———. "Maladies mentales: Conférences cliniques sur les maladies mentales et les affections nerveuses. Folle du jeune âge." *L'union Médicale,* June 27, 1872.

Warlomont, Evariste. *Louise Lateau: Rapport sur la stigmatisée belge de Bois-d'Haine.* Paris: J. B. Baillière et fils, 1875.

Wenegrat, Brant. *Illness and Power: Women's Mental Disorders and the Battle Between the Sexes.* New York: New York University Press, 1995.

Wong, Edward. "Doctor Carved His Initials into Patient, Lawsuit Says." *New York Times,* Jan. 22, 2000.

Wood, Gaby. *Edison's Eve: A Magical History of the Quest for Mechanical Life.* New York: Knopf, 2002.

Zola, Émile, and Ernest Alfred Vizetelly. *Lourdes.* Amherst, N.Y.: Prometheus, 2000.

INDEX

Page numbers in *italics* refer to illustrations.

A NOTE ON THE AUTHOR

Asti Hustvedt is an independent scholar who has written extensively on hysteria and literature. She has a PhD in French literature from New York University and is the recipient of numerous grants and awards, including a Phi Beta Kappa Fellowship. She is the editor of *The Decadent Reader: Fiction, Fantasy and Perversion from Fin-de-Siècle France* and has published many translations. She lives in New York City.